IN THE FOOTSTEPS
OF THE VICTORIANS

IN THE FOOTSTEPS
OF THE VICTORIANS

*Aspects of change in the Wrey Valley
and surrounding area*

1837–1901

ISBN: 978-0-9957122-1-8

Cover illustration: *Lustleigh Cleeve*, (1844) William Spreat. *The tourist's companion: A guide book to Chudleigh, the Rocks ...* Crook's "Weekly Express" Office, 1870. Second Edition. (Courtesy South West Heritage Trust)

Typeset, printed and bound by Short Run Press Ltd, Exeter

Contents

This book comprises the work of researchers involved in *In the footsteps of the Victorians*, a heritage project investigating Victorian influence on Dartmoor. It is funded by *Moor than meets the eye* and supported by the Heritage Lottery Fund. Through *Moor than meets the eye* people have explored Dartmoor's rich past, worked to conserve its wildlife and archaeology, improved understanding of the landscape and developed and shared the skills needed to look after it for generations to come. Active over a 280 square km area, *Moor than meets the eye* has told The Dartmoor Story of the last 4000 years.

In the footsteps of the Victorians has seen volunteers from communities across Dartmoor, research and write about the history of the Wrey Valley and surrounding area on the eastern edge of Dartmoor during the nineteenth and early twentieth century, with a particular focus on the social and economic changes brought about by the arrival of the railway in the 1860s. During this time and beyond, artists came to Dartmoor in search of 'the picturesque' and through their artwork, captured the changing attitudes to wilderness and the outdoors. This element of the project inspired an exhibition at the Royal Albert Memorial Museum between December 2017 and April 2018.

Acknowledgements

In addition to the authors of the essays in this book we would like to thank the following for additional information and research: George Black, Paul Brassley, Simon Butler, Stuart Drabble, Tom Greeves, James Gregory, Bill Hardiman (Moretonhampstead History Society), Hazel Jones, April Marjoram, Dr Phil Newman, Karen Stevenson (Lustleigh Community Archive).

Particular thanks go to Emma Stockley, Community Heritage Officer (*Moor than meets the eye*) for her invaluable support and guidance throughout the project.

Thanks to National Lottery players and funding made available through the Heritage Lottery Fund, without which, this project would not have been possible.

Thanks to the *Moor than meets the eye* Landscape Partnership.

Foreword

In their magnificent celebration of local distinctiveness, *England in Particular*, Sue Clifford and Angela King, founders of Common Ground, wrote: 'Everywhere is somewhere. What makes each place unique is the conspiracy of nature and culture; the accumulation of story upon history upon natural history.'

A key feature of the Heritage Lottery Fund's (HLF's) landscape partnership (LPS) programme is that it empowers communities to explore and celebrate what is unique, important and valued across a defined locality. By identifying a shared vision, as well as a geographical area, LPS projects create a context in which curious-minded and enthusiastic volunteers are supported to, sometimes literally, unearth 'the accumulation of story upon history upon natural history'.

Moor than meets the eye exemplifies this way of working, having at its heart a wealth of community initiatives in which people have energetically researched, recorded and shared the special qualities – the landscape features, historic events and stories – that have shaped this part of Devon.

This volume is testament to the resourcefulness and commitment of volunteers. It makes a significant and lasting contribution to the historic record and to public awareness of the heritage. I am delighted that, thanks to National Lottery players, HLF has been able to support such a worthwhile and well executed project.

Stephen Boyce
Chair, Heritage Lottery Fund, South West

The history of Dartmoor's Wrey Valley during the reign of Queen Victoria

An introduction

In 1837, at the start of Queen Victoria's reign, a resident of this remote, deeply agricultural valley on the eastern fringes of Dartmoor could scarcely have begun to imagine the changes and experiences that would have become embedded in daily life by 1901, when her son, King Edward VII, ascended the throne. Some things, such as the rural backcloth, would still be familiar but our resident would, from the mid-nineteenth century onwards, have become very aware of the encroachment of the outside world into many aspects of family and working life. Given the significance of this background, it is the aim of this book, a collection of essays produced by local amateur historians living in and close to the Wrey Valley, to paint a multifaceted picture of just how life did change over the Victorian era. The output, under the title *In the footsteps of the Victorians*, is a fully researched contribution to the *Moor than meets the eye* scheme, in which we have benefited greatly from the resources of local history societies, including the Lustleigh Society, the Bovey Tracey Heritage Trust, and a range of other groups such as the Kelly Mine Preservation Society.

The coming of the railway to Bovey Tracey, Lustleigh and thence to Moretonhampstead in 1866 clearly had a remarkable influence on all aspects of life in the Wrey Valley. This was not only in terms of its physical impact on the countryside, but on the local population – who they were, how they lived and the type of work they did, on settlement patterns and architecture, trade and industry, who was visiting the area, and how it was portrayed in art and literature. Our study also looks at how leisure time, sports and social activities changed over Victoria's reign, what it was like to be a child at school, and how the valley had its own 'movers and shakers' – important local and incoming families, exercising philanthropy and leading the valley into the brave new Victorian world. In all of this, the railway's arrival was a critical catalyst but, as each essay highlights, there were many other cross-connecting factors giving rise to profound changes such that, by the dawn of the twentieth century, previously remote villages such as Lustleigh could aptly be described as taking their place in the wider world. Perhaps above all, it was the access to Victorian imperial, industrial and technological progress, allied with continuing robust Christian morality and social reform, which proved such an intoxicating and irresistible influence.

There is, of course, always more to research and we are conscious that this anthology has gaps in relation to a detailed analysis of agricultural history, of changes in religious life and practice, on law and order, and in population health – although these subjects are touched on tangentially in a number of the essays. A word of definition is also required in relation to the geographic area which our work aims to cover. The Wrey (or 'Wray' – the two spellings continue to be used interchangeably to this day) Valley covers that area on the eastern edge of Dartmoor through which the railway line used to run. It covers the stretch from Bovey Tracey via Lustleigh to the town of Moretonhampstead, including all places in between such as Wrey Barton, and others nearby which, in their history, are essentially inseparable from that of the valley. Examples include the beautiful Lustleigh Cleave, beloved of the growing band of Victorian tourists, and important industrial locations such as the Kelly Mine. Although the railway terminated at Moretonhampstead, we have also included other nearby villages outside the Wrey Valley, such as Chagford, which showed some similar patterns of development and whose history has strong parallels with it.

In overall context, the county of Devon saw significant net outward rural migration between 1841 and 1901[1] at a rate which peaked at almost 2 per cent in each decade, with farm labour falling from 81,000 (1851) to just 44,000 (1901). Whilst the Wrey Valley certainly reflected this county-wide picture, there were important differences in population trends as revealed by census data in places only a short distance apart. During our period, the town of Bovey Tracey thrived as the railway arrived, a decline in its agricultural population more than offset by growth in craft and industry. This included the important pottery and associated businesses, where incoming businessmen and other middle-class people

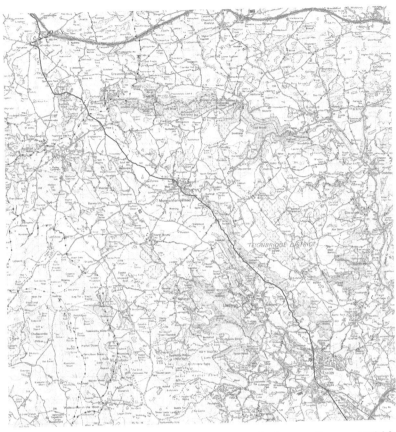

Crown copyright and database rights 2018 Ordnance Survey 100024842

seeking a rural life with good external communications were driving up demand for domestic services, which also surged. Along the valley, Lustleigh also saw agricultural decline but similar growth in those people of 'independent means', many born outside Devon, and in the service occupations which accompanied their arrival; tourists also start to feature in the census record. By contrast, Moretonhampstead's population declined from 1841 to 1901, its agricultural workforce roughly halving despite a growth in shops and services. A similar pattern was also generally reflected in Chagford, where growth in the 'high street' and its lodgings helped the town to hold its own, while the wider rural parish witnessed a contraction. Analysing the detailed reasons for these various contrasting fortunes would be a fruitful area for further study by others.

The enthusiastic support of the aristocracy and gentry was pivotal to the successful planning and realisation of the railway line along the valley, with names of influential gentlemen such as John Divett of Bovey Tracey, and George and Thomas Wills of Lustleigh cropping up in a number of the essays. These people were certainly local Victorian polymaths, pursuing their commercial interests but demonstrating significant philanthropy and having a pronounced impact on all areas of life and work in the Wrey Valley. It is instructive to note that the goals set out in the railway's original prospectus – related to its potential for improved trade, industry, tourism and communications – came largely to pass, duly opening up the valley and its environs to the Victorian world's trade, technology and ideas. This impact worked, of course, in both directions, with agricultural produce, mineral ores and manufactures leaving the valley, and with the flow of an established middle class of incomers, both permanent residents and tourists, in the other direction. These changes enabled the area gradually to shed its epithet of 'dreary' as it began to spark the wider imagination, becoming increasingly associated with being 'picturesque' and 'romantic', with all that implied for the growth of Victorian tourism.

In the 'high streets' of Bovey Tracey and Moretonhampstead, these changes had a clear impact. Pubs continued in their established role as the venues for social occasions of various types and often as the centres of commercial activities such as auctions, but as the Victorian era progressed, a wider variety of lodgings sprang up to cater to the new tourist trade, along with enterprises offering excursions onto the moor. In addition, as more well-heeled permanent residents moved in, a wider diversity of shops became established to meet their sartorial and more upmarket day-to-day needs as the social milieu gradually evolved. Along with this, the traditional population itself found more outlets for its leisure time, with a wider social participation. Various traditional activities and sports continued to be popular whilst others waned, and fierce local village pride was invariably combined with enthusiastic celebration of national events. From the 1870s, we see the impact of muscular Christianity and the later Victorian urge for social and moral improvement of the working man taking effect through the temperance movement and a wide range of 'self-development' activities, championed by well-meaning local philanthropists, encountering varying degrees of enthusiasm and success.

In the working context, mining and quarrying were important industries in the Wrey Valley, albeit not employing large numbers of people. The export of the local 'shining ore' and the economics of this business certainly benefited from the railway, but also from the advances in broader Victorian technology which expanded the market for its industrial applications. The quarrying of the heavy local granite, by contrast and for obvious economic reasons, saw its use predominantly in local construction and so did not contribute to the railway's revenues. But there were some fascinating new opportunities brought about by the opening up of the valley, a newspaper report of 1889 noting that 84,000 pairs of clog soles cut from local alder trees were being sent by rail to Manchester for 'Lancashire operatives'.[2] Not only was the export facilitated by rail, but so too was the original idea for the business opportunity, 'the principals [from Lancashire being] two brothers, named Goodfellow; [both] very intelligent men'. Not unexpectedly, all this development of activity was leaving its mark on the built environment, the size of which increased significantly and where the original vernacular architecture was increasingly supplemented by a planned architectural style. This represented a radical design shift from what had gone before. Some of the cross-cutting influences here included the railway, the incoming of a wealthier middle class, the availability of new materials and that of Victorian values and aspirations, the latter evidenced in the construction of a new school building in Lustleigh. Similar echoes are evident in the example of the village's Church House which, having been used as a Poor House was then, from 1840, serving as cottages for agricultural labourers of a prominent local gentleman farmer, Thomas Wills of East Wrey.[3] In line with the late Victorian *zeitgeist*, the Church House then saw a further change in form and function in its subsequent incarnation as the Parish Reading Room.

The national political discourse and focus on social 'improvement' had resulted in the Elementary Education Act (1870) making school attendance compulsory for children aged from five to 12. Prior to construction of the new Board School building in Lustleigh, there had been an Endowed School in the 'Old Vestry', a tiny building hosting some 40 children in often insanitary conditions. Actively promoted by the clergy and farming landowners, the Board School system of funding based on children's attainment faced numerous challenges, not limited to the sheer number of children, absenteeism, indiscipline, frequently low attainment, continual financial struggle and childhood illness and disease. Here again, we therefore see significant developments during the Victorian era and a range of resulting childhood experiences as education was balanced with farm work, and sickness took its toll. Underpinning almost all the changes which we have been studying, the role of local gentry is ever-present and influential. The case of John Divett of Bovey Tracey provides an illuminating example. A Cambridge graduate from a Quaker family, Divett co-founded the Bovey Tracey Pottery Company, an enterprise that was influential in the town's economic and social development throughout our period; he went on to become a central figure in its life, as landowner, mine shareholder, magistrate, a prime mover in bringing the railway to the Wrey Valley, and philanthropist. Such men were the facilitators, providing the spark igniting many of the changes within the valley and opening it up to a wealth of Victorian technologies and ideas from around the empire.

Having provided this background to the subject matter of the essays which follow and the many interlocking themes that run across them, it is, perhaps, entirely forgivable that the resident we figuratively 'met' at the outset may have been bemused and unable to grasp how their world might have changed by the end of the nineteenth century. Their working and social life, the physical changes in their small world, the people with whom they were sharing life in the valley, and the education their children received, had all changed markedly. The railway had been a key facilitator of that change – but not the only one. Had they thought deeply about it, our resident would also have been compelled to acknowledge the part played by the local and incoming gentry, the national and imperial developments in industry, trade and technology, and the evolution of political, economic and social thought. And, it is fair to assume, their feelings and reflections would doubtless have comprised a broad mix of markedly differing emotions.

Notes

1. Finch, G., in Bliss, J., Jago, C. and Maycock, E., eds, 2012. *Aspects of Devon History*. Exeter: Devon History Society.
2. *Western Morning News*, 10th May 1889.
3. Johnson, H., 1926. *Some Account of the Church House at Lustleigh*. Cambridge: Cambridge University Press.

1.   The coming of the railway

Mike Lang

When Queen Victoria acceded to the throne, in 1837, the only railways of any significance in Devon were the Haytor Granite Tramway and the Plymouth and Dartmoor Railway, opened in 1820 and 1823 respectively. Both of these, however, were operated using horse-drawn wagons and it was to be a further seven years before the first steam train reached Devon. At 12.30 p.m. on 1st May 1844, vast crowds at Exeter welcomed the engine *Actaeon* drawing the six carriages which comprised the train. After a great lunch in the goods shed at St David's, the return journey to Paddington commenced at 5.20 p.m. Among the passengers on the train was Sir Thomas Ackland, MP; at 10.30 that evening he rose in the House of Commons to say that he had been in Exeter little more than five hours earlier. The Bristol & Exeter Railway had arrived. It had been authorised by Parliament in May 1836, at the instigation of a group of Bristol merchants. In the meantime, no sooner had the Act of 1836 been passed than a group of enterprising Plymouth men proposed another railway, to link up at Exeter. Nothing became of this proposal, however, due to lack of support by the Devonshire people to subscribe the necessary capital, and, similarly, several other schemes brought before the public over the next six years met with the same fate. By then Isambard Kingdom Brunel had long since surveyed the countryside, and the Haldon range of hills, south-west of Exeter, had compelled him to plan for a line from Exeter to Starcross and along the coast to Dawlish and Teignmouth. Initially, it would then have continued over the River Teign to the neighbourhood of Torquay, thence over the Dart and into the South Hams. But, when the locomotive had shown its capabilities for hill climbing, he had abandoned the idea for a direct run from Teignmouth to Torquay, which would have involved many expensive works, in favour of a line running alongside the Teign estuary to Newton Abbot, and thence over the southern spurs of Dartmoor to Totnes, Ivybridge, Plympton and Plymouth.

Finally, in 1843, the Bristol & Exeter and Great Western Railway companies, together with the Bristol & Gloucester Railway, took up the matter and agreed to subscribe liberally to Brunel's project. This set the project on its feet; in October the prospectus of the Plymouth, Devonport & Exeter Railway – soon to become the South Devon Railway – was issued and the construction of the broad-gauge (7 ft 0¼ in.) line was authorised the following July. Furthermore, in less than two years, on 30th May 1846, the line was open for traffic as far as Teignmouth and, by the end of that year, it had reached Newton Abbot. Work proceeded, and Plymouth (Laira Green) was reached on 5th May 1848, but this was not its terminus. Mutley Tunnel had to be completed before it reached Millbay, in April of the following year.

In the wake of the railway reaching Devon, many other schemes were brought before the public, for by then it was already evident that a rapid means of communication was essential in the interests of commercial well-being. Indeed, such was the excitement and interest that many writers have referred to the mid-1840s as a period of railway 'mania'. A large number of these schemes, however, were destined for failure for one reason or another, and one of the earliest to fall into this category was a proposed railway from Torquay Harbour to Aller Barn (Newton Abbot) on the South Devon Railway – under the auspices of the Torquay and Newton Abbot Railway Company. In this instance, following the issue of a prospectus in 1844 and plans being deposited, the scheme was killed off by objectors, who felt that a station at Aller was close enough for Torquay.

Following hard on the heels of this proposed line from Torquay Harbour came another proposal, from a group of local gentlemen, for a broad-gauge line from Dartmouth to Aller (and a branch to Ashburton, which was later deleted). It was proposed to work this line on the atmospheric method, and the engineer was to be W.R. Neale (an assistant to the London & South Western Railway's engineer, Joseph Locke). In July 1845, however, this proposal, and a separate plan for a South & North Devon Junction Railway from Newton (Abbot) to Crediton, was swept into the 'narrow-gauge' (4 ft 8½ in.) camp by Joseph Locke, with a promise of support from London. The Dartmouth, Torbay & Exeter Railway began with separate branches from Dartmouth and Brixham, which combined at Galmpton and continued via Torbay, Newton Abbot and Moretonhampstead. At Exeter it would have joined up with intended 'narrow-gauge' lines via Yeovil and Salisbury to London.

At last disturbed by these attempts at competition, the South Devon Railway presented a Bill to the 1846 Session of Parliament. This proposed a branch from the South Devon Railway at Aller to Kingswear routed through Torquay, Paignton, Churston and Brixham Quay. Some £45,750 was paid into the Court of Chancery in support of the Bill on 3rd February 1846. On the following day the competing 'narrow-gauge' Dartmouth, Brixham, Torbay, Exeter and North Devon Junction Railway (to quote its full title) deposited £24,500 in the same Court on account of its Bill. However, the 'narrow-gauge' interest was defeated on technical objections; the Bill had been completed with too much haste. The South Devon Railway (Amendments and Branches) Act, on the other hand, received the Royal Assent on 28th August 1846, but strong opposition from Paignton and Goodrington residents (who feared loss of access to the beach) had foreshortened the line and the Act showed it to terminate in field no. 23 in the parish of Tormohan (Torquay). The station was to be under Chapel Hill, at 'St Michaels' (Torre), but was named Torquay: this was to remain its name after the line was opened, on 18th December 1848, until 1st August 1859. It was then, because of a new station being opened at Livermead in conjunction with the Dartmouth and Torbay Railway's line to Kingswear, which on that date became operational as far as Paignton, that the original station was renamed Torre. This latter company, incidentally, had been set up in 1856 under the direction of Charles Seale Hayne and received the Royal Assent to its Act on 27th July 1857.

Returning now to 1846, one of the consequences of the failure on the part of the Dartmouth, Brixham, Torbay, Exeter and North Devon Junction Railway Company in obtaining Parliamentary approval of its Bill was that any hopes that the local populace in and around the Moretonhampstead area may have had of having a railway connection nearby were dashed. Whether or not this led to another scheme being proposed at about this time is pure conjecture but, in his book *Small Talk at Wreyland*, Cecil Torr states that there was a project for a railway here (Wreyland, Lustleigh) as soon as the main line had reached Newton.

He then quotes from a letter written to his father by his grandfather on 25ᵗʰ April 1847, as follows:

> The surveyors have been from Newton to Okehampton, marking out a new line. They seem to be guided by the stream, and (if it takes place) they will go right up the meadows under here ... I cannot fancy it will take place, for people are a little cooled down, and not so mad for speculation. Had it been projected some little time ago, no doubt it would have taken.

Unfortunately, apart from stating that the project came to nothing, Cecil Torr makes no further comment about this particular scheme, and, despite extensive research, no documentary evidence of it has come to light. This, in itself, seems to suggest that it was an entirely local promotion arising from discussions within the trading community, something that would have been in common with many other short-lived schemes of this period.

Moving on to near the end of the 1840s, the country entered a period of sustained economic recession and, locally, the South Devon Railway Company fell into dire financial straits due to the amount of money spent on its ill-fated atmospheric system of propulsion on the main line between Exeter and Newton Abbot. As a result, the next ten years or so saw only a very limited number of railway schemes being proposed and only two of them in Devon reaching fruition – the Plymouth to Tavistock line and the Torquay to Paignton line (as part of the Dartmouth and Torbay Railway's line to Kingswear, already mentioned above). However, during the latter part of the 1850s, one of the schemes under consideration was for a railway to link Moretonhampstead to Newton Abbot. In this instance the promoters were a small group of individuals who owned land between these two locations and who were keen to improve the means by which their produce could be taken to the markets of Newton Abbot and Torquay. One of them was the Rector of Stokeinteignhead, the Reverend John Nutcombe Gould, and on 18ᵗʰ August 1858 he addressed an inaugural public meeting about the proposal at the Globe Hotel in Newton Abbot, a meeting presided over by Samuel Trehawke Kekewich – the Lord of the Manor of Stokeinteignhead and one of South Devon's newly elected MPs.

Eight days later a full account of the meeting appeared in the columns

Figure 1.1: *Bovey Station* Glass slide c.1900.
(Courtesy Carrett Collection)

of the *Exeter Flying Post*, and it was reported that during his address the rector had stated that he 'did not believe there was another line in England that could be made so cheaply' and 'that the engineering difficulties were comparatively trifling'. It was also reported that he had not hesitated to assert that the first week the railway was opened the traffic that would go upon it would pay every expense and give every shareholder a fair and profitable return. From this it can be gleaned that the rector had been carried away somewhat by his enthusiasm, but at least it had achieved the desired effect: a resolution had been passed at the meeting 'approving of a Line of Railway from Newton Abbot to Moretonhampstead through the Bovey Valley'. At the same meeting another resolution had also been passed whereby a committee was appointed, 'with power to add to their number', under the chairmanship of the Reverend J.N. Gould. Among the persons named were George Bragg (a Moretonhampstead solicitor), the Reverend William Charles Clack (Rector of St Andrew's Church, Moretonhampstead), Elias Cuming (of Linscott), John Rowell (a farmer at Teigngrace) and George and Thomas Wills (farmers at Kelly and East Wray respectively). The others were Messrs John Courtier (of Wray), John Drew (of Peamore, near Exeter), William Harris (of Plumley), Thomas Hatch (of Newton Abbot), Charles Langley (of Chudleigh), Alfred Puddicombe (of Moretonhampstead) and another member of the Wills family at Kelly.

In the months that followed, the Committee met on six more occasions in fairly quick succession. Meanwhile, certain members of the Committee were requested to canvas the landowners and others in the neighbourhood of the intended line for subscriptions in aid of preliminary expenses, and a Mr Thomas Whitaker of Exeter was paid the sum of £50 for carrying out a preliminary survey of the proposed line, which included preparing plans of the land required and an estimate of the cost. In addition, discussions took place between Lord Courtenay (the son of the 10th Earl of Devon), on behalf of the Committee, and Edward Adolphus Seymour (the 11th Duke of Somerset, who had purchased the Stover Estate, along with the Haytor Granite Tramway and Stover Canal, from George Templer in 1829) on the basis that 'the Committee will be quite prepared to entertain the question of compensating the Duke of Somerset for the value of his Canal – either by absolute purchase or by way of annual Rent Charge in the event of his Grace assenting to the formation of the intended Railway through his Lands'. However, despite a favourable outcome to these discussions, which were reported to the Committee at a further meeting held on 26th January 1859, the entire project was abandoned – for the time being, at least. The reason for this was not any lack of enthusiasm, but almost certainly the poor level of response to requests for subscriptions. Indeed, apart from a sum of £61. 14s. 0d. mentioned at one of the earlier committee meetings, no money at all appears to have been forthcoming and the balance in hand was just £1. 12s. 0d.

It was not until 31st October 1860 that anything further was heard on the matter. Then, at long last, another meeting of the Committee did take place, although the only persons present, apart from the Reverend J.N. Gould, who took the chair, were Messrs Drew, Langley and J. Harris. Furthermore, the only resolution passed was:

> that the Hon. Secretary be requested to watch the progress of Mr Toogood's Scheme for a Line down the Teign, to call a special meeting

of the Committee when necessary and at present to let all proceedings in opposition to the proposed line stand over till further information be obtained.

'Mr Toogood's Scheme' was, in fact, part of the Devon Central Railways Company's plan. This, in simplistic terms, was connected with the arrival, in Exeter, of the London & South Western Railway Company's 'narrow-gauge' line from Salisbury, in July 1860, and the desire on the part of Sir Lawrence Palk of Haldon House to have a railway link to his estates in the Teign Valley and Torquay, in the interests of commercial gain.

In order to try to achieve these aims, Palk had secured the services of William Toogood (a parliamentary agent with interests in railway promotion generally) and persuaded a number of other local notables to join him, including Lord Courtenay – now the 11th Earl of Devon, following the death of his father in 1859. On the face of it the new earl's involvement was a surprise, as he had once been a director of the South Devon Railway Company and, more recently, had joined the Newton & Moretonhampstead Railway Committee. However, as part of its overall scheme, the Devon Central Railways Company was proposing to build several other lines, one of which would commence from a junction with the proposed Teign Valley line at Leigh Cross (near Dunsford), pass near Moretonhampstead and continue to Chagford. It was this, in fact, that had persuaded the earl to join the 'narrow-gauge' camp: he owned estates in the Moretonhampstead/Chagford area and had become frustrated by the failure on the part of the South Devon Railway Company, still hard-pressed financially, to promote a railway link to his property from Newton Abbot, or to support the Newton & Moretonhampstead Railway Committee's project.

Suffice to say, the plans of the Devon Central Railways Company were to end in failure. Petitions against the scheme were lodged by both the South Devon Railway Company and the Bristol & Exeter Railway Company, and after the Devon Central had presented its Bill to Parliament – with the London & South Western Railway Company also in opposition – it was eventually rejected in its entirety by a House of Commons Committee on 28th May 1861. This, of course, threw everything back into the 'melting pot'. However, the chairman of the South Devon Railway Company, Thomas Woollcombe, responded immediately by entering into a series of discussions with his consultant engineer, John Fowler, and others to determine the best way forward as regards pre-empting any further opposition from within the 'narrow-gauge' camp. At this time the company was still in no position financially to promote any new lines, although it was agreed that it could at least offer favourable working agreements for any promoted by nominally independent companies and that efforts should be made to secure the promotion of two lines in particular. One would be from Tavistock to Launceston via Lydford, and the other would be either from Newton Abbot to Dunsford via the Teign Valley or from Newton Abbot to Moretonhampstead; eventually, on the recommendation of John Fowler, it was agreed that it should be the latter.

Quite apart from anything else, this proposal to support a line from Newton Abbot to Moretonhampstead fulfilled the aims and ambitions of the Earl of Devon. As a result, he was now enticed back into the broad-gauge camp, where many thought that he rightfully belonged, and on 11th September 1861 took the chair at the next meeting of the Newton & Moretonhampstead Railway Committee. Held once again at the Globe Hotel in Newton Abbot, the committee members on this occasion consisted of the Reverend J.N. Gould, Thomas Wills, John Rowell, John Drew Jr, Elias Cuming, William Harris and Charles Langley. Of even greater significance, however, were some of the persons who had been invited 'to meet the Committee', for these included Thomas Woollcombe, representatives of two influential landowners (the Duke of Somerset and William Hole of the Parke Estate in Bovey), John Divett (the owner of Bovey Pottery), John Hayman Whiteway (a local clay trader) and John Wills (a farmer of Higher Hisley, Lustleigh).

It is recorded that during this important meeting, when the Earl of Devon called upon him as the representative of the South Devon Railway Company to state the assistance that might be expected from that company to the proposed line, Mr Woollcombe responded with a speech. This included the following comments:

Subject to proper co-operation on the part of the Landowners for the purpose of forming an Independent Company the Directors of the South Devon Railway Company would be prepared to recommend their Shareholders to agree that the South Devon Railway Company should work the line for 50 per cent of its gross receipts, and also to give a rebate of 25 per cent upon Passenger traffic passing from the new line over the South Devon line and vice versa. That the cost at which the Goods traffic could be worked and any rebate to be granted in respect thereof would require further consideration.

The South Devon Railway Company would not subscribe any of the Capital, but [he] would not object as an individual to subscribe £500 provided that the Landowners acted in a liberal spirit in giving their lands on easy terms, and taking their proper share in raising the Capital. [He also thought that] if £1000 a mile was raised locally there ought to be no difficulty in carrying the matter out.

Other extracts from the minutes of this same meeting include the following:

The Revd. J. N. Gould consented to give the Land required [at Knowle]. Mr Thos. Wills consented to have his Land valued by Mr Hooper of Chagford at an Agricultural Value and to take it out in paid up Shares. He was also authorised to state that Mr George Wills of Kelly would do the same. Mr Wm. Harris consented to sell such Land as required at an Agricultural Value and to take payment in Shares. [It was then resolved] that a Sub-committee be appointed consisting of Messrs. Thos. Wills, Mr Courtier, Wm. Harris and John Drew Junr. for the purpose of ascertaining,

1st. From the Landowners on the Line on what terms they are disposed to part with their Land for the purposes of the intended Railway.
2nd. From the Public generally what amount of Shares [are] likely to be taken.
3rd. What amount each Subscriber is prepared to give towards the necessary preliminary expenses, the amount Subscribed to be allowed in Shares, – such Sub-committee to report at the earliest practicable period.

It was now over three years since the first meeting of the Newton & Moretonhampstead Railway Committee had taken place, but, at long last, it seemed that real progress was being made as regards achieving its aims. A fortnight later, at the next meeting of the Committee (and various landowners, or their agents), this was confirmed still further when it was reported by the Sub-committee that 14 'Gentlemen' had, between them, already consented to take shares to a total value of £1,675, and that two more landowners, George Wills of Narracombe and John Nosworthy of Steward Wood, would consent to sell their land at an agricultural value; the former 'to be paid in a Rent Charge on Condition of a Station being at Lustleigh'. Moreover, during the meeting, the Committee also obtained the consent of Messrs Divett, Amery, White and Stevens 'to part with their Lands upon an Agricultural Valuation and to accept payment by a Rent Charge'. Finally, before the meeting ended, it was agreed to take up a written offer received from a Newton Abbot surveyor, Mr John Adams, to prepare maps and plans of the railway, and a recommendation was made 'that Public Meetings be held at Chagford, Moreton Hampstead, Bovey and Newton Abbot and that a Prospectus be issued giving full particulars of Capital, Cost of Construction, terms with the South Devon Railway Company etc.'.

These meetings, of course, were necessary to try and encourage the public to subscribe for shares and subsequently took place on 7th/8th October. In addition, on the morning of the same day as the first public meeting held at Chagford, a separate meeting took place there and those recorded as being present were the Earl of Devon (chairman) and Messrs John Drew, Thomas Wills, Elias Cuming, Thomas Woollcombe, C.C. Whiteford, W. Carr, G. Pridham, J. Belfield, P.J. Margary & Lloyd, during the course of which the following resolutions were passed:

> That the undertaking commenced in 1858 under the title of the Newton and Moreton Hampstead Railway up the Bovey Valley be henceforth designated the Moreton Hampstead and South Devon Railway and a Company be formed to carry the same into effect.
>
> That the Capital of the Company be £100,000 in 4,000 Shares of £25 each and a deposit not exceeding £1 per Share be paid.
>
> That John Fowler and P. J. Margary be the Engineers of the Company.
>
> That Messrs. Whiteford & Co. be the Solicitors of the Company.
>
> That Messrs. Watts, Whidborne and Moir and the Devon and Cornwall Bank be the Bankers.

That Mr Josiah Harris be the Hon. Secretary.

That a Committee Meeting be called for at an Early Day to appoint Provisional Directors.

For reasons unknown the original promoter of the scheme, the Reverend J.N. Gould, did not attend this meeting and appears not to have had any further involvement in the matter. Another absentee was John Adams, the Newton Abbot surveyor appointed to prepare maps and plans of the railway. However, according to Thomas Woollcombe, doubts had arisen over whether he could complete the survey and sections in time to comply with the Standing Orders of the House of Commons and, as a result, 'an arrangement had been made with Mr Margary that he would complete all Engineering and Surveying including Lithographing Plans and every other expense for £375 a mile, payment to be made one third in Cash, one third in Debentures and one third in Shares'.

Figure 1.2: *The "Aurora", a 4-4-OST locomotive allocated to Moretonhampstead during the mid-1870s.*
(Courtesy J.B.N. Ashford)

Just over three weeks later, on 30th October, the first 'proper' meeting of the Moretonhampstead & South Devon Railway Committee, which was really no more than a continuation of the former Newton & Moretonhampstead Railway Committee, took place at the Globe Hotel in Newton Abbot. It was attended by the Earl of Devon (chairman), Thomas Woollcombe, John Drew, Thomas Wills, William Harris, John Rowell, John Fowler and Peter Margary – by now, all familiar names – and the main business to be conducted concerned the appointment of provisional directors of the proposed company. In the event this was dealt with by three separate resolutions. The first was that there should be five provisional directors, 'with power to add two to their number'; the second was a requirement that each director should hold shares in the company to the value of £500; and the third was that the Earl of Devon, Thomas Woollcombe, John Divett and Thomas Wills should be the provisional directors of the company, 'with power to add three to their number'. Three of the newly appointed provisional directors (John Divett was not present) then held a separate meeting immediately afterwards to confirm the appointments made by the Committee at the earlier meeting held at Chagford on the morning of 7th October.

The next important development came on 14th November, when a working agreement was drawn up in the form of a 'Heads of Arrangement for Working the Line by the South Devon Railway Company, and for Rebates to be allowed to the Moreton Hampstead and South Devon Railway Company'. This, it stated, was 'between the Moreton Hampstead and South Devon Railway Company (hereinafter called "The Moreton Company") of the first part; the South Devon Railway Company (hereinafter called "The South Devon Company") of the second part; and each of the Great Western Railway Company, the Bristol and Exeter Railway Company, and the Cornwall Railway Company (hereinafter called the "Three Companies") of the third part', and amongst its many clauses (or 'Heads') were the following:

1. These Heads to be subject to the Sanction of Parliament.
2. The Moreton Company, at their own expense, to make and complete the intended Moreton and South Devon Railway from Moreton Hampstead to Newton (hereinafter called the 'New Line'), according to their Act, as a Single Line, but with Land and Overbridges for a Double Line, with Double Line where requisite,

and all proper and sufficient Works and conveniences, including a Junction at Newton with the South Devon Railway; and all to the reasonable satisfaction of the South Devon Company's Engineer.

3.   All Contracts affecting the working of the Line, or involving conditions or engagements to be carried out either directly or indirectly by the South Devon Company, are to be made subject to approval by them.

4.   The New Line and Works to be maintained by the Contractor for making the railway, for Twelve Months after completion, to the satisfaction of the South Devon Company's Engineer.

5.   After the New Line is authorized to be opened for Public Traffic, the South Devon Company at all times, at their own expense, to maintain (without prejudice to the fourth head), stock, work, and use the New Line so as properly to develope and accommodate the local and general Traffic of the District.

6.   If, and whenever after the opening of the New Line, it shall be required, in consequence of increased Traffic or for the Public safety, to make additions to the Stations or Works, such additions as shall be reasonably required by the South Devon Company's Engineer shall be made at the expense of the Moreton Company, who shall provide Capital for the purpose, not exceeding the amount authorized by their Act.

This somewhat lengthy document also made provision for 'Fifty per cent of the gross traffic receipts for all traffic conveyed over the New Line to be paid to the South Devon Company for their expenses of maintaining, managing and working the line and traffic, and the other fifty per cent to be paid to the Moreton Company' and contained numerous other clauses, several of which related to the granting of rebates by the 'South Devon Company' and the 'Three Companies' in respect of any through traffic to, or from, any of the stations on the new line.

As recorded in the minutes, the document was read during a meeting of the provisional directors of the Moretonhampstead & South Devon Railway Company held at the Globe Hotel in Newton Abbot on 12th December 1861 and duly approved: by then it had already been signed by the Earl of Devon and Thomas Woollcombe (on behalf of the Moretonhampstead & South Devon Railway Company and the South Devon Railway Company respectively) and also by the chairman of the

'Three Companies'. The minutes of this same meeting also include the following other items of note:

> The Chairman [the Earl of Devon] reported that he had communicated with Mr [William] Hole and Mr Hames [the Reverend Hayter George Hames, Rector of Chagford] with reference to their becoming Provisional Directors, and that Mr Hole in reply had consented to join the Board but Mr Hames had declined.

> Mr Whitcford submitted a print of the Bill for the Incorporation of the Company and the Board proceeded to discuss the amount of Capital to be raised, the nominal value of the Shares & the qualification of Directors ...

> The Petition for the Bill was then signed by the Directors present, and the Secretary was instructed to arrange with the Devon and Cornwall Bank or Messrs. Watts & Co. [bankers of Newton Abbot] for a loan of Stock to meet the required Parliamentary deposit.

> Mr Woollcombe referred to the necessity of appointing a Surveyor to negotiate for the purchase of the land. Resolved that Mr Hooper [of Chagford] be requested to act as the Surveyor of the Company and to proceed as far as possible to arrange the necessary purchases.

Within just a few weeks of this meeting the Bill referred to above (with the Heads of Arrangement annexed to it) had been deposited and was first read in the House of Commons on 10th February 1862. After two further – unopposed – readings it was then referred to the House of Lords, where, apart from one or two minor amendments being found necessary by a Lords Committee, it again had a smooth passage and the resulting Act received the Royal Assent on 7th July 1862. It authorised 'the making of a Railway from the South Devon Railway, near to the Newton Station thereof, in the Parish of Wolborough in the County of Devon to Moretonhampstead in the same County' and was cited as 'The Moretonhampstead and South Devon Railway Act, 1862'. It also authorised a share capital of £105,000 in £10 shares, with borrowing power to the extent of £35,000, and contained a number of stipulations. These included a figure of £300 being quoted as a qualification for directorship; the number of directors being six; the named directors – The Right Honourable the Earl of Devon, Elias Cuming, John Divett, William Robert Hole, Thomas Wills and Thomas Woollcombe – being obliged to remain in office until 'the first ordinary meeting' of the company; the various categories of traffic that could be carried over the line and the tolls relating to each of them; and the maximum tolls to be charged for passengers conveyed in first, second and third class carriages (3d., 2d. and 1½d. per mile respectively).

Having obtained their Act, the promoters now arranged for the circulation of a new prospectus and for the 'first ordinary meeting' of the newly incorporated company to be held at the Union Hotel in Bovey Tracey on 4th August 1862. During this meeting, which was chaired by Thomas Woollcombe, the six directors named in the Act were formally elected as the first directors of the company, speeches were made outlining the benefits of the proposed railway and the amount of progress made to date, and a resolution passed that 'local Committees be formed at Moretonhampstead, North Bovey, Chagford, Lustleigh and Bovey Tracey for the purpose of canvassing additional shares'. Afterwards, at the Commercial Hotel in Bovey Tracey, the 'new' directors also held their first meeting, at which the main business to be conducted was the appointment of Alexander E. Lloyd as the company secretary.

As regards the prospectus, this contained details of the share capital, the names of the company's directors, engineers, secretary, solicitors and bankers, a 'Sketch of Arrangements with the South Devon, Great Western, Bristol and Exeter, and Cornwall Companies', a form of application for shares and a commentary, as follows:

The population of that portion of Devonshire which includes the Towns of Newton and Torquay, has increased since the Census of 1851 in a greater proportion than in any other part of the county, excepting Plymouth and Devonport, and the consequent increase in the demand for supplies of all kinds at the local markets, and in the trade and business of the District has induced a general requirement for extended railway communication.

In 1858, a Line was projected to proceed from Newton through the Pottery District of Bovey to the rich Agricultural tract which centres in Moretonhampstead, and this design being fully matured, and the promoters having secured the cordial support of the landowners, and obtained promises of material assistance from the Broad Gauge Railway Companies, application has been made to Parliament in the present Session (1862), for an Act of Incorporation, which has been passed without opposition.

The wild and beautiful country near Moretonhampstead on the borders of Dartmoor, – the picturesque old Stannary Town of Chagford, and the romantic scenery in the vicinity of Lustleigh, are celebrated in Guide Books, and well-known to Artists and Tourists; and the pure and invigorating air of this elevated country attracts annually numerous Visitors, to whom, and especially to Invalids suffering from the relaxation of a warmer climate, it offers all the natural advantages which have conferred such celebrity on Malvern.

The Country surrounding Moretonhampstead and along the upper portion of the Line is remarkably fertile, and large quantities of agricultural produce will be brought over the Line to the Markets of Newton and Torquay.

There is every reason to believe that the District is rich in Minerals, including Copper, Tin and Iron, and the Shipment of Ores can at present be effected with facility and economy at Torquay and Teignmouth; Dartmouth, by the completion of its Railway, will afford another port, and from all these places the Moreton District can be supplied with Coal, in addition to that which is brought by land over the Bristol and Exeter and South Devon Railways.

The Extensive Pottery Works at Bovey, and the Smelting Works in course of construction in that locality, in connexion with the well-known Bovey Coal-field, may be expected to contribute largely to the Traffic of the Line.

The arrangements concluded by the Company with the South Devon, the Great Western, the Bristol and Exeter, and the Cornwall Railway Companies, are set forth in the Act of Incorporation.

The particulars and practical effect of these arrangements are briefly stated at the foot of this Prospectus.

It may be fairly presumed that with such large additions to the actual proceeds of the New Line as must result from the rebates granted by the Companies, the undertaking, besides conferring great advantages on the locality, will be highly remunerative to the Shareholders.

The Directors have obtained from Messrs. BRASSEY AND OGILVIE *a guaranteed contract* for execution of the whole of the works, except stations, for a gross sum of £88,500, and these gentlemen have evinced their sense of the value of the undertaking by agreeing to take Shares for the sum of £29,500.

The Directors have also made arrangements with His Grace the DUKE OF SOMERSET for the purchase of his Canal and the Land required for the undertaking. A large majority of the Land-owners on the Line have agreed to accept the Agricultural Value of their land, the amount to be fixed by Mr. JOHN HOOPER, of Chagford, who commands the confidence of all parties.

The Directors have been met in the most liberal manner by the Engineers and Solicitors, who have agreed to become Shareholders to a considerable amount.

Taking into account the nature of the arrangements already concluded, which the Directors feel warranted in describing as being of a very satisfactory description, they see no reason to doubt that the Line can be completed at a cost within the Capital of the Company, leaving a margin applicable for future improvements, consequent on the development of the general traffic.

As can be seen from the above, the promoters had, by now, also secured the services of one of the best-known railway contractors in the country at that time, Thomas Brassey of Messrs Brassey & Ogilvie, who had agreed to construct the line for £88,500 (payable in cash, debentures and shares in three equal proportions). In addition, they had entered into tentative arrangements with a number of landowners to acquire the land needed for the railway at an agricultural value and, after protracted negotiations, agreed to purchase outright such land belonging to the Duke of Somerset as was required: this included the lower section of the Haytor Granite Tramway (much of this was to be used to form part of the route of the new line) and, at the duke's insistence, the whole of the Stover Canal. Although not mentioned in the prospectus, the total purchase price was to be £8,000 and the agreement had been made on the understanding that a siding would be installed at the junction of the duke's tramway near Bovey Pottery so that granite quarried on Haytor Down could still be transported out of the area, using the surviving section of the tramway for the initial stage of the journey.

At this point in time, apart from what had already been achieved by the promoters, it was clear that, locally, enthusiasm for the proposed railway had reached an all-time high. Indeed, the townspeople of Bovey Tracey had already indicated this fact by setting aside an entire day (Tuesday, 1st July) on which to celebrate the then imminent passing of the Act; celebrations which had included the flying of flags, music being provided by the town's brass band, bell-ringing and an open-air tea for around 500 people. However, over the ensuing weeks it soon became apparent that this enthusiasm meant very little when it came to the more serious business of subscribing for shares. Instead, in November, when the interest became payable on a loan of £8,500 taken out to pay the parliamentary deposit, the company's finances were in such a parlous state that the directors had to dig into their own pockets and negotiate a temporary loan from the South Devon Railway Company. The second half-yearly meeting of the shareholders was also notable for its lack of support, but behind the scenes the promoters were already working in collaboration with the South Devon Railway Company to try to devise a means of raising a sum of £25,000, the amount still needed before work could commence on the construction of the line. Ultimately, this led to supplementary Heads of Arrangement being agreed upon between the two companies during a specially convened conference held in London on 23rd March 1863, which were recorded in the form of a memorandum; this included mention of the fact that it was 'Proposed that with consent of the Ordinary Moreton Shareholders the South Devon shall guarantee that in addition to the dividends on the Ordinary shares any deficiency not exceeding 5 per cent per annum upon an amount of £25,000 shall be paid by the South Devon Company, the South Devon taking the whole of the rebates'. The guarantee mentioned was also 'conditional on the sanction by the South Devon Shareholders', which resulted in 'Special Meetings' being held on consecutive days at the end of May in order to obtain formal approval by the shareholders of both companies to the proposed arrangement. That achieved, the promoters were then able to concentrate their efforts on making final arrangements for work to be started on the construction of the line, and on 10th August the first sod was finally cut, a ceremony performed on Bovey Heath by William Crosley in his official capacity as the engineer and manager for Messrs Brassey & Ogilvie, the contractors.

According to a contemporary report 'the works were [then] vigorously commenced', and would, in the opinion of the directors, be completed in about eighteen months. In the event, this timescale was somewhat over-optimistic due, in no small part, to local people being slow to subscribe and thereby causing the company to run into more financial difficulties. These, in fact, became so dire that in the autumn of 1864 work on

Figure 1.3: *View from the Pound, Lustleigh, with the newly formed railway cutting in the background.*
(Courtesy Lustleigh Community Archive)

constructing the 12¼-mile-long broad-gauge line actually stopped for
a short while – because of 'the inability of the Company to meet their
engagements with the Contractors'. Only after new Heads of Arrangement
had been agreed upon in December 'for the disposition of the Special
Shares [the 'guaranteed' shares referred to in the memorandum dated
23rd March 1863, mentioned earlier] and the general settlement of the
Company's affairs' did the work resume. By then discussions were taking
place concerning the possibility of extending the line to Chagford, but,
despite surveys having been undertaken, nothing further was to become
of the matter. Instead, the promoters knew only too well that they had
to direct all available resources towards getting their line completed to
Moretonhampstead, which was proving to be difficult enough in itself.
Although there was little in the way of major engineering works, the
contractors were also experiencing unforeseen problems, one of which
had been delays in starting work between Newton Abbot and Bovey
Heath due to difficulties in establishing the Duke of Somerset's legal title
to the land required from him. In addition, they had been obliged to
make a long diversion of the road on Bovey Heath in order to pacify
the landowners, the Enclosure Commissioners, and, to the south of
Lustleigh, Yeo Farm became a casualty of the railway due to the lie of the
land and the extremely hard nature of the rock in the locality rendering
it impossible to make a deviation. The contractors also ran into one or
two other unexpected problems. These included having to make a deep
cutting at Caseley Hill rather than curve round its outer slope – because
the curve was condemned as dangerous on so steep a gradient – and also
having to contend with very wet weather during the winter of 1864/65
followed by an even wetter, and stormier, winter in 1865/66, which led
to flooding at Teignbridge and part of an embankment being washed
away; this then had to be restored with larger flood openings.

The construction of the line also caused a few problems among some
of the indigenous population, especially in the Lustleigh area where there
was a large concentration of navvies. For example, in his book *Small
Talk at Wreyland*, Cecil Torr states the following:

> The navvies made things unpleasant here, while the line was building.
> My grandfather writes to my father on 17 November 1864: 'More than
> a hundred discharged on Monday, and a pretty row there was: drunk
> altogether, and fighting altogether, except one couple fought in the

meadows for an hour and got badly served, I hear. The same night the villains stole all poor old *****'s fowls. He had them under lock and key, but they broke in and took the whole, young and old ... There is not a fowl or egg to be got hereabout.' Writing on 29 March 1865, he describes a visit from a drunken navvy the day before –'about as fine a built tall likely a fellow as you ever saw, and nicknamed the Bulldog.' He asked for meat and drink, and was sent empty away. 'I learnt that he worked Saturday and Monday, and received 5s. 6d. for the two days, slept in a barn and spent all his earnings at the public house ... Not long after I saw the policeman who belongs to the line – not the Lustleigh man – and he said, "If anything of the kind occurs again, send for me, and I will soon put all right." But he spends all his time on the line keeping the navvies in order; and before he can be got mischief may be done.' One of the dogs here had been poisoned by meat thrown her by a navvy, 22 September 1864. After that, he kept a revolver.

Despite the various difficulties described above, the engineering work and the laying of the permanent way was almost complete by the early spring of 1866. In addition, having obtained the plans from Peter Margary, the contractors had commenced work on the construction of the platform walls and station foundations at Bovey, Lustleigh and Moretonhampstead, and were now reported to be making good progress. The directors, meanwhile, had accepted a tender from Messrs Call & Pethick of Plymouth for erecting the station buildings above the level of the platforms at a cost of £3,136. Earlier in the year the directors had also made arrangements for other matters to receive attention, such as the installation of the telegraph wires and signals, and were now hoping that the line could be opened to passenger traffic towards the end of May. Indeed, with this in mind, it was not long before they instructed the company secretary to send a preliminary notice to the railway department of the Board of Trade, stating that it was the company's intention 'to open for the public conveyance of Passengers after the expiration of one Calendar month from this date [26th April 1866] their Railway ...'.

It soon became apparent, however, that the proposed opening date could not be met, due to the work on completing the line taking a little longer than at first anticipated. As a result, the required Board of Trade inspection had to be deferred, and it was not until 20th June that the matter arose again. Then the company secretary was instructed to send another letter, giving notice 'that in the opinion of the Moretonhampstead and South Devon Railway Company their Railway … will on the Second day of July next be sufficiently completed for the safe conveyance of Passengers, and is now ready for inspection'. In the meantime, at least two trains were reported to have passed over the entire length of the line, for testing purposes and for the benefit of the local press, and the directors, rather than await the outcome of the Board of Trade inspection, had publicly announced their intention to hold an official opening ceremony on 26th June. Although it is no more than pure conjecture, the reason for this apparent lack of patience appears to have been that the directors, no doubt eagerly awaiting the first traffic receipts in order to ease the company's financial position, wanted to dispense with the formalities as soon as possible. In this way a public service could then be instigated immediately after the line had passed its inspection. Whatever, both the company and the inhabitants of Moretonhampstead were now busy making preparations for the event, which was to be celebrated with a local public holiday.

On the opening day a special train carrying the directors of the Moretonhampstead & South Devon Railway Company, together with others involved in the promotion and construction of the line, left Newton Abbot Station at 11.15 a.m. – amid the sound of loud cheers from an enthusiastic crowd that had gathered there. More of the same followed at Bovey and Lustleigh, as well as at other vantage points along the line, and, when the train reached Moretonhampstead (just before 12 noon), it was reported that over a thousand people had gathered there to await its arrival, many of them having come into the town from neighbouring parishes. The directors, on alighting from the train, were then formally welcomed, an address was read and, after that, they went into what was a well-decorated town to attend a pre-arranged luncheon for some 200 people, during which further speeches followed, along with numerous toasts. The day's celebrations also included a public tea for women and children, refreshments being provided for the men and various sports taking place, and it was subsequently reported that 'In every respect the holiday passed off well and the inhabitants of Moreton will for many years to come regard the 26th of June, 1866, as a red-letter day in their existence'.

There were no such demonstrations at Bovey Tracey as it was proposed to await the opening of a new town hall at the end of July and then to celebrate the opening of the railway at the same time. Demonstrations did, however, take place at Lustleigh – although not until 31st July. Then, after having been arranged by Thomas Wills and several other local farmers and landowners, two fields adjoining the station were 'set apart for rural sports of all kinds, which were indulged in by a large number of persons of both sexes', a specially-prepared luncheon was held in two marquees for the villagers and, later, a tea was provided for 'all-comers'. These included visitors arriving in trains from Moretonhampstead and Bovey Tracey, 'who prolonged the festivities until a late hour'.

Almost before the last cheers from the opening day celebrations had subsided Colonel N. Yolland arrived to carry out the official inspection of the line on behalf of the Board of Trade. This actually commenced on the very next day (Wednesday, 27th June) and just one day later the inspector was able to submit a written report to the Board, which included a recommendation that the opening of the line be sanctioned as soon as the turntable at Moretonhampstead was in working order. Then, over the weekend, the company received official notification from the Board authorising the opening of the line for public traffic, subject to the same proviso as mentioned by the Inspector. By that time the turntable in question had already been put into working order and, had it not been too late to publicise the fact, the public timetable could have been brought into operation on the following Monday, as originally contemplated. As it was, the decision was made by the company to place advertisements in the local newspapers as quickly as possible, these stating that the railway would be opened for passenger traffic on Wednesday, 4th July and accompanied by a timetable showing that there would be three trains running in each direction on weekdays and two on Sundays.

Unlike the excitement and celebrations of the previous week, the first day of the public service proved to be a rather low-key affair, although it was reported that 'the whole of the carriages of the first train, the 9.50 am [from Moretonhampstead] were full and at every station large wondering crowds were gathered to witness the arrival of the train'. Meanwhile, although the line was now at long last open for passenger traffic, there was still much to be done. For a start, there was a need to attend to additional requirements being demanded by some of the landowners from whom land had been purchased for the railway, such as extra accommodation works, and even to arrange for the completion of legal formalities in one or two instances. However, the main priority of the directors at this time was, undoubtedly, arranging for the station buildings to be completed, which, at Bovey and Moretonhampstead, included substantial goods sheds so that goods services could be introduced. As this work continued over the ensuing weeks, ultimately leading to the introduction of goods services on 8th October, the single junction with the main line of the South Devon Railway at Newton Abbot was necessarily replaced by a recommended double junction, and arrangements were also put in hand for the provision of a siding near the Bovey Pottery. According to the Duke of Somerset, 'Haytor Granite Quarry was now being worked' and, in consequence, he had demanded that the company should fulfil its obligations by constructing and maintaining a siding and crane near the point at which the tramway diverged away from the railway; this was duly carried out to completion either towards the end of the year or in the early part of 1867. When completed, the siding became known as Bovey Granite Siding or, in its shortened version, as Granite Siding.

Almost concurrently with the duke's demand, a request for another siding was made by John Divett, of the Bovey Pottery. In this instance, he advised the company that he 'was desirous of having a siding into the Potteries', so that completed earthenware products could be despatched direct by rail. During the discussions that followed, including working arrangements being agreed with the South Devon Railway Company, John Divett also managed to persuade his fellow directors to make a contribution of £175 out of company funds towards the installation costs of the siding. It was then opened a few months later than its nearby counterpart and was known as Bovey Pottery Siding – more often referred to as simply Pottery Siding.

During the summer of 1867 the company received another approach from the Duke of Somerset, requesting that a station should be built at Teigngrace. Once again discussions followed, and it was agreed that the construction costs, estimated at £200, 'would be paid for out of Special Shares to be subscribed for by the Duke of Somerset and others in the neighbourhood'. The work then commenced shortly afterwards and was completed in time for the station to be opened on 16th December of the same year. By then the company had already received a request for another station to be erected. On this occasion it had come from a representative of the inhabitants of Chudleigh, who wanted a station at Jews Bridge (the name of a bridge over the River Bovey on the turnpike road between

Plymouth and Exeter, situated just to the north of the railway line in the vicinity of what would later become known as Heathfield). However, after leaving the matter in abeyance for around six months, until being pressed for a decision, the directors resolved to instruct the Company Secretary to inform the representative of the Chudleigh inhabitants 'that the Board had given the matter careful consideration but were not prepared at present to undertake the cost'.

This negative response was, without doubt, attributable to the company's ongoing financial problems. These, in fact, were highlighted during a meeting held on 16th April 1868 when the company's solicitor, Mr Whitehead, submitted a 'rough estimate' showing that the outstanding liabilities of the company amounted to £26,980. 4s. 10d. and the assets to £10,930. Moreover, the estimate also revealed that there was a deficiency of income to meet the annual charges of £627, so from this it was clear that the railway was not proving to be the financial success that the directors had originally anticipated. In part, at least, this was due to outside influences and their effect on traffic receipts, as explained in the following extract from the Directors' Report that had been submitted to the twelfth half-yearly general meeting of the shareholders held on 28th February 1868:

> A slight decrease is shewn in the amount of receipts [£2,167. 10s. 11d.], as compared with the corresponding period of the previous year, but this reduction is not more than may be accounted for by the falling off of Tourist and pleasure Traffic occasioned by the Paris Exhibition, and the continued Commercial depression by which the Railway Interest generally has been so much affected.

At this meeting in February, however, some of the shareholders had put forward other views on why the traffic receipts had decreased and, essentially, blamed what they considered to be inadequate and poorly scheduled train services. In fact, one of the shareholders had even presented a memorandum to the Earl of Devon, setting out his observations and thoughts on the matter with the request that he lay it before the directors of the South Devon Railway Company. However, in essence, it failed to achieve the desired effect except that during the following year the South Devon Railway Company finally adopted one of the suggestions by providing an early morning train on all weekdays rather than just on Tuesdays and Wednesdays. In the meantime, the traffic receipts were still showing little sign of improvement, remaining at around the rate of £4,000 per annum, of which sum, of course, 50 per cent was retained by the South Devon Railway Company for working the line. Furthermore, this was to remain the pattern until eventually, with the company's financial position still deteriorating, albeit only marginally, the Earl of Devon entered into negotiations with the Chairman and Secretary of the South Devon Railway Company on the subject of amalgamating the two companies. This was at the beginning of 1871, and, after prolonged negotiations and obtaining the approval of both sets of shareholders to the terms proposed, the two companies were formally amalgamated on 1st July 1872. As a result, the Moretonhampstead line became part of the South Devon Railway system. However, this was to prove a somewhat short-lived situation, as less than four years later, on 1st February 1876, the South Devon Railway Company was itself absorbed by the Great Western Railway Company (GWR), prior to the two companies being formally amalgamated on 1st August 1878. During this relatively brief period there were few noticeable changes, certainly from an operating point of view, but one significant development was the construction of the long-awaited station near Jews Bridge: this was opened as Chudleigh Road Station on 1st July 1874, but was to be renamed Heathfield Station on 1st October 1882 immediately prior to it becoming the junction for the Teign Valley Railway.

Initially, in what effectively was the beginning of a new era for the line, no major changes were made, and the train service continued to consist of just four trains in each direction on weekdays and two on Sundays. As before, no separate goods trains were provided beyond Bovey – all goods traffic between there and Moretonhampstead was attached to the aforementioned services as and when required – and the locomotives employed to haul the familiar six-wheeled coaches of the day were almost certainly confined exclusively to the same Daniel Gooch-designed 4-4-0 saddle tanks that the South Devon Railway Company had probably been relying on ever since the line opened.

Over the course of the next five years or so there is little to record except that the GWR gradually began introducing different types of locomotives to the branch and some attempt was made to improve the level of service by an extra afternoon working being added to the summer timetable, an arrangement that took effect in 1877. However, in 1882, the year during which the daily goods train eventually started covering the entire length of the line, came the first major event of historical importance for the branch under GWR ownership – the opening, on 9th October, of the independently owned Teign Valley Railway; this was a standard-gauge line that ran from Heathfield to Ashton before continuing, as a goods siding, to Teign House (Christow). After that, apart from the installation of a private siding for Candy & Co. on the western side of the line at Heathfield in April 1888 – to serve the rather grandiosely named Great Western Pottery Brick and Tile Works (opened in 1874) – the only change of any significance to occur over the next ten years was when all the remaining broad-gauge lines west of Exeter were converted to standard gauge over the momentous weekend of 21st/22nd May 1892. Up until then the broad-gauge Moretonhampstead line and the standard-gauge Teign Valley Railway merely existed side by side with no physical connection between them, and goods had to be laboriously transhipped from wagon to wagon. However, the standardisation of the gauge now presented an opportunity for the two lines to be connected, and during the following year this was finally done. Meanwhile, elsehere

Figure 1.4: *Moretonhampstead Station 1865/1875.*
(Courtesy of Bovey Tracey Heritage Centre)

along the Moretonhampstead branch the gauge conversion produced no appreciable changes, both as regards the layout at each of the other four stations and the train service on offer. It did, however, lead to the introduction of an increasing variety of locomotives and rolling stock over the ensuing years, although initially the typical motive power for passenger and goods workings alike was provided by 0-6-0 saddle tanks.

By now, of course, the branch had become well established and not only were the levels of passenger traffic improving as the result of more and more visitors becoming aware of the attractions of Dartmoor and its many picturesque villages, but also the amount of freight being carried over the line. Coal formed the bulk of the incoming goods traffic, while outward goods traffic included frequent consignments of timber from the surrounding woodlands, cattle (particularly from Moretonhampstead), large hampers of rabbits and farm produce, as well as general merchandise of widely varying types from such sources as the Bovey Pottery and the Great Western Pottery Brick and Tile Works at Heathfield. Increasing amounts of ball clay were now also being transported out of the area by rail and, in 1893, the loading facilities that already existed at Heathfield and Teigngrace for this commodity were supplemented by the opening of a purpose-built siding at Teignbridge; the result of an Agreement made between the GWR and Mr William Herbert Whiteway-Wilkinson of Whiteway & Co.

The opening of the clay siding at Teignbridge was to be the last item of note in the history of the line until the end of Queen Victoria's reign in 1901. It had certainly been a chequered history, but most of what the directors of the Moretonhampstead & South Devon Railway Company had set out to achieve had come to fruition, albeit over a much longer timescale than anticipated. For the indigenous population, life had been transformed for many and, like it or not, they had become part of a new era.

References

Harris, H., 1994. *The Haytor Granite Tramway and Stover Canal*. Newton Abbot: Peninsula Press.

Kingdom, A.R. and Lang, M., 2004. *The Newton Abbot to Moretonhampstead Railway*. Newton Abbot: ARK Publications (Railways).

Minutes of meetings of the Newton & Moretonhampstead Railway Committee and of the provisional directors/directors of the Moretonhampstead and South Devon Railway Company.

Pomroy, L.W., 1995. *The Heathfield to Exeter (Teign Valley) Railway.* Newton Abbot: ARK Publications (Railways).

Reports from the half-yearly meetings of the shareholders of the Moretonhampstead and South Devon Railway Company.

St John Thomas, D., 1981. *A Regional History of the Railways of Great Britain – Volume 1: The West Country.* Newton Abbot: David & Charles.

The Book of Reference (Landowners).

The Moretonhampstead and South Devon Railway Act, 1862.

The Prospectus issued by the Moretonhampstead and South Devon Railway Company.

Torr, C., 1996. *Small Talk at Wreyland.* Newton Abbot: Forest Publishing.

Various newspaper/magazine articles.

2.   Eastern Dartmoor in the Victorian guidebook and newspaper

Peter F. Mason

Regarded as a mountain district, Dartmoor is one of the dullest and dreariest uplands of any extent in Great Britain; ... In describing Dartmoor it is customary to generalize freely on its 'sternness', 'sublimity', and 'poetic delight.' If long lines of bare hill, scarcely undulating as much as a league-long roller of the Atlantic, fitly illustrate sternness, then Dartmoor is stern; if peat-bog, partly covered with cotton-grass vegetation, be sublime, then Dartmoor is sublime; and, lastly, if floundering about for several successive hours in an alternation of ruts, morasses, and scrub heather represent 'poetic delight', we obtain that feeling to perfection on Dartmoor. Otherwise it is what we have described it to be – in itself the quintessence of unlovely dreariness ...

However the writer of this guide book goes on to talk about the river valleys on Dartmoor's fringes which are 'scenes of beauty formed by cultivated peninsulas of land thrust into its bosom'.[1]

Until the second half of the eighteenth century Dartmoor was somewhere to be shunned. Well known to miners and to Devon farmers who pastured their sheep and cattle on the moor in summer months, the moor was a place to be avoided by everyone else.[2] In the sixteenth century William Camden called it 'squallida Montana Dertmore'.[3] Richard Gough in the eighteenth century, writes of 'the dreary mountainous tract ... Dertmore' and for a long time 'dreary' becomes a key word in the Dartmoor writers' vocabulary.[4]

The Reverend Richard Warner was an early visitor to the eastern fringes of Dartmoor. In 1799 he made a journey from his home in Bath through Somerset and Devon. Having visited the North Devon coast he travelled to Lydford and Okehampton before visiting Chagford and Moretonhampstead. With the assistance of a guide, who he engaged at Chagford, he found his way from Moretonhampstead to Bovey Tracey:

> Our route ... conducted us along a true Devonshire Road, running between high banks and canopied over-head by the trees that intermingle their branches from the opposite sides. Gateway or accidental aperture in the hedges, let in the surrounding country and afforded us a view of the lofty hills to the left, and the rich valley to the right which accompanied our progress. At Bovey Tracey I had intended to sleep, and therefore parted with Spindle [his guide] as soon as the town was in view; but the wretched appearance of the village, and the melancholy exterior of two hovels which the people of the place called inns, determined me to proceed to Chudleigh, in spite of rain and darkness.[5]

The author of a guide published in 1851 cautiously advised the visitor to stay at the Union Inn in Bovey Tracey (or South Bovey as it was sometimes called at the time) 'where a man may "rough" it'.[6] Warner was not the only visitor to the eastern fringes of Dartmoor to use a guide. In the 1840s a guide was recommended if the visitor wanted to extend a walk to Widecombe via Haytor and on to Becky Falls as the route 'over the open down ... is somewhat perplexing'.[7] The most famous of the guides was James Perrott of Chagford who placed the first of the Dartmoor 'letterboxes' at Cranmere Pool (in his case a jar) in the 1850s. He ran a successful business in Chagford making fishing tackle, supplying carriages and guiding visitors not only onto the moor itself but also to nearby places of interest such as Gidleigh Park, Spinsters Rock and Fingle Gorge. Among those that he guided were Charles Dickens, Charles Kingsley and R.D. Blackmore.[8] As late as 1889 the author of another guide suggested that tourists should use a guide to take them from Chagford to Fingle Bridge.[9] However, Perrott was not the only guide. Throughout most of the nineteenth century there are examples of visitors being led by guides.

The Reverend Edward Giddy from Cornwall was another early visitor to eastern Dartmoor. He travelled through the area sometime between 1812 and 1817 and wrote the following in his journal:

> Beyond Bovey Tracey the country becomes very hilly; and the scenery is
> extremely picturesque and romantic. The Hills inclose [*sic*] long winding
> vallies [*sic*], their sides frequently covered with woods, and their
> summits crowned with rocks. The fields are at various places thickly
> strewed with blocks of granite. The road leading to Moreton-Hampstead
> affords a great variety of beautiful scenery, it is carried through a fertile
> valley, inclosed [*sic*] with a succession of rocks and woods with a few
> breaks which open towards the downs. This road has of late been much
> improved, and the ride from Bovey Tracey to Moreton-Hampstead has
> been pronounced by some persons to be the finest in the county, it is
> about seven miles in length.[10]

His mention of the road having been improved refers to work that
was done by the Moretonhampstead Turnpike Trust at that time. The
artist Francis Stevens, who had settled in Exeter in 1817, visited eastern
Dartmoor on 5th and 6th July 1819. He wrote the following about his
visit:

> Went from Moreton to Lus[t]leigh Cleve found it much more beautiful
> than the description given to me. The day was remarkably fine for
> effects and the colouring good and mellow. Lustleigh Cleve is one of the
> places strangers ought to see when they visit Devon Shire – the whole
> valley from North Bovey is worth exploring and there are many points
> … worth studies which I have not drawn or sketched. Moreton should
> be the point of [departure] or the village of Manaton or North Bovey.[11]

One of the earliest guide books to the area, published in 1826, was
written under the pseudonym of 'A Devonian' by T.H. Williams. The
writer describes the bracing air that will be enjoyed when Haytor has
been reached by way of the granite railway. From there the visitor is
advised to visit 'the romantic spot' at Becky Falls and return to Bovey
Tracey, through the Bovey Valley. For this journey the writer suggests
that:

> it is *possible* for a car or gig to pass from Manaton to South Bovey,
> but horses, particularly those of a small hardy breed, accustomed to the

part, would ensure safety, even in such a descent as from this point to Becky bridge.[12]

These are examples of how the area was perceived at the time when Victoria came to the throne in 1837. It was only in the 1840s that tourist guide books which we would recognise as such became widely available and it was no coincidence that they began to appear at this time. The first through train reached Exeter on 1st May 1844 and the railway network was extended to Dartmoor in the coming years. The impact this had on accessibility to Devon is illustrated by Cecil Torr writing in *Small Talk at Wreyland* about contrasting journeys made by his grandfather from London to Exeter. In 1841 the journey by coach had taken him eighteen hours. Just five years later the journey made by express train took him only four and a half hours.[13]

This was a time of change and the beginning of the opening up of Dartmoor. On 22nd June 1841 Cecil Torr's grandfather wrote that:

> Moreton, they say, is all alive: there are three vehicles they call Omnibusses. Wills goes from Exeter (through Moreton) to Plymouth, Waldron and Croot to Exeter and Newton ... All grades appear to go by this means, even the farmers go instead of horseback.[14]

Henry Besley published his *Route Book of Devon* in c.1845 and the first edition of Murray's *Handbook for Travellers in Devon and Cornwall* was published in 1851. Interestingly Murray's *Handbook for Travellers in Northern Italy* had been published nine years earlier. The author of Murray's guide described Dartmoor in poetic terms and particularly recommended the valleys on the fringes of the moor:

> the barren and elevated moors ... delight the eye by wild and imposing prospects ... For those who relish less cultivated scenes, Dartmoor presents a waste of rock-capped heights and dark morasses, most truly forlorn and wild. But the tints of the moor are of surpassing beauty, the air most exhilarating, and the grandeur of its lonely hills calculated to impress the most apathetic tourist. The finest scenery of Devonshire is to be found [among other parts] on the skirts of Dartmoor, which on every side are pierced by deep romantic glens, leading to a desolation, but clothed themselves with golden gorse and oaks.[15]

In 1883, Richard Nicholls Worth wrote that 'there are no fresher and greener nooks in all England than some of these border valleys where nestle, quaint and grey, amid their cluster of trees, not a few ancient homesteads'.[16] In 1827 and 1828, Samuel Rowe, vicar of Crediton, historian and antiquarian, travelled extensively around Dartmoor conducting research that was to lead to the publication of *A Perambulation of Dartmoor* in 1848. Travelling west from Dunsford he described reaching the area around Moretonhampstead in glowing terms:

> Following the turnpike as it winds down the hill towards Moreton one of the finest of our moorland border landscapes expands before us. The greater portion of the amphitheatre which sweeps around the town is seen from a most favourable point of view. The huge dorsal ridge of Hamildon stretches far across the western horizon while along the Bovey vale southward the eye looks down a long drawn vista where the picturesque forms the ground and the rich variety of foliage irresistibly attract the attention and make us resolve to obtain a nearer view of this charming scene assured that they will lose nothing of their attractions on closer inspection.[17]

The railway line from Newton Abbot to Moretonhampstead opened to the public on Wednesday 4th July 1866. Prior to this, access to the area had only been on foot, horseback or by cart. In *Worth's Tourist Guide to S. Devon* published in 1878 the author writes that:

> Within living if aged memory, the only approach to Moreton was on foot or by pack-horse; and no wheeled vehicle larger than a wheelbarrow had ever been seen in the neighbourhood. Now it has a station of its own, and is a place of resort.

Surprisingly, six months after the line opened, in January 1867, a Mr Horace Waddington who was working in Exeter chose to travel to Chagford by cart, departing at five in the morning and not reaching his destination until quarter past ten in the evening, having reached Cheriton Cross at eight o'clock and then walking the rest of the way.[18] His journey would probably have been a great deal quicker if he had taken the train to Moretonhampstead, via Newton Abbot, and then hiring a carriage to complete the journey.

The principle places to stay in the area were Bovey Tracey, Moretonhampstead and Chagford. Bovey Tracey was described as 'a quiet town ... lying among pastoral scenery, but well placed for making excursions to Dartmoor'.[19] It was also described as being 'a good centre, as long or short walks will take the visitor to scenes of striking character'.[20] Baring Gould recommended the town for the view it commanded of Haytor Rocks and Dartmoor.[21]

The author of Murray's guide described Moretonhampstead as being a

> small place, situated in a wild and beautiful country on the border of Dartmoor, and swept by the purest and most invigorating breezes, is remarkable for its salubrity, which the stranger may infer from the healthful looks of the inhabitants, particularly of the women who are quite Amazons in appearance.[22]

The reference to Amazons had been dropped by the 1860s. Ward Lock thought that Moretonhampstead had 'nothing to detain'[23] the tourist, and the author of *Black's Guide* described the inhabitants of Moreton as having

> a primeval simplicity in their manners and customs, and gave way to certain little superstitions which were evidence of their exceedingly secluded lives. Even now there are few towns in England which retain more of the calm and contentment of antiquity.[24]

In 1899, Baring-Gould thought that although Moreton had 'a primitive appearance' it did have 'a look of cleanliness' and although he commented on it being the fashion to stay in Chagford, 'which has been much puffed', he thought that 'Moreton makes quite as good a headquarters for Dartmoor excursions'.[25]

By 1900, *Pearson's Gossipy Guide* was describing Moreton as 'a good place to work the moor from. It is small and primitive in character, but the coming of the railway, and its fine bracing climate, are adding to its prosperity'.

Chagford was described as being 'charmingly placed on a hill surrounded by hills, on the very verge of Dartmoor'[26] and Warden Page was very taken with the place:

Of all the towns on Dartmoor's verge, none approach Chagford in picturesque situation. Deep in the valley, yet raised on its hill above the river-mists, it nestles, having on the one hand the emerald meadows where the Teign flows onward to the wooded gorge of Fingle; on the other Milldown, Nattadon, and more distant Kestor, the vanguard of the wild Moor, shielding it from the boisterous winds which sweep across the waste.[27]

Several guide books, including Black's, describe Chagford as being: 'in summer ... a Devonshire Elysium; in winter a Devonshire hades' – a difference which is vividly expressed in the local sayings: In summer it is 'Chagford, and what d'ye think of it?' In winter, 'Chagford! Good Lord!'[28] By the beginning of the twentieth century Baring Gould was drawing attention to the fact that Chagford had become a tourist resort:

Chagford was but a moorland village, but by means of clever advertising the place, and pushing it in various ways, a former rector managed to get for it a name as a health resort, and a place suitable to holiday takers and trippers, which it has maintained and is likely to maintain.[29]

Baring Gould described North Bovey as 'a picturesque village situated high upon the confines of the Moor'[30] and Manaton was 'a beautifully situated, ... peaceful, delightful English village'[31] – 'the very picture of rural peace.[32] However, the author of Murray's guide was concerned that 'a poor public-house is the only accommodation for those who hunger and thirst'.[33] There was also accommodation at Becky Falls but this only

afforded visitors ... a table and a few chairs, and an occasional kettle of hot water, if required: therefore it behoves the picknickers to come provided with a few of the creature comforts ... to fortify against the bracing and appetising air of this moorland region.[34]

Samuel Rowe wrote the following about Lustleigh: '[the] Church is placed on the pleasant slope of one of our deepest coombs, where the most pleasant features of village scenery are happily combined'.[35] In 1894 Worth described Lustleigh as 'the most charmingly situated village in Devon'.[36] However, most early guide books had little to say about the village concentrating instead on Lustleigh Cleave which Rowe described

Figure 2.1: *Lustleigh Cleave from the Old Manaton Road.*
(Courtesy Lustleigh Community Archive.
Reproduced from a F. Frith & Co Postcard)

as being 'far-famed'[37] and another author called it 'the lion of Lustleigh'.[38] One author even went so far as to write that 'some places can boast but of one or two spots of pictorial beauty or grandeur, but here, where our mother earth appears like the oriental goddess of many breasts, nature abounds in loveliness'.[39]

Throughout the nineteenth century, guide books were recommending tourists to visit the same places many of which are still extensively visited today. Principal among these were Haytor, Lustleigh Cleave and Fingle Gorge. Others such as Bottor Rock near Hennock and Blackingstone near Moretonhampstead are less popular today. Interestingly, as early as 1851 there was concern about the numbers of people visiting Haytor. Steps had been cut into the rock and an iron hand rail added leading one writer to allude to this as 'the unsightly stair step to enable the enervated and pinguitudinous scions of humanity of this wonderful nineteenth century to gain its summit'.[40]

Bovey Tracey was a favoured place for trips around the area, 'since here, daily in summer, starts two sets of five-shilling circular coach excursions, so arranged to allow passengers from Exeter, Torquay, etc., to visit the best parts of the moor and return in the evening'.[41] In the 1880s, for example, J.L. Joll was running trips on three days a week in the summer from the Dolphin Hotel taking passengers who had arrived on the 12.16 train from Newton Abbot on Mondays through the 'Lustleigh Valley to Moreton, Blackingstone Rock, Tottiford, and Kenwick Reservoir ... via Canonteign and the Valley of the Teign. On Tuesdays to Haytor, Houndtor, Manaton, and Becky Falls'. And on Thursdays to 'Rippon Tor, Widecombe-on-the-Moor, Leusdon, Spitchwick (by kind permission of Dr Blackall), [and] Holne Bridge'. Box seats were available at an extra charge, and tea, either 'meat or plain', was provided at the Dolphin Hotel at the end of the trip.[42] A Mr Wolf Allen was also running trips from Bovey Tracey to Haytor, Becky Falls and the Teign Valley.[43]

Figure 2.2: *A coach party organised by J.L.Joll about to leave Bovey Tracey for a tour of the moor, 1880s.*
(Courtesy of Bovey Tracey Heritage Centre)

Within three years of the railway line opening, Thomas Pollard, proprietor of the White Hart Hotel in Moretonhampstead, was advertising to:

Parties availing themselves of the Cheap and other Trains to Moreton that he has Large and Small Wagonettes and other Carriages and Horses ready at the shortest notice to convey them to Cranbrook Castle, Fingle Bridge, Holy Street Chagford, Whiddon Park, Gidley Castle, Blackingstone Tor, Wooston Castle, Haytor Rocks, Becky Falls, Lustleigh Cleave, Horsham Steps, or any of the other numerous places of note in the neighbourhood of the Moor, at moderate charges.[44]

At a later date, Great Western Railway ran their own trips eight times a day in July, August and September to Haytor, Widecombe, Grimspound, Manaton and Becky Falls.[45] The first highlight on this trip were the views from Haytor: 'Three or four miles westward rises one of the most famous points of this region, Hey Tor, conspicuously crowned by the largest mass of rocks on Dartmoor … commanding a splendid panorama southwards'.[46]

Tours also took in Grimspound which was 'the most remarkable of the walled villages or "pounds" on Dartmoor'.[47] In the summer, Becky Falls, whilst providing the visitor with a scene that was 'at all times romantic and delightful', was not dramatic, the stream only being heard beneath the rocks. In winter 'the cascade' would have presented 'an imposing spectacle, thundering in volume over the steep, while icicles hang from the trees and wave in the wind which is raised by the rushing water'.[48]

Trips by coach were still in favour at the beginning of the twentieth century, as is evidenced by this quote from *Pearson's Gossipy Guide* published in 1900:

> Coaching is in high favour in Devon, because of the contour of the country and the charm of Devonshire lanes. These coaching trips wind in and out of highways and byways with never-ending variety, taking the visitor over hill and dale, by riverside, woodland, and rugged Dartmoor tors, through quaint old villages, and past churches that have stood sentinels for centuries.[49]

Visitors to Manaton were recommended to climb 'the wooded rocks of Manaton Tor … for the view, opposite which will be noticed the tall pile of rocks known as Bowerman's Nose, so like a human figure that it has been taken for a druidical idol'.[50] Lustleigh Cleave was described as being 'a bold, bare ridge covered with the most picturesquely confused piles of rocks to be found within the circuit of Dartmoor'.[51] It was sometimes even suggested at the time that the distribution of the rocks was the act of giants. As early as 1840, the Cleave was being described in a national publication as 'remarkable for the romantic beauty of its scenery'[52] and, in 1852, J.G. Crocker described it in a way that was to be reflected in other guides in the Victorian era:

> Lustleigh Cleave [is] generally considered one of the most romantic spots in this mountainous region; the wide expanse of its rocky steep terminates in a wide sweeping brow, below whose highest verge may be discovered the romantic Mill of Foxworthy, surrounded by wood and a few green fields extending up the side of the adjacent hill; the long low thatched roof of the Mill might often escape observation, were it not for the blue smoke curling upward from its quiet hearth, affording the most perfect idea of solitude and seclusion. Close by Foxworthy the river Bovey forces its way over a bed of huge detached rocks, beneath which it is at one place quite lost, flowing for several hundred feet in a subterranean passage; a visit to this romantic spot, and the adjacent nook of 'Little Silver' would well repay the admirer of the picturesque in rock, wood and water.[53]

The principle target for visitors to Chagford was Fingle Gorge.

> FINGLE BRIDGE is a point no tourist should fail to visit ... The road sweeps down an embowered descent to the river, which is crossed by a narrow, time-worn bridge, covered with ivy and lichens, and supported by numerous arches. Its eddying and whirling stream is pent up between precipitous banks, which throw a peculiar shadow upon its waters, and enforce, as it were, a strange and impressive silence ... Having refreshed himself at the mill, a short distance below the bridge, where a couple of rooms are placed at the disposal of visitors, the wayfarer will proceed up the Teign, passing between some formidable crags, and winding with the sinuous course of the river, to the LOGAN, or ROLLING STONE.[54]

Figure 2.3: *Fingle Mill, River Teign, c1880*. Stereoscopic Gems, English Scenery (Courtesy Tom Greeves)

Warden Page was another writer to wax lyrical about the Fingle Gorge:

What a lovely spot it is! How clear the rushing waters gliding between the three grey arches! How rich in colouring have the lichens and ferns rendered its hoary walls! and, whether we look up-stream to the hills, softly meeting one another with foliage changing from bright green in the foreground to misty blue in the distance, or downward to where the old mill, with its moss-grown water-wheel, nestles beneath the woods, and Prestonbury rises mountainous over all, we shall confess that a scene of greater beauty it has never been our lot to view.[55]

Just as it is a popular spot for picnics today, so it was in Victorian times:

This is a great place for Pic-Nics [*sic*], indeed it is a pretty sure 'find' on any day from the middle of May to the middle of August. We were there in July and found two Pic-Nics going on at once to the tune of a hideous German band the winding of whose melodious (?) horns was far more out of place, if not quite so unbearable as in those would-be quiet streets whence the magic of Brass' is driving them. Some premonitory drops had been warning of what to expect, and very shortly the rain came down in torrents, and we were fain to seek shelter with the dripping Pic-Nicers [*sic*] and draggle-tailed musicians in the picturesque old mill that lies below the bridge. The Pic-Nicers, though damp, were affable and most kindly insisted on our drinking several glasses of their sherry.[56]

The popularity of the area led to a proposal by the Excter, Teign Valley and Chagford Railway Company to create a railway line from the Teign Valley to Chagford through the Fingle Gorge:

affording direct railway communication with Chagford, Fingal [*sic*] Bridge, and the romantic scenery of the District, which is rapidly coming into popularity as an important health and pleasure resort ... The connection with the existing Teign Valley line will have the effect of placing Chagford within easy reach of Torquay and other South Devon watering places, and there can be no doubt that Chagford, with its mild bracing moorland air, and its abundant natural attractions, with direct access by Railway from the south and east, will rapidly increase in importance, and develop a considerable traffic ... Fingal Bridge is now resorted to by great numbers of holiday makers in the summer time, and the traffic in this season to this spot when the line is open will doubtless be greatly increased.[57]

Whilst in the area the visitor was also recommended to visit Spinster's Rock, Cranbrook Castle and 'the Celtic camps of Wooston and Prestonbury'.[58] Gidleigh Castle and the surrounding antiquities were also on the menu. Gidleigh Park was described by Baring Gould as 'a most romantic domain – the very sovereignty of the Fairy Queen – where the Teign rushes over rock and crag, and, swollen by the waters of the Wallabrook, rolls majestically through shadowy hollows'.[59] All the guide books recommended the visitor not to miss Holy Street Mill which was repeatedly painted by artists. The adventurous tourist would also be guided to Cranmere Pool by Perrott or another guide. As the author of Worth's *Guide* advised: 'This is one of the most desolate spots in all of England. It will not be advisable to undertake the search without a guide – easily procured at Chagford – for the pool is environed by bogs'.[60]

Just as they do today, newspapers in the Victorian era carried articles featuring places to visit. As early as 1861 an Irish newspaper was singing the praises of the south eastern corner of Dartmoor:

> The prettiest scene in all England – and if I am contradicted that assertion, will say all Europe – is in Devonshire, on the southern and south eastern skirts of Dartmoor, where the rivers Dart and Avon and Teign form themselves, and where the broken moor is half cultivated, and the, wild looking upland fields are half moor.[61]

The *Western Times* was enthusiastic about the railway line to Moretonhampstead when it opened in 1866:

> Thence it enters the picturesque valley leading to Lustleigh Cleeve [*sic*] and Becky Falls – beloved of artists. As it advances, it develops to view romantic moorland scenery – beautiful as the fancy can imagine – for which Moreton is famous in these parts. It halts, for the present, in the heart of this glorious scenery near Moreton, and it must be confessed that no tourist in lovely Devon will have seen the choicest of its beauties who fails to make acquaintance with the route of the Moretonhampstead and South Devon Railway.[62]

By 1869 the newspaper was also suggesting that Lustleigh was taking its place in the wider world:

> This old fashioned village which has been isolated from the world for centuries, is, thanks to an enterprising public and the Railway Company, just emerging into life again. It still retains its ardent and romantic appearance, but nature having lavished upon its suburbs inimitable grandeur, especially at the Cleeve [*sic*], numerous visitors resort thither during the summer season to enjoy it's [*sic*] refreshing breezes and a pleasant day's outing.[63]

By 1886 'many thousands' had visited Lustleigh Cleeve and the area was being promoted in newspapers across the country. In 'Rambles About Dartmoor' in the *Gloucester Journal*, for example, the author writes about the area and recommends that:

When, weary with the world of busy men and busy life, the poor jaded mind seeks perfect change, we know of a place where you may get thoroughly away from the world in the region of Dartmoor ... From Newton Abbot Station, a point easily reached from almost any part of the land by Great Western and South Devon Railway, we took the branch line for Moreton – the town in the moor – passing through the charming scenery around Bovey Tracy and Lustleigh, with its magnificent 'Cleave'. Many tourists take their quarters here, whence the wild yet beautiful scenery of Manaton and Becky Fall is easily reached; but we preferred journeying some four miles to Chagford, which forms an advantageous centre for the country on this edge of the moor. Hotels and lodging-houses at moderate charges are to be found in this quaint little town of some 1600 inhabitants, with its white-washed cottages and green wooden market-house in the centre.[64]

In 1873 the author of an article in the *London Evening Standard* wrote that:

It is only of late years that the wild district of Dartmoor, with its picturesque border country, has become much known even to English travellers and tourists ... although railways have produced their usual effects, and although many a once primitive village at the foot of the highland is alive in summer with a population 'not its own,' it may well

Figure 2.4: *Visitors picnicking on Haytor, 1865/1875.*
(Courtesy of Bovey Tracey Heritage Centre)

be doubted whether, except in some special corners, the district is much better known now than it was thirty years since.[65]

The writer goes on to recommend the visitor spends time exploring the valleys around the edge of the moor including Lustleigh Cleave and in 1871 the *Burnley Gazette* was another paper to recommend the Cleave as a place to visit when in Devon.[66]

In 1885 the *Pall Mall Gazette* was recommending Chagford as a destination:

> While jaded Londoners are panting in the heat crowded streets, there lies nestling under the granite tors of Dartmoor a cool and breezy village where the life giving air from the moors brings back the colour to the worn faces of those wanderers who by lucky chance or more fortunate design, have already taken up their quarter there.[67]

As the nineteenth century came to an end the United Devon Association was formed 'for the purpose of improving the accommodation and facilities of the county of Devon as a place of residence and as a touring ground'.[68] Dartmoor was no longer a place to be shunned and, in the words of the author of the United Devon Association guide:

> No county in England other than Devonshire can boast of such a region as Dartmoor ... it comprises within its limits the most grand and sublime scenery, and offers a field wherein a vast variety of tastes may be gratified such as is rarely to be found.[69]

It is worth finishing with the words of the 'Gentleman' who undertook a walking tour of Dartmoor in 1864:

> It is a surprising thing that so few Englishmen, comparatively speaking, appreciate the beautiful scenery of their native land ... Why go to Switzerland at no small expense, and hazard your lives, and put yourself to no inconsiderable inconvenience for the sake of seeing sunrise from the peak of an almost inaccessible mountain? ... Have you been to Westmoreland? No! Land's End? No! The Highlands? No! Up Snowdon? No! Down the Dart? Though Wales? Over Dartmoor? No, no, no! Well then, take my advice and try some of these places ... Four days is hardly

enough to 'do' Dartmoor thoroughly and we found ourselves obliged to leave many interesting spots unvisited. But a week will give a good walker ample time to do justice to all that is worth seeing on the Moor, and the pure bracing air will invigorate his frame in a marvellous manner.[70]

Notes

1. Baddeley, M.J.B. and Ward, C.S., 1884. *South Devon and South Cornwall including Dartmoor and the Isles of Scilly.* London: Ward Lock. p.78.
2. See the history of transhumance in Devon in Fox, H., 2012. *Dartmoor's Alluring Uplands: Transhumance and Pastoral Management in the Middle Ages.* Exeter: University of Exeter Press.
3. Camden, W., 1586, 1594. *Britannia: Siva Florentis Imorum Regnorum Angliae, Scotiae, Hiberniae, et Insularum Adiacentium Exintima Antiquitate.* p.135.
4. Milton, P., 2006. *The Discovery of Dartmoor, A Wild and Wondrous Region.* Chichester: Phillimore. p.20.
5. Warner, R., 1800. *A Walk through Some of the Western Counties of England.* Bath. p.177.
6. 1851 *A Handbook for Travellers in Devon and Cornwall.* 1st ed. London: John Murray. p.56.
7. 1846 *The Route Book of Devon.* 2nd ed. p.258.
8. [Online] <http://www.legendarydartmoor.co.uk/james-perrot.htm> [Accessed 15th August 2017].
9. Warden Page, J.L., 1889. *An Exploration of Dartmoor and its Antiquities.* London: Seeley. p.179.
10. Moretonhampstead History Society (Transcribed 2015). *The Travel Journal(s) of Reverend Edward Giddy.* Cornwall Record Office, ref. X539/6.
11. Stevens, F., *Sketches of Devon scenes, 1819–23.* Devon and Exeter Institution.
12. Williams, T.H., 1827. *Devonshire Scenery, or directions for visiting the most Picturesque Spots on the Eastern or Southern Coast from Sidmouth to Plymouth.* 2nd ed. Exeter: W.C. Pollard, p.64.
13. Torr, C., 1918. *Small Talk at Wreyland.* 1st series, Cambridge: The University Press, p.69.
14. Ibid., p.70.
15. 1851 *A Handbook for Travellers in Devon and Cornwall.* 1st ed. London: John Murray. p.xliv.

16. Worth, R.N., 1886. *Tourist Guide to South Devon*. 4th ed. London: Edward Stanford. p.117.

17. Rowe, S., 1848. *A Perambulation of Dartmoor*. 2nd ed. p.145.

18. *Exeter and Plymouth Gazette*, 10th January 1867.

19. 1898. *Black's Guide to Devonshire*. 16th ed. Edinburgh: Adam & Charles Black. pp.154-155.

20. 1900. *Pearson's Gossipy Guide to South Devon*. London: C. Arthur Pearson Ltd. p.140.

21. Baring Gould, S., 1907. *Devon*. London: Methuen & Co. p.111.

22. 1851. *A Handbook for Travellers in Devon and Cornwall*. 1st ed. London: John Murray, p.72.

23. Baddeley, M.J.B. and Ward, C.S. *Guide to South Devon and South Cornwall*. 9th ed. London: Ward Lock. p.151.

24. *Black's Guide to Dorset, Devon, Cornwall*. 5th ed. Edinburgh: Adam & Charles Black. p.250.

25. Baring-Gould, S., 1899. *A Book of the West*. London: Methuen & Co. p.225.

26. Worth, R.N., 1886. *Tourist Guide to South Devon*. 4th ed. London: Edward Stanford. p.78.

27. Warden Page, J.L., 1889. *An Exploration of Dartmoor and its Antiquities*, London: Seeley. p.176.

28. Worth, R.N., 1886. *Tourist Guide to South Devon*. 4th ed. London: Edward Stanford. p.78.

29. Baring Gould, S., 1907. *Devon*. London: Methuen & Co. p.33.

30. Ibid., p.135.

31. 1913. *Dartmoor*. 5th ed, London: Ward Lock & Co. p.39.

32. Worth, R.N., 1886. *Tourist Guide to South Devon*. 4th ed. London: Edward Stanford. p.77.

33. 1865. *A Handbook for Travellers in Devon and Cornwall*. 6th ed. London: John Murray. p.122.

34. 1846. *The Route Book of Devon* 2nd ed. p.260.

35. 1848. Rowe, S., 1985. *A Perambulation of Dartmoor*. Reprint. Exeter: Devon Books. p.136.

36. Worth, R.N., 1886. *Tourist's Guide to South Devon*. London: Edward Stanford. p.76.

37. Rowe, S., 1848. *A Perambulation of Dartmoor*. 2nd ed. p.118.

38. Worth, R.N., 1886. *Tourist's Guide to South Devon*. London: Edward Stanford. p.76.

39. Halle, Fraser D., 1851. *Letters Historical and Botanical [...]*. London: Houlston & Stoneman. p.14.

40. Dr Crocker quoted in *Crossing's Guide to Dartmoor*. 1912 edition. Reprint. Newton Abbot: David & Charles. p.300.

41. 1898. *Black's Guide to Devonshire*. 16th ed. Edinburgh: Adam & Charles Black. p.154.

42. *Western Times*, 20th July 1888.

43. *Western Morning News*, 18th July 1887.

44. *Exeter and Plymouth Gazette*, 6th August 1869.

45. Baddeley, M.J.B. and Ward, C.S., 1884. *South Devon and South Cornwall including Dartmoor and the Isles of Scilly*. 9th ed. London: Ward Lock. p.151.

46. 1898. *Black's Guide to Devonshire*. 16th ed. Edinburgh: Adam & Charles Black. p.155.

47. 1865. *A Handbook for Travellers in Devon and Cornwall*. 6th ed. London: John Murray. p125.

48. Ibid., p.123.

49. 1900. *Pearson's Gossipy Guide to South Devon*. London: C. Arthur Pearson Ltd. p.xix.

50. 1898. *Black's Guide to Devonshire*. 16th ed. Edinburgh: Adam & Charles Black. p.155.

51. Worth, R.N., 1886. *Tourist Guide to South Devon*. 4th ed. London: Edward Stanford. p.76.

52. Lewis, S.L., 1840. *Topographical Dictionary of England*. London: S. Lewis & Co.

53. Crocker, Reverend J.G., 1852. *A Guide to the Eastern Escarpment of Dartmoor*. London: Kirkman & Thackray. pp.13-14.

54. 1862. *Black's Guide to the South Western Counties of England (Dorset, Devonshire, Cornwall)*. Edinburgh: Adam & Charles Black. p.200.

55. Warden Page, J.L., 1889. *An Exploration of Dartmoor and its Antiquities*. London: Seeley. p.182.

56. Butler, S., 1986. *A Gentleman's Walking Tour of Dartmoor, 1864*. Exeter: Devon Books. p.53.

57. Exeter, Teign Valley and Chagford Railway Company Prospectus issued on 31st July 1894.

58. *Dartmoor*. 8th ed. London: Ward, Lock & Co. p.69.

59. Ibid., p.70.

60. Worth, R.N., 1886. *Tourist Guide to South Devon*. 4th ed. London: Edward Stanford. pp.78–79.

61. *Kings County Chronicle*, 13th March 1861.

62. *Western Times*, 29th June, 1866.

63. *Western Times*, 25th June 1869.

64. *Gloucester Journal*, 2nd July 1870.

65. *London Evening Standard*, 22nd July 1873.

66. *Burnley Gazette*, 29th July 1871.

67. Quoted in the *Western Times*, 15th August, 1885.

68. 1899/1900. *The Fair Book of Devon*, Exeter: United Devon Association. p.3.

69. Ibid., p.38.

70. Butler S., 1986. *A Gentleman's Walking Tour of Dartmoor, 1864*. Exeter: Devon Books. p.56.

All newspaper articles cited in the notes are available at: <www.britishnewspaperarchive.co.uk> [Accessed between January 2016 and June 2017].

3   Population changes in the Wrey Valley

Clive Pearson

Introduction

The coming of the railway must have been the event that had the greatest impact on the Wrey Valley in the Victorian period. Quite remote villages, particularly at the head of the valley, were suddenly open to easy access. But other pressures, social, economic and technological must also have

Figure 3.1: *General view of Lustleigh.*
(Courtesy of Lustleigh Community Archive)

played a part in changing the character of the area. At what point and in what way did these pressures inflict change on the valley?

This essay looks at how the population of the Wrey Valley changed during the Victorian period. The findings are based on the censuses of 1841, 1861, 1881 and 1901 for Moretonhampstead and Lustleigh and 1861, 1881 and 1901 for Bovey Tracey. It looks not only at the changes in total numbers but also at how the pattern of employment and the make-up of society in the three locations changed over the period. It will raise a number of questions, mainly in the form of 'why?', but although some speculation will be indulged in, it will not provide answers. To try to do so would need detailed cross-referencing of some 15,000 entries and a wide-ranging study of social trends over the period. It sets the scene for other reports in the study which will cover some of the matters raised.

Difficulties and assumptions

The 1841 census was little more than a headcount of the various occupations. No marital status was given and descriptions of employment were often rather sketchy. Also the ages of all over 15 were rounded down to the multiple of five years below. Although not a part of this essay it would make a comparison of ages difficult. Not that it would be easy in any case. It was noted that between ten-year censuses other than 1841 the age of the same person in the same property could increase by anything between eight and thirteen years.

A big problem was the lack of consistency in the categories of employment. This occurred not only between the different districts and the different censuses but also within the same censuses. The large range of occupations presumably self-described by servants was no problem, they were easily classified. But when a census starting with a category of 'Agricultural Labourer' becomes 'Farm Labourer' and ends as 'Labourer' there is a problem. There is no distinction in the type of labourer so the only choice is to put all into the largest category, Agriculture. Similarly, different enumerators in Moretonhampstead seem to have had different ideas of what 'Independent' meant. In one census it seemed to be largely applied, but not consistently or solely, to those above what we would call retirement age who did not specify an occupation. In another it seemed to imply private means.

A separate category to include those with apparently private means has been inserted in the analyses of occupations. Although this refers to people who were not working they are an important aspect of the economic picture of the area and need to be identified separately.

Apart from this use of the description 'Independent', there are few instances of men of working age, and even beyond, not showing an occupation. There are examples of 80-year-old agricultural labourers. This raises the question of whether the entry of an occupation necessarily meant that the person was actually in that occupation at that time. There were several other individual problems where a rather arbitrary decision regarding the category to be allocated had to be made.

Lack of detailed knowledge of the time did not help. What in 1841 was the occupation MSL? What sort of establishment in 1881 was Banner House which had a manager and a cook? Possibly a hotel or hostel so Food & Lodging was assumed. What was the status of a Governess in 1841 and was it the same in 1901? And most of all, what should be made of the great majority of married women for whom no occupation was shown?

It seems probable that the wives of farmers would have been involved in the work of the farms. Accordingly they have been included in the numbers employed in agriculture. But what about the wives of agricultural labourers, tradesmen and other employed men who are not shown as having an occupation? True, several had a number of young children to care for, six or more not being uncommon. They must surely have had to contribute to the household income in some way. The censuses have nothing more to say about them.

This analysis is, therefore, far from a scientific study of population changes in the Wrey Valley. But it should give a broad impression of how the population was changing in total numbers, patterns of employment and social diversity.

Moretonhampstead

The most significant change revealed by the Mortonhampstead censuses is the reduction of almost 29 per cent in the total population between 1841 and 1861. In fact the fall was even more sudden. Of the 580 total reduction, 401 occurred in the ten years from 1851 to 1861. There was a slight recovery in numbers over the next 20 years, but a further small

Table 3.1: *Moretonhampstead Census summaries*

Classification	Code	Includes	1841	1861	1881	1901
Agriculture	Ag	Farmers, Ag Labourers/Other farm workers	414	277	239	203
Commercial	Bs	Shops and Traders not in Fl	12	23	25	30
Church	Ch	Clergy, Organist, Lay church people	4	4	4	3
Dress	Dr	Makers & sellers of Cloth/ clothing inc shoes	72	71	55	42
Food & Lodging	Fl	Bakers, Butchers, Innkeepers	25	32	49	57
Gov & Prof	Gp	Lawyers, Police, Teachers	26	20	29	37
Mining	Mn	Mining & Quarrying	10	0	1	17
Non-specific/Craft	Ns	Carpenters, Masons, Smiths, Gen Trades	85	73	109	126
Textiles	Tx	Weavers, Spinners etc	42	4	0	0
Service	Sv	Domestic Service, Laundry	161	146	155	93
Transport	Tr	Railway workers, Carriers not in other classes	3	13	17	19
Independent	In	Private means	–	17	22	40
Total			854	680	705	667
Total number in Census			2029	1449	1572	1529

drop meant that by 1901 the total was only just over 75 per cent of the 1841 figure.

What caused this? There was an agricultural recession in the 1840s and this may have thrown many agricultural labourers out of work forcing them to leave the area in search of work. But one change may be significant. In 1841 there were 42 people employed in the textile industry. Of these 29 were serge weavers, all of them women. By 1861 four people were working in textiles, none of them serge weavers. Perhaps a small-scale operation was wiped out by competition from larger firms in the towns and cities. Or perhaps the weavers thought their skills might be better rewarded in a larger town. If they were, this could have persuaded others to follow them. The question is whether the exodus was forced or voluntary.

Agriculture of course was most affected by the decline, with employment numbers falling from 414 to 277 in 1861. By 1901 the figure was less than half the 1841 total, at 203. Over that period the number of farmers fell from 60 to 35. It is not possible to judge merely from census figures whether this resulted from a shortage of labour, a reduction in demand for local produce, improved farming methods or other reasons.

Despite the fall in population, there were increases in employment in other areas. The railway brought jobs and, although coal mining disappeared, 17 men were employed in quarrying in 1901. Commercial activity rose. While enterprises such as tallow chandler and fellmongers disappeared, by 1901 there were more drapers and the appearance of ironmongers, coal merchants, a newsagent, a hairdresser and a chemist. The traditional craftsmen such as masons, blacksmiths and wheelwrights increased slightly and crafts such as plumbing, house painting and glazing appeared. But the number of thatchers reduced from eight to one. There were six men who had set themselves up in the new business of road contractor, indicating a desire to improve the infrastructure of the village. In the food and lodging sector from 1841 to 1901 the numbers employed in baking went up from two to fourteen, in grocery from none to nine and innkeepers from three to nine. Government and Professional jobs expanded with the opening of a Post Office and such new professions as insurance agent, photographer, estate agent, bank manager and even a university tutor resident in the village.

As stated above, the category 'Independent' caused a problem. In 1841 it was widely applied to men over 65, making it impossible to make any useful estimate of how many had private means. By 1901 there was a more reasonable assessment and 40 people were given this description. Many of these were still over the age of 65 and, while they may have had some savings to make them independent, it seems the majority were not wealthy. So the comparatively small number of people of substance, the limited professional class and the reduction in the number of farmers may partly explain the second most notable figure in the chart, the slump in domestic servants to only 93.

On the other hand this was still a time when quite modest households might well employ a servant. Rather than a lack of would-be employers, perhaps there was instead a lack of supply of servants. The reduction in population might suggest the latter. But the number of servants fell by 42 per cent compared with the 29 per cent fall in population, a disproportionate reduction. The figures could be used to argue either way.

The 1881 and 1901 censuses added an extra item of information, a note of disabilities suffered. In 1881 eight people were recorded as blind and one as deaf and dumb. By 1901 there was only one blind person but four were recorded as deaf and dumb and one as feeble-minded.

Moretonhampstead clearly suffered a severe recession in the 1840s and 1850s. Even though there was a slight recovery in population by 1881, it was still struggling to maintain its size at the end of the period. The problem was that apart from a few weaving and craft jobs there was no alternative to agriculture. If this industry hit trouble there would have been no option for people put out of work but to leave to find employment. This may have caused others to think that moving on would offer better prospects. Whatever the cause and effect, recovery seemed far off.

Even so the character of the village had changed by 1901. There were more shops, and professional services were becoming available. The beginning of consumerism and what we would recognise as a business community can be discerned.

Bovey Tracey

By contrast Bovey Tracey seems to have thrived during the Victorian period. An increase in employment of 34 per cent between 1861 and 1901 is pretty impressive. But the expansion was not evenly spread over the whole period and over all sectors.

Agriculture lost ninety-one jobs in the twenty years to 1881. There was also a reduction in the number employed in pottery, which is rather surprising as the arrival of the railway since the previous census may have been expected to help the industry by taking its products more quickly, and presumably more cheaply, to its markets.

Other sectors compensated for these losses so that total employment did not fall. An increase in the craft and general trades sector was largely down to more general labourers being employed and a new industry emerging, that of brickmaking, which employed 16 people. A tripling

Table 3.2: *Bovey Tracey Census summaries*

Classification	Code	Includes	1861	1881	1901
Agriculture	Ag	Farmers, Ag Labourers/Other farm workers	263	172	217
Commercial	Bs	Shops and Traders not in Fl	25	17	26
Church	Ch	Clergy, Organist, Lay church people	8	23	20
Dress	Dr	Makers & sellers of Cloth/clothing inc shoes	79	64	63
Food & Lodging	Fl	Bakers, Butchers, Innkeepers	21	49	77
Gov & Prof	Gp	Lawyers, Police, Teachers	28	32	56
Mining	Mn	Mining & Quarrying	38	7	32
Non-specific/Craft	Ns	Carpenters, Masons, Smiths, Gen Trades	111	151	174
Pottery	Tx	Working at Pottery	180	142	188
Service	Sv	Domestic Service, Laundry	112	206	223
Transport	Tr	Railway workers, Carriers not in other classes	0	10	32
Independent	In	Private means	6	10	72
Total			871	883	1180

of bakers and grocers and a doubling of innkeepers and lodging-house keepers also were seen. The large rise in the church community did not stem from a revival of religious fervour in Bovey Tracey. Rather, it was the result of a dozen Sisters of Mercy opening a home for unmarried mothers in Devon House. We must assume that with the number of Sisters in attendance their catchment area was not restricted to Bovey Tracey.

But the sector that did most to prevent a fall in employment was domestic service. The rise over 20 years was over 80 per cent and the increase was mainly made up of women. Perhaps the fall in employment in the chief industries in the village had made it necessary for more women to find work.

By 1901 agriculture was recovering, with an increase of 45 in the numbers employed in the sector. Employment in the pottery industry recovered to its 1861 level. Employment in the brick-making business had risen to 57, bringing further diversity in the work available. Almost all other sectors either maintained or expanded their size, with a large increase coming in the government and professional category. But by far the biggest proportionate rise came from those classed as independent.

In 1881 there were ten people classified as fundholders or landholders. By 1901 the number of fundholders had risen to 72. The cause of such expansion must surely be the railway. The easy access it offered would have encouraged people from the towns to come for their recreation on days out to the countryside. To those with money it must have seemed an ideal place to live, particularly to retire to. They had the benefits of a rural life yet with good access to Torquay, Newton Abbot, Exeter and even London. In effect tourism turned into colonisation.

Bovey Tracey was a prosperous place in 1901. There was an established middle class and some families of real substance. This would have created a virtuous circle, more demand for goods and services creating more employment for the providers of these. But it raises an interesting question of what it was that prevented the railway from bringing similar benefits to Moretonhampstead.

Lustleigh

The first important point to make is that at the time of these censuses Wreyland, Knowle Road and Brookfield were all under the administration of Bovey Tracey. The occupants of these areas were, therefore, included in the Bovey Tracey censuses.

In 1841 Lustleigh was greatly dependent on agriculture, with only domestic service providing a substantial other form of work. The village suffered a slump in agricultural and total employment between 1841 and 1861 but on nothing like the scale of Moretonhampstead. Domestic service was also down, but these reductions were offset to some degree by more craftsmen and clothing workers. The total population scarcely changed. Over the rest of the century agriculture declined, domestic service and the total population increased, but the nature of the village changed.

The number of under-fourteens shown under 'No occupation' rose between 1841 and 1881 from 82 to 118. This may show a rise in the birth rate, or perhaps a fall in infant mortality, but this is not the only reason. In 1841, nine 10-year-old boys were being employed as agricultural

Table 3.3: *Lustleigh Census summaries – occupations*

Classification	Code	Includes	1841	1861	1881	1901
Agriculture	Ag	Farmers, Ag Labourers/Other farm workers	96	86	70	67
Commercial	Bs	Shops and Traders not in Fl	1	1	2	2
Church	Ch	Clergy, Organist, Lay church people	2	1	2	1
Dress	Dr	Makers & sellers of Cloth/ clothing inc shoes	6	10	12	4
Food & Lodging	Fl	Bakers, Butchers, Innkeepers	6	3	2	7
Gov & Prof	Gp	Lawyers, Police, Teachers	0	2	5	11
Mining	Mn	Mining & Quarrying	0	0	0	7
Non specific/Craft	Ns	Carpenters, Masons, Smiths, Gen Trades	5	14	12	10
Service	Sv	Domestic Service, Laundry	33	25	42	56
Transport	Tr	Railway workers, Carriers not in other classes	0	0	3	1
Independent	In	Private means	3	0	0	28
Total			152	142	150	194

Table 3.4: *Lustleigh Censuses – no occupation*

	1841	1861	1881	1901
Married/Widowed	56	55	61	67
Unmarried, 16 and over	14	8	7	26
14 & 15	3	5	7	6
5 to 13	42	56	66	54
2 to 4	23	26	34	20
1 & under	17	17	18	17
Totals	155	167	193	190
Visitors	0	3	13	15

labourers or agricultural apprentices. In total there were 15 under-14s in work. By 1881 no one under 14 was working in agriculture and only four girls as domestic servants. The 1870 Education Act may well have led to this, but that will be covered in another essay. Also, the arrival of the railway made the village more accessible to the outside world. In 1861 three visitors were recorded but, in 1881, 13 visitors were resident for the night of the census. This tourism probably led to an important change over the next 20 years.

As with Bovey Tracey, the total in occupations in Lustleigh in 1901 is swollen by the category independent, but to a proportionally greater extent. No fewer than 27 declared themselves as 'Living on own means' and one as 'Retired Farmer' (at the age of 30). Of these, 23 were women and 15 were widows. Only six could be traced on the 1891 census and only seven were born in Devon. They could have come to Lustleigh with their husbands or after they were widowed. Either way, Lustleigh had clearly been discovered as a good place to retire to, in the same way as had Bovey Tracey.

This influx probably accounts for the rise in the number of domestic servants. On the other hand, there was a sharp reduction in the clothing business. Only two dressmakers and two shoemakers were left in the village by 1901. Perhaps people preferred to use the easier access provided by the railway to shop for more fashionable clothing in the larger towns. The increase in the number of 'Unmarried, 16 and over' with no occupation is in part accounted for by the daughters of those of independent means. But a new entry was being recorded in the census, that of 'Retired'. Perhaps there were always some retired people in the village but now they were describing themselves as such.

In 1841 Lustleigh was a rustic, largely self-contained village dependent on agriculture. Only one resident was born outside Devon and not many outside a 10-mile radius. By 1901, 79 out of a population of 384 people in the census were born outside Devon. Agriculture was still important, but there was a much greater mixture of society. Lustleigh had been transformed, it seems, by the railway bringing in the outside world.

Conclusion

This is a brief review of information revealed by the censuses and speculation about why changes happened and what their effect was. To perform a full comparative analysis of all aspects of the details collected would require the digitisation and computerised study of the censuses. To understand fully the causes and effects of the changes revealed would need a big sociological examination based on a thorough knowledge of the period. But this report may have suggested areas which are worth further investigation. Perhaps even the big question. Why did the opposite ends of the Wrey Valley experience such different fortunes during the Victorian period? And why did Moretonhampstead not benefit from the same improved transport as Bovey Tracey?

4. Occupational survey of Chagford 1851–1901

Judith Moss

This essay provides some comparison with the population profile of the Wrey Valley. Chagford became one of the original three stannary towns in 1305, and continued as a market town since then.[1] It lies 6.5 kilometres north-west of Moretonhampstead in the adjacent River Teign valley. The town is surrounded by agricultural land which extends onto common land on Dartmoor in the vicinity of Kestor.

The Chagford censuses have been analysed for the years 1851, 1881 and 1901.[2] It has been much debated that women's work was under-recorded in the Victorian censuses. This current analysis has taken the approach of including women in a work category (though none was recorded on the census) where the family business would imply their participation and the number of children and their age ranges would have permitted it. Though it may be argued that this approach involves subjectivity, it is not without precedent.[3] Also, people recorded as 'Independent' are interpreted as living on their own means, and therefore having no occupation.

1851

Town

Chagford Town consisted of eight streets or areas: Fore Street (from the Globe Inn to the bowling green), Mill Street (leading from there down to Chagford Bridge), New Street (from the corner at the Globe Inn out towards Meldon Hall), Pie Corner, Dicker's Row, Lower Street (from The Square down towards Easton Cross), and The Island (including the current triangle of buildings on the north side of The Square, but extending to include the houses north of the current Spar shop).

Apart from the three public houses which still bear the same names (The Globe Inn, The Three Crowns, and the Ring of Bells on what was then called Fore Street) there were three other inns in Chagford in 1851. Among the 32 houses along Mill Street there was the Baker's Arms (later the Buller's Arms and now the Chagford Inn); The Royal Oak was among the 17 houses in Pie Corner, and there was a King's Arms among 20 houses recorded in The Island.

The 1851 census shows that western streets, Mill Street and Fore Street, housed predominantly artisans. Innkeepers generally had two occupations, being also butchers or coopers. Two saddlers resided near the Fore Street inns. Turning the corner at the Globe Inn into New Street, it is noticeable that the further out of town to the south, the greater the occupation of houses by agricultural labourers. Travelling north down Lower Street, there is a similar pattern though less accentuated, of more agricultural labourers, with paupers also particularly occupying this street.

Some of the shopkeepers are difficult to classify, because several were dual purpose, for example 'Grocer and Draper', 'Grocer and Postmistress', 'Linen Draper, Grocer and Artist, Portrait Painter' (this was William Morrish, a well-known painter).

There were three farmers living in town, farming 11, 12, and 25 acres each.

Some of the more unusual occupations were:

Dealer in Marine Stores

Chelsea Pensioner

Hawker of Nuts etc.

Veterinary Surgeon

Mantua Maker

Hawker of Books

Watchmaker

The town's population was 897; that of the parish as a whole was 1521. The number of paupers was 62: this dropped significantly for the later sample census years, 25 in 1881 and one in 1901.

Farms

Out of town, in the rural areas of Chagford parish, lay the farms. Of the six households at Westcott, only two were of agricultural labourers, with one weaver: the rest of 'middling sort', annuitants and landed proprietors. Little and Great Week were farming communities, two farms and six agricultural labourers' households. Drewston consisted of three farms, all with farm and house servants living in, and no labourers' households.

Easton was a mixed farming community similar to the Weeks: three farms, four labourers' families, and one out-of-town butcher. One of the sons at Forder Farm was also a butcher. At the Whiddon Park estate, the farm included live-in farm servants, and the house was occupied by an annuitant widow born Hungerford, her daughters and a house servant.

Perhaps the largest farm in Chagford parish was at Rushford Barton, the 644 acres requiring a bailiff and 14 labourers. Rushford Mill itself was headed by a widow, who was both farming and milling with a miller son and mill servant; her daughter's family with three toddler grandchildren were part of this household. Two agricultural labouring households also had addresses here at the Mill.

At Higher Withecombe was another smaller farm, with two agricultural labourers' households. Lower Withecombe was a sizeable holding of 165 acres also requiring a bailiff on account of the farmer running another business, that of land agent, surveyor and auctioneer. This is John Hooper, whose name appears throughout this period letting and selling farms and land; he employed a live-in clerk to assist with this. He acted as surveyor to the consortium of railway companies which set up the Moretonhampstead and South Devon Railway Company to construct the Newton Abbot to Moretonhampstead railway line.[4] Apart from his wife, the household consisted solely of employees, six farm and house servants in addition to the clerk and bailiff. By 1881 he was a widower aged 80; his acreage had risen to 256 acres employing nine men and a boy, but he was no longer a land agent.

It seems that with four houses uninhabited at Lower Factory, this must have been closed by 1851, the owner John Berry having died in

1848.[5] All the people registered as wool combers were in Chagford Town, one of whom was a master employing seven people. There was some evidence of wool-working out of town: one spinner at Thorn, and another at Coombe.

To the south-west of the town, what is now merely a very attractive house, Hole Farm, was a significant operation of 100 acres headed by a couple in their seventies. There were three middle-aged daughters (one a dressmaker) but the other two, a son-in-law and a granddaughter were obviously doing farm duties. In addition, two waggoners and three farm and house servants were part of the household, with one younger granddaughter aged 7 a scholar.

Collihole Farm was also a large and well-to-do operation. James Rowe was one of the monied Throwleigh and Gidleigh Rowes. His own household included seven children ranging in age from 8 to 28 years. The youngest two were scholars, and it is most unlikely that the other children were doing manual labour. Three farm servants were in this household. The bailiff was housed separately in the Collihole complex. There was another farm at Collihole, with the more modest arrangement of family sons, daughters and father doing most of the work.

These examples serve to form a benchmark for the range of occupational arrangements in farming households. In general, through examination of the other farming communities to the south of Chagford Town it appears that farms of under 100 acres used family labour with a servant or two. Rarely does one find a young man running a farm single-handed. A few agricultural labourers' households are scattered in this area. One 150-acre farm was unoccupied (probably Lincombe). It was not unusual to find families housing elderly relatives, sometimes annuitants, but often paupers. When the farmer's wife is obviously coping with a shower of young children (for example, Mrs Holmes at Hurston with six children under 11 years), then there are more servants and sometimes another farm-skilled relative helping out.

There are a handful of farmers who are noted as freeholders: Mr Nosworthy's 11 acres at Broadalls, Mr Ellis's 60 acres at Stiniel, Mr Collins' 161 acres at Lower Batworthy, and Henry Hooper's 300 acres at Yellam.

The hamlets to the south-east of Chagford at Woodtown, Horselake and Cleave appears to have been a poor area, housing mainly agricultural labourers around the small 30-acre farm itself at Cleave.

Mills

The mill at Dogmarsh Bridge (Mill End Hotel today) was called Sandy Park Mill in 1851, with another mill close by at Rushford. Another mill, difficult to locate, was run by the sons of an annuitant, employing a waggoner: this could either have been Holy Street Mill or a mill below Beechlands. The mill at Higher Batworthy appears to have been the biggest operation locally, father and son working as millers and employing another miller, a waggoner, a grist gatherer and an errand boy. There was also a 44-acre farm to run here, and retired father and mother had a household on the premises.

Tin mining

Five tin miners lived on the outskirts of the parish, on the side of the moor at Jurston and beyond, three of them born in Cornwall. There were a further two living in Chagford town. The Jurston men may have been workers at Golden Dagger mine, just south of Warren House, and there may still have been tinning going on out at Week to the east of Chagford town. By 1901 there was only one tin miner in the parish.

1851 occupational statistics

Figure 4.1 is presented to demonstrate that about 50 per cent of the population had no occupation recorded in the 1851 census. Figure 4.2

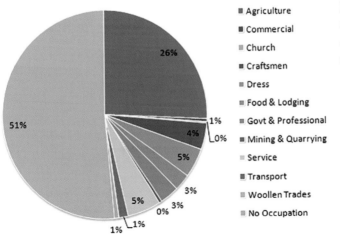

Figure 4.1: *Chagford 1851 occupations, including 'No Occupation'*

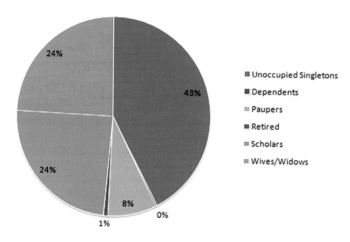

Figure 4.2:
*Chagford 1851
'No Occupation'*

- Unoccupied Singletons
- Dependents
- Paupers
- Retired
- Scholars
- Wives/Widows

gives the analysis of those unoccupied people. About a quarter of this population were children at school, and a further quarter were wives and widows. The 43 per cent 'Unoccupied Singletons' consist of all children not 'Scholars', and people of any age unmarried and unoccupied.

Figure 4.3 gives the distribution of occupations in the working population.

Over half are employed on farms, and includes farming wives, sons and daughters. The next tier of workers are in 'Service', 'Dress' and 'Craftsmen'. Chagford had 28 dressmakers and 21 shoe and boot makers. The majority of 'Craftsmen' were carpenters, blacksmiths and masons.

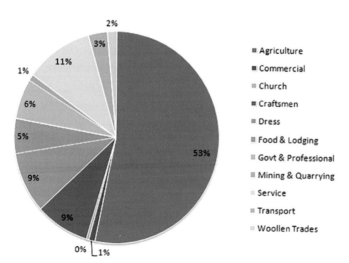

Figure 4.3:
*Chagford 1851
occupations,
excluding 'No
Occupation'*

- Agriculture
- Commercial
- Church
- Craftsmen
- Dress
- Food & Lodging
- Govt & Professional
- Mining & Quarrying
- Service
- Transport
- Woollen Trades

1881

Notes on categorisation of occupations in 1881

Wives deemed to be working were:

> Draper/grocer's wives (this classed as 'Commercial')
>
> Butcher's wives ('Food & Lodging')
>
> Baker's wives ('Food & Lodging').

A gas maker has been classed in 'Craftsmen'.

There are eight machinists which have been classed in 'Agriculture'. John Dicker and George Henry Reed are two of them, the latter employing four men and two boys. A later hand on the census annotates some of these machinists 'Ag Mac': Price and Rhodes describe the working relationship between Reed and Dicker and the type of machinery they built, corroborating the 'Agriculture' categorisation.[6]

All occupations relating to milling have been classed in 'Food & Lodging'.

Included in 'Transport' are occupations that 'keep the wheels turning', such as farriers and wheelwrights; also (h)ostlers – those who look after horses at inns. Masons have been categorised as 'Craftsmen', with lesser skilled quarrymen in 'Mining & Quarrying'.

'Agricultural' workers include farmers' wives, sons and daughters (and other relatives in some cases) where it is obvious that they must have been working, for example, where no other labour is included in the household and the farm acreage would necessitate it, and/or the childrens' ages would imply it.

Town

By 1881, the eastern section of Fore Street had been re-named High Street, and Mill Street extended replacing the western section of Fore Street. 'The Square' had replaced Pie Corner and The Island.

Unusual occupations were:

> A 15-year-old described as a page.
>
> A woman combining being a barmaid with book keeping
>
> A pork dealer

Two men are described as husbandmen. They were probably agricultural workers with particular responsibility for livestock, possibly with breeding.

The population of the town had dropped only slightly (3 per cent) since 1851, to 870. The whole parish population was 1,444, a 5 per cent drop since 1851.

Two cottages were occupied at Factory, not by factory workers but by a granite mason and a gas maker. A gasworks was started in 1869 on the site of another mill[7].

There were only farming people living in the Whiddon Park properties.

Little had changed at Week, though it provides an example of farm engrossment. In 1881 there was just one much larger farm, by then in the hands of one of the previous farmer's sons, and prosperous enough to employ a governess.

1881 occupational statistics

Figure 4.4 shows that the unoccupied proportion of the population remained at about half in 1881, and the farming community had dropped from 26 per cent to 19 per cent. Figure 4.5 gives a full analysis of the 'Unoccupied' population in 1881. 'Unoccupied Singletons' had reduced from 43 per cent in 1851 to 28 per cent, scholars had increased from 24 per cent to 42 per cent, and wives and widows were down a couple of

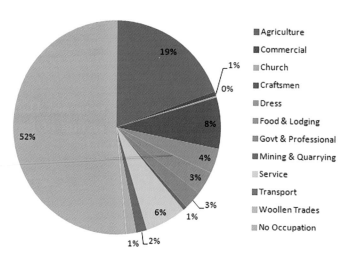

Figure 4.4: *Chagford 1881 occupations, including 'No Occupation'*

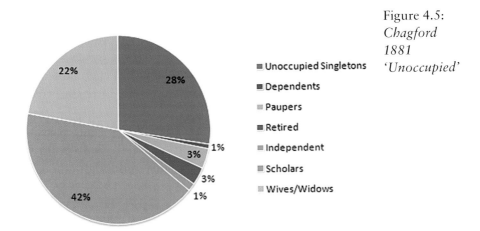

Figure 4.5:
*Chagford
1881
'Unoccupied'*

- Unoccupied Singletons
- Dependents
- Paupers
- Retired
- Independent
- Scholars
- Wives/Widows

percentage points. The number of 'Paupers' had more than halved. The number of 'Retired' had trebled; this could have been due to increased life expectancy, or more families being able to afford to look after their relatives (and thus fewer recorded as 'Paupers').

The number of farmers rose from 58 in 1851 to 62 in 1881, suggesting that Chagford was not affected by the nineteenth-century agricultural crisis, but the fall in the number of agricultural workers offers a different picture. Comparing Figure 4.6 with Figure 4.3, the percentage of the working population in this sector reduced from 53 per cent to 40 per cent, which is a numerical drop of 30 per cent (388 workers down to 273). Only further study would determine the reason for this. Greater

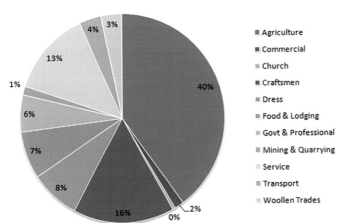

Figure 4.6:
*Chagford 1881
occupations,
excluding 'No
Occupation'*

- Agriculture
- Commercial
- Church
- Craftsmen
- Dress
- Food & Lodging
- Govt & Professional
- Mining & Quarrying
- Service
- Transport
- Woollen Trades

efficiency brought about by the development of farm machinery is likely, change to the proportion of arable versus stock raising could reduce the need for workers, or people left the land for better opportunities.

Referring again to Figure 4.6, the 'Craftsmen' and 'Service' categories of occupation remained the next most frequent employment, with increased percentages over 1851, 'Service' now 13 per cent, up from 11 per cent and 'Craftsmen' 16 per cent up from 9 per cent, possibly to serve the modest increase in 'Govt & Professional' and 'Food & Lodging' numbers: there were now nine hotels, inns and lodging houses, and a coffee tavern. The rector, Hayter George Hames, 1852–1886, was instrumental in the promotion of Chagford as a resort, by entertaining the editors of journals and magazines who wrote, among other aspects, of the 'ready hospitality' of Chagford. 'The lodging-house keepers know how to make visitors comfortable, and to charge for so doing' reflected Baring-Gould.[8]

1901

Notes on categorisation of occupations in 1901

The 1901 census did not record scholars, presumably since education had become compulsory. To provide some comparison with earlier years, those in the age range 5–13 years have been categorised as scholars.

There were several people with dual occupations which crossed the categories of our survey. Two examples are 'Coal Merchant and Farmer' and 'Postman Saddler'.

With the rise of boarding houses and hotels, a judgement has been made as to whether the occupation was probably of someone working locally, or a visitor. In cases such as someone classed as 'Living on own means' the accompanying staff have been categorised as 'Visitors'. Service staff in hotels have been categorised as 'Service', though there is an argument for them being 'Commercial'.

As in 1881, any occupation to do with horses (in town) has been categorised as 'Transport', for example wheelwrights, farriers, harness makers, grooms.

Errand boys have been classed according to which business they are running for, thus a postal errand boy is within 'Govt & Professional'.

Under 'Mining & Quarrying', stone masons and stone cutters have been included, but wall masons and masons are in 'Craftsmen', along with builders.

Town

There are noticeably more people from further afield making their living in Chagford by 1901, in particular wives or husbands from outside the West Country: Jersey, Leicestershire, Suffolk, Kent, Northumberland, Norfolk (a widow with two children born in China), Berkshire, London, Gloucestershire, Warwickshire, Hertfordshire, Australia, Wiltshire, Hampshire, Isle of Wight, and Cambridge. This possibly indicates that men had either travelled away to learn a trade and returned with a 'foreign' wife, or women had moved away to find service positions, married, and the partnership returned to Chagford to take advantage of the commercial opportunities. The population had dropped a little further since 1881: there were now 854 people living in Chagford town (down 2 per cent) and 1,391 in the whole parish (down 3.5 per cent).

This was compensated for commercially by the number of leisured, monied and professional people now in the parish, requiring support services. There were small families of independent means, with full complements of cooks, parlour maids, housemaids and so forth. For Chagford, many of them would have seemed exotic: a retired surgeon living with his 83-year-old mother of independent means, he (noted in the margin) suffering from cirrhosis of the liver; Freya Stark age 8, living with her mother (artist and sculptor) and sister at Ford Park; a lady and daughter from Glasgow, at Thornworthy, listed with 'husband in Africa'. These 'incomers' and those staying in hotels, would have used the coaching and carriage businesses (there were five coach builders in Chagford), had supplies delivered from the bakers, grocers, fruiterers and butchers, had their horses shod by the farriers, hired grooms, and used dressmaking and tailoring services. There were two businesses in particular to supply the higher classes, a licensed victualler and a wine agent. There was a public reading room attended by a 14-year-old carpenter's son.

Many of the houses in town now had names, for some probably in support of their business as lodging houses or to reflect their improved station in life. Incomers and professionals also generally lived in named houses, though a retired milliner and her sister from Islington, aged 26 and 17 respectively, the latter funded by an allowance from her father, living together in a house called The Jungle, is a surprise.

Farms

There were 54 farmers and farm bailiffs in 1901. This census does not give farm acreages nor record how many men and boys a farmer employed (unlike in 1881 and 1851), so though it is possible to identify engrossment between the earlier years, this is not at all clear for 1901. The majority of farmers were born in Chagford or neighbouring parishes, two from further away were married to Chagford-born wives, and there were only four farming families from further out in Devon, the farthest being Bovey Tracey; there were none from out of the county.

1901 occupational statistics

Figure 4.7 illustrates that the number of people with 'No Occupation' had dropped to 50 per cent from 52 per cent in 1881; in terms of actual numbers, this category had dropped 20 per cent since 1851, and 11 per cent since 1881.

The number of 'Scholars' indicates a significant drop over earlier sample years, but since the 1901 census did not record scholars, and this author uses an arbitrary measure of 'all children between age 5 and 13' to be scholars, this may simply be under-recording. The rise in number

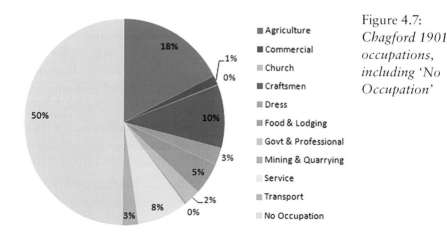

Figure 4.7: *Chagford 1901 occupations, including 'No Occupation'*

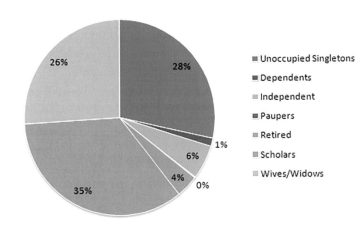

Figure 4.8:
*Chagford 1901
'Unoccupied'*

- Unoccupied Singletons
- Dependents
- Independent
- Paupers
- Retired
- Scholars
- Wives/Widows

of 'Wives/Widows' (compare Figures 4.8 and 4.5) might be attributed to working families becoming more affluent and/or the higher proportion of leisured and affluent 'incomer' families whose wives did not work.

The combined proportion of 'Dependents' and 'Retired' was 5 per cent in 1901, with 0 per cent paupers (Figure 4.8). This is a significant difference from 1851, when there were 1 per cent 'Retired' and 8 per cent 'Paupers'. This drop in the presence of paupers in Chagford could be attributed to such people being sent to the Okehampton Union Work House. Alternatively, these statistics may be indicating that greater affluence allowed working families to look after their elderly relatives.

By 1901, only one-third of the population was involved in agriculture (Figure 4.9), down from 40 per cent in 1881, and down from over half in 1851. The farming pattern had altered to a greater proportion of pasture, and this together with mechanisation would have reduced the number of agricultural labourers and farm servants.[9] 'Services', on the other hand, had been a growth sector, rising from 11 per cent in 1851 to 16 per cent at the beginning of the twentieth century. This was most likely caused by the rise in 'Govt and Professional' and 'Independent' categories who would seek to employ maids, cooks and grooms: between 1881 and 1901 the former grew from 3 per cent to 5 per cent, and 'Independent' people, that is, 'living on own means', expanded from 1 per cent in 1881 to 6 per cent in 1901. Another burgeoning sector was 'Craftsmen'; in 1901 standing at 20 per cent this was the second largest occupational category. It included the building trades: carpenters, labourers, masons, a house painter, two plumbers, stone masons, wall masons and trowel masons, and builders. Together these numbered 102 out of the 136 in the 'Craftsmen' category, three-quarters of this category. The built environment in and around Chagford would have been expanding and upgrading significantly to meet the demands of incomers and more prosperous locals.[10] Occupations relating to 'Dress' had contracted, perhaps most significantly affected by the reduction to zero of the number of boot and shoe makers, who had formed 30 per cent of this sector in 1851. The 'Food & Lodging' category continued to expand (from 5 per cent in 1851, to 7 per cent in 1881 to 10 per cent in 1901), once again reflecting the growth of the visitor and incomer population.[11]

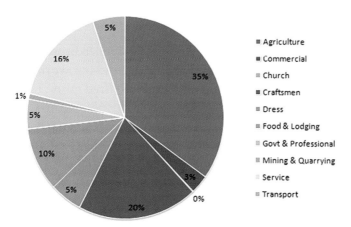

Figure 4.9: *Chagford 1901 occupations, excluding 'No Occupation'*

The 'Transport' sector had risen modestly but steadily, from 3 per cent in 1851 to 5 per cent in 1901. In the early years the sector was dominated by carriers and waggoners, with one coachman. By 1881 there were two coachmen. Sources other than the census inform that in 1868 one Henry Aggett, proprietor of the Three Crowns, had set up an omnibus service to transfer passengers between the terminus of the railway line at Moretonhampstead and Chagford (though his entry in the 1871 census gives only 'Innkeeper'). The Great Western Railway (GWR) absorbed the South Devon Railway Company in mid-1878:[12] There was a horse bus subsidised by the GWR operating from the Chagford Globe Family Hotel in 1889.[13] The 1891 census for Chagford gives one bus proprietor (a widow), two bus drivers, a cab driver and one coachman. In 1901 there were six coach builders, three coach proprietors and seven

Figure 4.10: *The Chagford to Moretonhampstead horse bus outside the Globe Family Hotel, Chagford, circa 1890.*
(Courtesy of the Globe Hotel, Chagford)

coachmen; there were also three jobmasters (providers of horse and carriage with driver for hire). It would appear that Chagford's transport entrepreneurs took full advantage of there being no railway line between Moretonhampstead and their town, and were instrumental in Chagford's growth as a tourist centre.

Notes

1. Hoskins, W.G., 1992. *Devon*. Tiverton: Devon Books. p.361.
2. Ancestry, <https://www.ancestry.co.uk/> [Accessed 20th August 2017].
3. Higgs, E. and Wilkinson, A., 2016. Women, occupations and work in the Victorian censuses revisited. *History Workshop Journal*, 81(1), p.22. [pdf] Available at: <https://academic.oup.com/hwj/article-abstract/81/1/17/2385582/Women-Occupations-and-Work-in-the-Victorian> [Accessed 23rd September 2017].
4. Kingdom, A.R. and Lang, M., 2004. *The Newton Abbot to Moretonhampstead Railway*. Newton Abbot: Ark Publications (Railways). pp.106, 301.

5. Price, S. and Rhodes, J., 2012. From wool to electricity. In Bliss, J., Jago, C. and Maycock, E., eds, *Aspects of Devon History: People, Places and Landscapes*. Exeter: The Devon History Society. p.323.
6. Ibid., pp.324–325.
7. Ibid., p.323; Hayter-Hames, J., 1981. *A History of Chagford*. Chichester: Philimore. p.88.
8. Baring-Gould, S., 1907. *A Book of Dartmoor*. London: Methuen. pp.157–158. Available at <http://www.gutenberg.org/files/51134/51134-h/51134-h.htm#Page_157> [Accessed 24th September 2017]; Hayter-Hames, p.79.
9. Hayter-Hames, pp.103–104.
10. Ibid., pp.107–108.
11. Hoskins, p.121.
12. Kingdom and Lang, Appendix VI: Some important dates, p.316.
13. Ibid., Appendix IV: The proposed extension of the line and bus services, pp.301–307 at p.302.

5.   The Victorian high street

Chris Wilson

It would be wrong to suggest that the high street did not change during Queen Victoria's reign, but it would be misleading to imply that it underwent major change. There were some developments in terms of technology – tinned food bringing additional convenience and choice to the grocers' shelves – and new Acts of Parliament dealing with food and drink adulteration, as well as curbing alcohol consumption. Shops and pubs naturally changed hands, sometimes from father to son and other times from husband to widowed wife, while yet others, as today, came and went. Of particular interest is the wide variety of roles to which pubs, inns and hotels were put.

Inquests

Turning back the clock 150 or so years, these licensed hostelries would regularly fulfil the function of inquest venue, for example, looking into deaths at work as well as other unexplained fatalities. One such case was related to a major symbol of the Victorian era, the coming of the railway: on 2nd June 1865, an inquest was held at the White Horse Inn, Moretonhampstead, into the death, a couple of days previously, of a railway worker. The newspaper report described how:

> two excavators named William Long and John Major were engaged 'damping hole' in a piece of rock between Lustleigh and Moretonhampstead, the powder suddenly exploded, blowing Long a considerable distance into the air. He was fearfully mutilated, and died

shortly afterwards. Major was seriously injured, having lost the sight of both eyes. Long was thirty-two years of age and leaves a wife and three children.

A verdict of accidental death was returned by the jury.[1]

Tragedy of a different sort befell William Bolestone, as revealed during an inquest held at The Gregory Arms Inn, Doccombe, in a story which reflects the harsh Dartmoor environment of the time. The 76-year-old beer-house keeper had left his home village of Dunsford for Moretonhampstead by donkey and cart with apples for sale; on his return, despite severe weather with 'snow falling fast', he refused a friend's invitation to stay the night in Moretonhampstead, preferring to press for home. While his donkey and cart made the return journey, William Bolestone did not and was found the following morning, after a lengthy search, buried in deep snow. The inquest concluded that he had died from exhaustion and the severity of the weather.[2]

Societies and celebrations

Pubs and hotels were, of course, much as they are today, venues for parties, celebrations and social gatherings but on a much greater scale and variety. Returning to the arrival of the railway, it is no surprise to find many of the pubs and hotels taking their part in marking this historic milestone. A newspaper advert in 1866 gave notice that, to mark the occasion,

> a luncheon will be provided at Moretonhampstead … for the Directors and others, the tickets for which will be 3s. 6d. each, or 6s for a Lady and Gentleman, exclusive of wine, to be obtained at the White Hart and White Horse Hotels.[3]

These hostelries also threw open their doors for many royal celebrations, perhaps most notably Queen Victoria's coronation and jubilees, but also, for example, the christening in 1842 of the Prince of Wales when

> a party of about 60 persons dined at the White Hart Inn; the dinner was served up in Mr. and Mrs. Cann's usually good style, and the wines

were excellent. Many loyal and appropriate toasts were drank, to which the band responded.[4]

The Prince of Wales was her first born and was to succeed her to the throne as King Edward VII.

Neither would major civic events pass without the intervention of licensed premises, although it is perhaps only to be expected that such a momentous occasion as the arrival of gas at Bovey Tracey in 1881, maybe equally as important as the arrival of the railway, would be celebrated throughout the town. Thus, 'in honour of the occasion the directors' of the newly opened gas works 'and their friends dined together in the evening at the Railway Hotel. Mr. Beer, the host, served up a capital dinner in a large room most tastefully decorated'.[5]

Many of the principal inns and hotels in the towns and villages held annual balls, regularly attracting large numbers. A throng of 80 squeezed into the Cleave Hotel, Lustleigh, in 1881 and

> all seemed to enjoy themselves. It may be remarked as a proof of the popularity of this annual gathering, that several came from long distances to attend. Dancing was kept up until daylight, to the strains of Tanner's Quadrille Band. Some capital songs were rendered during the evening. Too much praise cannot be given to host Henwood, and all concerned, for the able manner in which the arrangements were carried out.[6]

There were also juvenile fancy dress balls, tradesmen balls, an annual ball of the Yeomanry Cavalry,[7] masonic dinners and, for example, a fellowship dinner at which

> a large assemblage of gentlemen, farmers, and tradesmen of Bovey Tracey and its neighbourhood, numbering upwards of 120, dined together in the large room of the Union Hotel. The gathering was intended to express the friendly feeling existing between all classes.[8]

Indeed, tradesmen would regularly find reason to gather at these establishments, ranging from the meeting of the Western Counties Manure Company when 'a large party sat down to dinner' at the White Horse Hotel, Moretonhampstead,[9] to the gathering of the Early Closing

Association at the White Hart Hotel, also in Moretonhampstead, where 'there was a good attendance' and 'it was resolved to close the shops at seven p.m. every evening throughout the year, with the exception of Thursdays and Saturdays, on which days they will be closed at five p.m., and 9.30 p.m. respectively, as heretofore'.[10]

Workers also had their opportunity for repast and libation, such as the railway employees' annual supper at the White Hart Hotel during which 'the usual loyal toasts were honoured, and the healths of the host and hostess and others drunk in a hearty manner' and 'dinner was served up in the usual creditable style of the caterer. Extension of hours was allowed for the occasion'.[11]

In fact, it would seem that no end of excuses would be found to dine in one of the local hotels – after a day at the races or hunting, after wrestling matches and after farmer's society ploughing matches. Dinners would also be the culmination of rent audit meetings such as that connected with the tenantry of the Earl of Devon when 'between fifty and sixty sat down to a most substantial meal' at the White Hart Hotel in Moretonhampstead,[12] the same gastronomic venue on occasion for The Garden and Allotment Rent Audit and for the Tithe Rent Audit.

As further example, if ever it should be needed, of the scope of events and celebrations that took place in hotels and inns in the Wrey Valley, a dinner and presentation was held at Bovey Tracey's Dolphin Hotel to mark the departure of one of their medical practitioners after just four or five years' service. Presumably, he was quite a remarkable man, being honoured after such a short time and given a 'very costly, very handsome … old English bracket clock, the case being of ebony, enriched with gold'.[13]

Entertainment

As well as feasting and celebration, these hostelries would host a variety of entertainment, concerts being one example from the 'capital entertainment … given at the concert-room of the White Hart Hotel by the "Cremona Musical Union"',[14] a well-known group of eight brothers and sisters who performed around the country, through to more local affairs like the morning and evening concert given at the White Horse Rooms by an organist 'assisted by members of the Choral Society, and several gentlemen, amateurs of the neighbourhood'.[15]

Particularly representative of its time, was when 'members of Bovey Tracey Constitutional Club held a most successful smoking concert on Thursday evening at the Railway Hotel ... It is hoped that this is only the first of a series of similar meetings'.[16] Popular during the Victorian era, smoking concerts were men-only events at which they would smoke and speak of politics while listening to live music.[17]

Auctions

Auctions were regularly held at these licensed establishments with all manner of things being put up for sale. In 1892, The Cleave Hotel in Lustleigh held an auction for the sale of The Bridge Park Iron Works 'occupying an excellent situation on the main road, close to Lustleigh Railway Station, and where for a number of years a successful and increasing general smith's, sawyer's, and builder's and contractor's business has been carried on'.[18]

A rather different sale took place 20 years earlier at the same venue when '900 Oak, 287 Ash, 29 Elm, 7 Sycamore, 10 Cherry, 29 Holly, 352 Larch, and 175 Scotch Fir TREES with their Tops, Lops and Bark' went under the hammer, with the newspaper advertisement extolling the virtues of the oak for ship- and boat-building, other trees ideal for wheelwrights 'and the larch and scotch fir for railing, building, and mining requirements'.[19]

There would be auctions of land, property, household contents and even livestock, although on the latter occasions they were more likely to be a collection point before viewing the lots. A carriage was laid on, for example, from Moretonhampstead's White Horse Hotel to convey prospective buyers to Sanduck to view:

> surplus stock consisting of 46 excellent breeding ewes, 46 ewe and ram lambs, 30 store wether hoggets, 4 grazing heifers, 9 heifers from 18 to 24 months old, 5 steers, ditto, 11 yearling heifers and steers, 1 heifer and a bull calf, each six months old, 1 bull two years old ... The above is a very improving stock: the sheep have good conditions with plenty of wool and quality; the bullocks are mostly of the South Hams breed, and are in fine condition.[20]

Excursions

Of particular relevance during the Victorian era, as Dartmoor's reputation was growing and access to the moors improving, most notably following the arrival of the railway, are the excursions which took place from the hotels in the area. Two examples come from adjoining 1869 advertisements in which Thomas Pollard of Moretonhampstead's White Hart Hotel informs parties arriving by train that he has 'Large and Small Waggonetts and other Carriages and Horses ready … to convey them … [to] numerous places', while Jabez Mugford of the Union Family Hotel in Bovey Tracey promotes his 'large and suitable Four-in-hand Breaks, Waggonetts, and Carriages, to suit the convenience of large or small pic-nic [sic] or pleasure parties visiting the scenery of Dartmoor Hills'.[21]

Word began to spread as newspapers ran reports of these trips and talked about the beauty of the area. In 1886, one correspondent wrote about some of the key places to visit and concluded:

> 'I have merely suggested the best known, hoping that many who read these lines will, for their own sakes, visit a district which is rich in beauty – beauty equal to that which English people often go abroad to seek in their ignorance of what is within a few hours' reach by rail from almost any part of England'.[22]

Such excursions proved popular and an article in the *Western Times* in 1891 talks of 'the increased travelling facilities offered by the Great Western railway [which] will enable holiday seekers to spend a longer time on Dartmoor than hitherto'. It continues, referencing an improved train timetable, which

> will give two hours more to those who care to avail themselves of the privilege, and Messrs. Hellier and Joll, the enterprising coach proprietors, of the Dolphin Hotel, Bovey Tracey, have also arranged a somewhat more extended trip than either of those included in their ordinary programme.[23]

The number of excursions grew significantly over the closing 15 years of the nineteenth century. In 1885, for example, the Dolphin Hotel advertised their four-horse char-a-banc which would take passengers on Mondays and Thursdays to Heytor [*sic*] Rock, Houndtor, Manaton and Becky Falls, while on Tuesdays they would visit Chudleigh Rock, Haldon Racecourse, Beggar's Bush and Ugbrook Park.[24] The following year, they were running two four-horse char-a-bancs, the 'Original' and the 'Victoria'; they later ran three distinctive routes and by 1893 were advertising daily excursions during June to September, which included routes arranged 'by special permission along the private Moorland Road to Grimspound, the largest and most perfect Aboriginal Village left standing on Dartmoor'.[25]

Along with the Union and Dolphin hotels in Bovey Tracey, The Railway Hotel was also very active running such excursions and in just this one town 'there were soon over 100 horses engaged on the tours during the summer months'.[26]

New arrivals

There was some change in the stock of inns and hotels during the Victorian period, two of the most notable were both unquestionably driven by the

Figure 5.1: *The Cleave Hotel, Lustleigh.*
(Courtesy of Lustleigh Community Archive)

Figure 5.2: *White Hart Hotel, Moretonhampstead, 1900/1910.* (Courtesy of Moreton Archives)

arrival of the railway: The Cleave in Lustleigh and the aforementioned Railway Hotel in Bovey Tracey. The Cleave was previously a farmhouse owned by Thomas Wills, one of the directors of the Moretonhampstead and South Devon Railway Company, who lost no time in capitalising on his property when he advertised two years before the railway's arrival:

> To be LET with immediate possession ... all that large and commodious HOUSE now known as 'GATEHOUSE,' to be known as the 'CLEAVE HOTEL,' ... adjoining the proposed Lustleigh Station ... The fact of there being no licensed house within three miles renders this a desirable opening for an enterprising man.[27]

The Railway Hotel, as the name indicates, was also built as a consequence of the railway but came much later. It was built close to Bovey Tracey railway station (and converted this century into Dartmoor Court) around the same time that the Dolphin Hotel was rebuilt in a new location almost opposite its new competitor, the construction of both being welcomed at a time that other parts of the town were being redeveloped.

NO POSTAGE
STAMP
NECESSARY
IF POSTED IN
GREAT BRITAIN
OR NORTHERN
IRELAND

SECOND CLASS

BUSINESS REPLY SERVICE
Licence No. 9839

CO-OPERATIVE INSURANCE SOCIETY LTD.

MILLER STREET

MANCHESTER M4 8AA

POSTAGE WILL
BE PAID BY
CO-OPERATIVE
INSURANCE
SOCIETY LTD.

The Licensed Victuallers were not behind hand, and alterations on a large scale have been made at every hotel. Commencing at the bottom of the town, we have a new Railway Hotel instead of a beer-house, and further improvements are contracted for. The old Dolphin is no longer a licensed house, but has given place to a new building, which was opened a few days since. It is a gigantic structure, and near the Railway Hotel. Then comes the Union Hotel, which, though last, is not least.[28]

Lodging houses

Of course, these hotels were not just there as a base for day trippers wanting an excursion to the moors, they also provided accommodation to visitors seeking a longer stay in the area. At the same time, there would have been private houses offering lodgings, although it is difficult to quantify the precise numbers of homeowners providing such facilities: directories did not start listing lodging houses until 1866 when, for example, Kelly's directory names just a scattering in some of the Wrey Valley towns and villages.[29] There would undoubtedly have been private lodging houses before then, but perhaps this timing is a reflection of certain enterprising individuals (they probably had to pay for their directory entries) recognising the opportunity of reaching beyond passers-by and appealing to visitors being brought to the region by the new railway.

Somewhat oddly, it is Chagford which the directories seem to indicate was seizing this opportunity more than most – odd because the railway never extended that far; or maybe it was precisely because of this that they were driven to work harder to attract tourism business. An 1873 directory noted that in Chagford 'convenient lodgings are to be had both in the town and neighbourhood, and these are in great requisition during the summer'.[30] Throughout, much of the Victorian period, directories listed twice as many lodging houses here than its neighbouring towns of Moretonhampstead and Bovey Tracey. Another notable trend during this time was the shift from the tag 'lodging house' to the rather grander nomenclature 'apartment', perhaps to lure a better class of person and/or to draw a distinction between the image portrayed by the early nineteenth-century lodgings compared with the more salubrious accommodation available during the latter part of Victoria's reign.

There were also some home owners who would rent out their entire house, moving into smaller quarters for the duration, particularly ideal for those seeking an even longer stay in the area. One visitor, however, got more than he bargained for when he sought a two-month stay at the house of Ranulph Edward Glanville in Lustleigh who 'during the summer had been accustomed to let the front or practically the whole of the house as furnished apartments, whilst he lived at the back with his family'. However, what was described as 'an amusing case' played out at Newton County Court after a dispute arose when the visitor moved out and refused to pay any more rent on the account of the house being infested with beetles and woodlice.[31]

Licensing

There were also alternative places to buy drink other than the hotels, inns and pubs. On the one hand, there was a long tradition of beer or ale houses, but discovering exactly where and how many is difficult as they are rarely recorded, for example, in directories. Maybe this is because they served a largely local clientele to whom they were known and did not need to advertise. Occasionally, though, they appear in newspaper reports such as when the appropriately named 'Ann Beer, a widow, who keeps a beer-shop at Bovey Tracey' was charged with 'keeping open her house during unlawful hours'; with witnesses including the arresting policeman who 'gave the house a very good character and stated that he had never known anything against [the] defendant before', she was given a lenient fine of 20 shillings.[32]

On the other hand, grocers were becoming a new phenomenon in the licensed trade seeking to add to their wares with off duty sales. One such grocer was Percy William Henry Peters who, in 1883, applied for a 'grocer's license to sell wines, spirits, and ale in bottles off the premises' highlighting a hitherto unsatisfied demand with only one other off-licence in the town (Bovey Tracey) and stating that 'a great number of visitors lodged in the town during the summer, and very recently he had to refuse four applicants for bottled ale in one day'.[33]

Of course, such license applications were not without their objectors. The Victorian era saw a rise in the temperance movement, and Bovey Tracey had, indeed, just six years earlier, witnessed the building of a new Temperance Hall 'used for entertainments and the meetings of the Plymouth Brethren and … seat about 300 persons'.[34] At the above licence hearing, a Mr Frederick Kellock, of Totnes 'opposed the application on behalf – as he said – of the advocates of Temperance in the town', although it was really suspected to be on behalf of the other licensed victuallers.[35]

While the objection, in that instance at least, was rejected, the temperance movement did have an effect on the high street in another way, and that was the emergence of coffee houses. An interesting item appeared in the *Western Times* in 1878 when a letter was published in which the correspondent felt that:

> the use or abuse of intoxicating drinks has been more or less a problem afflicting the welfare of all nations, until it has reached such a climax in this country at the present day that the universal cry is 'something must be done'. One of the last, and I would fain hope not the least of the remedies propounded, is the establishment of 'Coffee Taverns', 'Cocoa Houses', Cafés, and the like – houses that shall offer all the comfort and accommodation of inns and hotels without the baneful influence of alcoholic stimulants.[36]

White's Directory of the same year indicates that there were already such establishments in Bovey Tracey and Moretonhampstead, while Chagford gained its equivalent a couple of years later when it was reported that:

> The Chagford Coffee Tavern was opened yesterday, and it being Fair-day the establishment had a large amount of support. The dinner was well attended, and a tea in the afternoon was patronised by many of the principal residents in the neighbourhood. The arrangements are complete within, and everything is carried out in a modern and improved style. Reading and smoking-rooms are provided. The Branch of the Church Temperance Society gave a concert in the evening in support of the institution.[37]

Returning to grocers, it was not just alcohol which began appearing on their shelves. Not only were the railways making the transportation of food easier, but so too was another major invention, canned food. Although food had been preserved in metal cans previously, and in glass jars, it was an expensive option, but in the 1860s huge canneries appeared, dramatically reducing prices and thereby opening up such food to a mass audience. This also facilitated the route for imports, with canned meat first arriving from Australia and then from America.[38] This was followed by freezing technology which saw meat imported from across the world and in 1882 'butter was shipped to the UK from New Zealand for the first time'.[39]

All was not rosy with Victorian food, however, and adulteration was a major issue: bread being bulked out with plaster of Paris[40] among other things, 'coffee was adulterated with acorns, sugar with sand, pepper with pea-flour, cocoa with brick-dust',[41] tea may have been recycled with the addition of 'floor sweepings'[42] or sheep manure[43] and cheese was sometimes dyed with red lead[44]. Back in the pub, wine and cider may contain lead,[45] while the beer might have been adulterated with rat poison to make it taste more bitter,[46] green vitriol to enhance the head,[47] or salt to make drinkers thirsty and drink more.[48]

Very little seems to have been done to tackle the issue of food adulteration until the 1860s, a key turning point being the 'Bradford Lozenge Scandal' of 1858 when a confectioner mistakenly added arsenic instead of 'daff' (the trade slang for plaster of Paris) which resulted in 200 poisonings and 20 deaths.[49] Various legislative Acts followed until the Sale of Food and Drugs Act 1875 which finally started to make a difference.

Other Acts of Parliament were introduced to curb alcohol consumption, which was on the rise and, according to Gladstone, 'the curse of the working man' and so he introduced the Licensing Act 1872 which 'gave magistrates the power to issue licenses to public houses; where it was thought that there were too many of these … and close down some of them' and to force pubs to close at midnight in towns and at 11 p.m. in the countryside 'so that agricultural labourers could walk home and arrive before midnight.[50] The Act also made it an offence to sell spirits to children under 16.[51]

Traditional shops

Returning to the non-alcoholic side of the Victorian high street, there were, of course, the expected staples of butchers, bakers, grocers, chemists, drapers, shoe-makers, tailors and watchmakers, some of whom changed hands throughout the era while others remained with one family for much of Victoria's 64-year reign. One of the longest

Figure 5.3: *Fore Street, Bovey Tracey, 1865/1875.*
(Courtesy of Bovey Tracey Heritage Centre)

established butchers was William Mann & Sons which began trading in Bovey Tracey in 1827 and continued into the twentieth century. For much of the period his chief competition in the town came from William Hamlyn, while in neighbouring Moretonhampstead, Peters (William, father and son of the same name, and nephew Frank) was the dominant family; an example of their wares can be garnered from the display put on by the latter at the 1886 Christmas market which included carcases of ox, heifers, hogs, sheep, wethers and a number of pigs.[52]

Despite similar populations, Chagford had only half the number of butchers as Moretonhampstead during the early part of the period, although from a high of around seven, numbers dropped to similar levels in both towns around the 1860s, and Bovey Tracey, to a stable two or three; meanwhile, the smaller villages would likely have just one butcher at most.

The numbers of bakers in the three towns were similar and again there were many families who spanned the era, more so in Bovey Tracey where names like Isaac Baker, James Cade, Samuel Murch, Charles Loveys and Thomas Weslford continued for more than two decades apiece, while the successful partnership of Helyer & Barkell continued for over 30 years. On the other hand, in villages like Lustleigh, the bakery was not simply another shop but an extension of the mill, indeed this was a Victorian addition to a centuries-old corn mill to produce bread for the local population.

The towns and larger villages had grocers, of varying quantity, most of whom would combine this line with something else; many were also drapers but among their number were also seed merchants, glass and china dealers, chemists and even a wool-comber. As already explained, as the century wore on, the range of groceries expanded and this is reflected in the appearance of the words 'stores' or 'provision dealers'. Towards the end of the century, directories were also starting to list separately greengrocers and fruiterers; many other miscellaneous shopkeepers were listed without specific mention of their wares except for some references to newsagents, stationers and fancy repositories.

One of the general shopkeepers, William Sercombe in Moretonhampstead, listed one of his specialities in 1857 as a shoe warehouse,[53] suggesting that he was not making footwear, just retailing such goods. Considering that this was before mass production (Clarks of Somerset, for example, did not start mechanised shoe production until the 1870s), he would seem to have been ahead of the curve. The main availability continued to be from the individual shoe- and boot-makers, of which there were many in the Wrey Valley – as numerous, for example, as butchers and bakers and every town and village had at least one. Again, many were permanent fixtures in their neighbourhoods: John & Susan Hamlyn and Thomas Prouse in Bovey Tracey; George Brown and John Lewis in Moretonhampstead; Edward and George Lydon, James and Thomas Aggett and Robert Holman in Chagford.

Equally numerous were the clothiers: in 1857, for example, *Billing's Directory* listed Chagford as having as many 16 dressmakers and milliners and Moretonhampstead only a few less (although these numbers were never repeated) alongside five and six tailors respectively; at the same time Chagford had one staymaker while Moreton had two.[54] Perhaps interesting to note is the emergence, towards the end of the era, of a new generation of clothier, that of the outfitter; for example, Walter Alfred Dodd and Ernest Parson in Chagford in 1893 and Edward Endacott in Bovey Tracey, who declared in one 1886 advert 'fit and style guaranteed' and also that he dealt in hosiery.[55]

One of the other major businesses of the era was that of watch- and clock-maker, the trade directories of the time suggesting that Moretonhampstead was the most thriving, being the only location listing such artisans at the beginning of Victoria's reign. Among the most noteworthy of their timepiece craftsman were the Treleavens, particularly father and son both named Silvester, who are said to be an important part of the town's history and involved in myriad other businesses including a hairdresser, bookseller, post office, stationer, druggist, baker and more. Another of their notable watch- and clock-makers was William Rihll, the son of a French prisoner of war, and whose son continued the business.[56] It is said that his original surname had just one 'l' but he added a second in order to match his name to the numbers on the clock face.[57]

Watch- and clock-makers, it would appear, were also not immune to having a second string to their bow; in Bovey Tracey, for example, Thomas Miles, also advertised his services as an oil and lamp dealer, while James Evans' sideline was as an umbrella repair shop.

There were various other traders plying their wares on the Wrey Valley 'high streets' including basket-makers, tallow chandlers and fancy repositories, while in the very last years appeared tobacconists and photographers. One of the most unusually named businesses, considering the inland location of the Wrey Valley, were marine store dealers which traded in all three towns; this was, however, another term for a junk shop or 'rag and bone' man.

Perhaps a useful snapshot of the Victorian high street, particularly towards the end of the era, is a newspaper description of the Christmas offerings at Bovey Tracey:

Every kind of good cheer for the Christmas season is provided. In the confectionery line, Messrs. Leaker, Darke and Godsland have a plentiful supply of cakes, and fancy sweetmeats. The grocers run each other close, Messrs. Turner, Sercombe, Peters, and Mrs Westwood vieing [*sic*] with each other in providing the best fruits for the Christmas pudding. Mr Alford stands alone in the outfitting business, and he shows a fine lot of hats, caps, ties and collars. Mr Heath of Town Place, has a splendid variety of fancy china, and with the bountiful provision made by the butchers – Messrs. Mann and Hamlyn – there need be no fear of any difficulty of ministering to creature comforts at Bovey Tracey. Seekers of jewellery souveniers [sic] should patronize Mr. Maye's establishment.[58]

Notes

1. *North Devon Journal*, 8th June 1865.
2. Moretonhampstead, an old man buried in the snow. *Woolmer's Exeter and Plymouth Gazette*, 4th January 1861.
3. Opening of the Moretonhampstead and South Devon Railway. *Western Times*, 15th June 1866.
4. Celebration of the christening. *Western Times*, 29th January 1842.
5. Opening of the gas works at Bovey Tracey. *Western Times*, 30th August 1881.
6. Lustleigh. Annual ball. *Western Times*, 24th February 1881.
7. *East and South Devon Advertiser*, 5th February 1898.
8. Good fellowship at Bovey Tracey. *Western Times*, 13th February 1863.
9. *Totnes Weekly Times*, 5th December 1891.
10. *Totnes Weekly Times*, 16th March 1889.
11. *Western Times*, 27th January 1890.
12. *Somerset County Gazette and Bristol Express*, 2nd February 1878.
13. Presentation at Bovey Tracey. *Western Daily Mercury*, 27th September 1883.
14. *Totnes Weekly Times*, 25th April 1891.
15. *Western Times*, 5th April 1856.
16. *Exeter and Plymouth Gazette*, 31st March 1894.
17. 'Smoking concert', Wikipedia. [online] Available at: <https://en.wikipedia.org/wiki/Smoking_concert> [Accessed 4th June 2017].
18. Absolute sale without reserve. *Western Times*, 22nd July 1892.
19. Prime timber for sale on Caseley and Willowray Farms. *Exeter Flying Post*, 22nd February 1871.
20. Auctions. *Western Morning News*, 24th May 1890.
21. *Exeter and Plymouth Gazette Daily Telegrams*, 'To tourist and picnic parties', 24th June 1869.
22. *Western Times*, 6th August 1886.
23. Dartmoor drives. *Western Times*, 26th May 1891.
24. Dartmoor excursions. *Western Morning News*, 27th June 1885.
25. Important alterations. *East and South Devon Advertiser*, 26th August 1893.
26. Kennedy, V., The Bovey Tracey Heritage Trust, 2005. *The Bovey Book: The Story of a Devonshire Town in Words and Pictures*. Bovey Tracey: Cottage Publishing, p.173.
27. *Western Times*, 7th October 1864.
28. *Western Times*, 26th October 1880.
29. *Post Office Directory of Devon & Cornwall*, 1866. London: Kelly & Co., pp.734, 755, 911, 912.

30. *Post Office Directory of Devon & Cornwall*, 1873. London: Kelly & Co., p.82.
31. The lodgers & the beetles. *East and South Devon Advertiser*, 24th October 1896.
32. Newton Abbot monthly sessions. *Western Daily Mercury*, 1st October 1862.
33. Newton. Petty sessions. *Western Times*, 24th August 1883.
34. *Kelly's Directory of Devonshire*, 1910. London: Kelly's Directories Ltd, p.90.
35. Newton. Petty sessions. *Western Times*, 24th August 1883.
36. Coffee taverns. *Western Times*, 24th October 1878.
37. *Exeter and Plymouth Gazette*, 29th October 1880.
38. Patterson, J., 2008. *Life in Victorian Britain*. London: Robinson. p.57.
39. BBC News, 7th January 2012 [online] Available at: <http://www.bbc.co.uk/news/business-16450526> [Accessed 26th April 2017].
40. BBC News 16th December 2013 [online] Available at: <http://www.bbc.co.uk/news/uk-25259505> [Accessed 8th June 2017].
41. Patterson, J., 2008. *Life in Victorian Britain*. London: Robinson. p.55.
42. Patterson, J., 2008. *Life in Victorian Britain*. London: Robinson. p.55.
43. Francatelli, C.E., 1861. The cook's guide and housekeeper's & butler's assistant. *Adulteration of Food* [online] Available at: <http://www.thecooksguide.com/articles/adulteration.html> [Accessed 10th June 2017].
44. Broomfield, A., 2007. *Food and Cooking in Victorian England*. [e-book] Westport: Greenwood Publishing Group. Available at: <Google Books https://books.google.co.uk> [Accessed 10th June 2017].
45. Artisan Food Law, 2014. *History of Food Law: The 19th Century* [online] Available at: <http://www.artisanfoodlaw.co.uk> [Accessed 10th June 2017].
46. Francatelli, C.E., 1861. The cook's guide and housekeeper's & butler's assistant. *Adulteration of Food* [online] Available at: http://www.thecooksguide.com/articles/adulteration.html [Accessed 10th June 2017].
47. Wilson, B., 2008. *Swindled. The Dark History of Food Fraud, from Poisoned Candy to Counterfeit Coffee*. Princeton, NJ: Princeton University Press. p.19.
48. Bloy, M., 2014. The Victorian web. *Victorian Legislation: A Timeline* [online] Available at: <http://www.victorianweb.org/history/legistl.html> [Accessed 6th October 2016].
49. Artisan Food Law, 2014. *History of Food Law: The 19th Century* [online] Available at: <http://www.artisanfoodlaw.co.uk> [Accessed 10th June 2017].
50. Bloy, M., 2014. The Victorian web. *Victorian Legislation: A Timeline*

[online] Available at: <http://www.victorianweb.org/history/legistl.html> [Accessed 6th October 2016].

51. Holdsworth, W.A., 1872. *The Licensing Act, 1872, with Explanatory Intr., and Notes.* [e-book] London: George Routledge and Sons. Available at: <https://books.google.co.uk> [Accessed 11th June 2017].

52. Christmas markets. *Western Times*, 23rd December 1886.

53. *Billing's Directory and Gazetteer* of *Devonshire 1857*, p.320. Birmingham: M. Billing.

54. *Billing's Directory and Gazetteer* of *Devonshire 1857*, pp.96, 319. Birmingham: M. Billing.

55. Public notices. *East and South Devon Advertiser*, 18th December 1886.

56. Moretonhampstead History Society, 2013. *Clock- and Watchmakers.* [online] Available at: <http://www.moretonhampstead.org.uk/texts/glimpses/occupations/clockmakers.ghtml> [accessed 16th June 2017].

57. Friend, G., 1989. *Memories of Moretonhampstead.* Tiverton: Devon Books. p.52.

58. *Totnes Weekly Times*, 24th December 1892.

All historical newspaper articles sourced from the British Newspaper Archive. Available at: <www.britishnewspaperarchive.co.uk> [Accessed between December 2016 and June 2017].

6.   Continuity and change
Social life, celebrations, and leisure activities in the Wrey Valley during the Victorian era

Alastair Camp

The period of Queen Victoria's reign (1837–1901) is remembered as a time when the *Pax Britannica* was at its peak, Britain's imperial standing buttressed by its naval superiority, its global economic and commercial power benefiting from its head start in the Industrial Revolution and the technological innovation which significantly underpinned it. Concurrently, whilst 'Victorian values'[1] emphasised Christian religious observance, respectability, freedom and progress, the challenge of Charles Darwin's *On the Origin of Species by Means of Natural Selection* (published 1859) was shaking the Christian world.

The Wrey Valley, between Bovey Tracey and Moretonhampstead, reflected these national developments to varying extents in its social and leisure activities and celebrations. Certainly, the coming of the railway to Lustleigh in 1866 opened the valley to visitors, ideas and activities from farther afield. Although many local leisure activities and sports remained rooted in a local and rural tradition, and continued with relatively little change over Victoria's reign, some such as wrestling declined, whilst others such as amateur dramatics opened up, providing opportunities to a broader range of participants. In class-bound Victorian Britain, the Wrey Valley saw traditional pastimes being enjoyed by many people, although the role of local gentry in funding various activities is clear, together with a trend from the 1870s onwards towards leisure time being seen as a vehicle for moral 'improvement' of the working man, of which the Temperance movement provides a prominent example. Moreover, at a time when Britain's state government remained relatively small, devolution of further power to local parishes gave increasing emphasis to poor relief, spawning an increasingly philanthropic dimension to social life as a conduit for fund-raising. An enduring feature across this era was a local reflection of national pride in Britain's global power, monarchy and patriotism, which saw its outlet in the many celebrations marking the way-points of Victoria's reign and where locally established sports, dancing and feasting gave their own flavour to a shared national euphoria. In its social and leisure activities, the Wrey Valley therefore demonstrated both continuity and change, as the advent of the railway, other new technologies and evolving political, economic and social factors brought their broad tapestry of influence to bear in various different ways.

In terms of local sports, the traditional rural sport of hunting maintained its attraction throughout the nineteenth century. In 1829, the *Sherborne Mercury* reported that 'two fine foxes were traced into Lustleigh Cleave by some labourers ... about a hundred sporting farmers assembled from adjoining parishes ... the gallant reynards were quickly destroyed by a discharge of musketry'.[2] Fox hunting continued its expansion during the nineteenth century, Robert Tombs[3] noting that it brought the gentry, farmers and increasingly the middle classes together – although the extent of the labourers' involvement in this Lustleigh hunt is perhaps debatable. Nevertheless, by 1866 the numbers involved in hunting were growing, 'Squire Bragg's excellent pack of hounds ... afforded the local farmers some first class sport. The two hundred sportsmen – "happy nimrods" – later assembled at Pollard's White Hart Hotel at Moreton, where they enjoyed a sumptuous repast'.[4] Toasts were made to 'the Army and Navy' and 'Agriculture and Commerce', while 'Mr Pollard spoke in the highest terms of Mr Bragg, [commending] his contribution to the sport of his friends', highlighting the traditional role of local gentry in facilitating such events.

After the arrival of the railway, there is evidence that the new transport links drew a wider cast of participants. In 1887, a report of an otter hunt in the tributaries of the River Bovey refers to the meet taking place at Bovey Tracey railway station, the hounds drawing up the Bovey, through Lustleigh and along the valley towards Wrey Barton. Although no otters were captured this time, it was noted that 'glorious river and moorland scenery ... made up for an otherwise tiresome journey',[5] indicating that the area's natural beauty was an important attraction in such sports. Similar evidence of the railway bringing new faces to local competition comes from a pigeon-shooting match in 1881 in a Lustleigh field 'belonging to Mr T Wills', in which participants came from Exeter, Newton Abbot, Bovey Tracey, Moreton and Chagford, 'the victor of a capital match being Mr T. Amery of Lustleigh, winning a prize of £5'.[6]

Sporting events, however, also continued to demonstrate a distinctly local flavour throughout Victoria's reign, the *Western Times* reporting in 1886 on 'an exciting horse race in Lustleigh ... a race for honour [which] shook the inhabitants out of their usual lethargy ... entering into the spirit of the contest with considerable zest.'[7] Sadly, 'Plucky Joe', despite being 'a spirited cob', failed to clear the church style at the first jump, effectively handing over the honours to his opponent, 'Cock of the Walk'. Wrestling, a traditional Dartmoor sport, did not, however, demonstrate the same longevity as some other sports. In *Small Talk at Wreyland* (1918), Cecil Torr of Lustleigh recounts his grandfather's tale of a party of parsons and doctors at 'Gidly' [*sic*] in 1843, where wrestling took place, one combatant suffering a broken arm. In the morality of the Victorian era, his grandfather noted that it was 'high time to do something with these fellows – how can people go to church and sit under them?'[8] But, writing in 1918, Torr observes that 'wrestling in this district died out fifty years ago' – supported by his grandfather's assertion in 1858 that he had just seen 'a grand wrestling match at Moreton ... but a few years earlier there was wrestling at Moreton every summer ... it was often that so-and-so had gone there instead of sticking to work'.[9] Some things seem, therefore, never to change, but it remains unclear exactly what mix of factors precipitated the demise of wrestling in the Wrey Valley, although the growing popularity of other team games doubtless played a part.

Rugby football and cricket were sports which remained popular during the Victorian era and appear to have appealed to a broad social spectrum, these robust team sports embracing moral exhortation and a degree of cultural unity, in which all classes took pleasure.[10] In 1861, Cecil Torr's grandfather noted that [rugby] football 'was a game much played in my youth, but cricket was my favourite'.[11] In 1901 it was still very popular even if local tactics were not necessarily the strongest. The

Lustleigh Parish Magazine of February that year noted a recently drawn game against Highweek Juniors of one try per side, with Lustleigh's Percy Wills being a 'tower of strength' – albeit rather wistfully observing that 'the players would soon improve if they had a few men who knew the game to assist them'.[12] A similar approach of keen amateurism saw the Lustleigh cricket team lose in September 1880 at Moretonhampstead by an innings and ten runs, after following on – 'a very poor show they made.[13] The team's fortunes, however, subsequently improved, for by 1888, Lustleigh was on a winning streak of eight wins to just one loss, with victories over Ashburton and Chudleigh. Moreover, in this most Victorian of all team games where practice took place most evenings in a field by the Cleave Hotel, youngsters were equally keen to get involved, the *Parish Magazine* reporting that the choir boys played every Saturday at the rectory.[14]

The arrival of the railway at Lustleigh in 1866 was itself marked by a heady mix of traditional feasting, sports and entertainments, with local rivalries still evident even as the brave new world was further opened up. Praising 'the yeomen of Lustleigh', the *Western Times* noted that 'a scheme [they devise] is sure to be carried out … when they have competing parties to contend with'.[15] Lustleigh's 500 parishioners raised £40 to fund the celebration, although one person refused to subscribe 'on the lame pretence that a general holiday would encourage the Bovey "roughs" to attend and cause a disturbance'. Fortunately, the newspaper was able to record that 'many good folks of Bovey were on the ground but did nothing to justify this aspersion on their character'. Mr T. Wills presided over the celebrations which took place in one of his fields, 'a cold collation being served up to all labouring men of the parish', with 'a splendid tea then later served to all comers free of charge'. Amusements included donkey racing, foot racing, wrestling, and dancing to the music of the Chagford Brass Band, with local pride in national technological progress being reflected in a hearty rendition of the National Anthem as 'red, white and blue floated in the breeze'. In these social celebrations we might therefore detect an echo of the Great Exhibition of 1851, which represented the nation's visible embodiment of commercial, technological and political progress.[16]

There followed a significant increase in visitors to the Wrey Valley, which became host to a variety of outside groups seeking new opportunities for their leisure. An example in 1871 was the visit on the Whitsun bank holiday of Newton Abbot's Methodist Free Church Mutual Improvement Society to Lustleigh on their annual outing, on a day when the railway's cheap tickets saw rail take the lion's share of excursion traffic.[17] It was noted that 'many had never previously visited the mighty Cleave', an indication of the attractions now being enjoyed in leisure time through a combination of rail communications and the allure of the natural landscape – but with traditional social ties and a strong moral focus remaining important factors. This blend remained typical – in 1888, a guild of over 50 people from Budleigh Salterton visited Lustleigh and its Cleave, their visit including a short church service held for them by the Reverend R.C. Price.[18] Here we see examples of 'the countryside' (a term coined in the nineteenth century) acquiring a central role as representing the true essence of England[19] and becoming a greater aspiration of leisure activity for town dwellers. Of course, the railway also opened up opportunities in the other direction and, in 1894, as a result of their own fund-raising through a concert they put on, a group of Lustleigh schoolchildren visited Teignmouth by train.[20] The trains also provided an innovative and convenient draw for leisure travel on a smaller scale – in 1872, children of the Moreton Wesleyan Sunday School had an excursion to Lustleigh by train, a large party of children and teachers singing for the local people before enjoying cakes and cream supplied by 'S. N. Neck Esq. and his kind and benevolent lady'.[21] The same year, Lustleigh Church hosted the annual festival of the choral associations of the deaneries of Moreton, Ipplepen and Totnes, a 'full congregation' contributing to the restoration fund for the church.[22]

The agricultural character of the Wrey Valley had long shaped many of its social activities, although it was not until 1844 that a meeting at the White Hart Inn in Moretonhampstead was held to set up a farmers' club for the town and adjoining parishes, including North Bovey, Chagford, Bovey Tracey and Lustleigh. Seventy farmers attended and it was agreed that the similarity of soil type would help assure fair competition for produce, while there would be cattle shows, too – another example of the inter-parish rivalry which prevailed in most social settings; annual subscriptions were set at 5 shillings. Interestingly, at a time when national political debate was focused on the arguments for and against free trade in the run-up to repeal of the Corn Laws (1846) and rural communities feared for the possible impact on produce prices, the club's rules specifically allowed for petitions to Parliament on issues such as local taxation, quarter sessions and 'anything intimately connected with farmers' interests'.[23] So, social life embraced an overtly political dimension, the inaugural meeting's minutes recording the view that there was 'no reason why the farmers' tongues should be tied'. By 1848, the club was firmly established and the fifth annual ploughing match had taken place in fields belonging to Messrs John and Thomas Amery in Lustleigh. There were 28 competitors, the principal prize – a plate worth 3 guineas – won by W. Webber, ploughman to Mr J. Strong of Drewinsteignton, although there was evidently a lighter side to the competition, with 'a prize of one pound going to W. Mardon, servant to J. Ponsford Esq., for the largest family'[24] (he had eight children). Sadly, it is not clear whether the family were present at the event, the details presented in the newspaper report focusing entirely on the adult male perspective. Again, there followed a dinner at Cann's White Hart Inn, Moreton, where toasts included 'The Queen', 'The Army and Navy' and 'Earl Fortescue, Lord Lieutenant of Devon'. Even in the social setting, deference and respect for national institutions were rarely overlooked.

The remote rural setting of Dartmoor inevitably influenced local social life, Brian Le Mesurier[25] noting that for centuries and well into the Victorian period, Dartmoor people had spent their limited leisure time making up their own entertainments to while away the evenings. Traditional tunes were played on an accordion, with some men being famed for 'dancing on the washboard, producing the steps that were displayed at fairs on the tailboards of carts'. Other variations included comedy skits and stories, and the tradition of making small articulated 'jig dolls' dance on a board to the accompaniment of an accordion. It is hard to find local references to these activities in the historical record, although a newspaper report in 1891[26] refers to a very successful entertainment in the Church House at Lustleigh. This included 'two dialogues by Mr & Mrs Engelbach and Mr Mainwaring' and 'songs, comic and otherwise, by the remainder of the party'. Whether or not these songs and comedy turns used long-established traditional material or not is unrecorded, but it does seem to be evidence of the continuation of a traditional Dartmoor entertainment format, towards the end of the Victorian era.

As Victoria's reign advanced, there is evidence of an increasing variety of social and leisure activities, embracing horticulture, amateur theatricals, dances and bazaars, with widening participation. Although there had been a 'Cottage Garden Society' in Lustleigh for some years, the first show of the Lustleigh Horticultural Society in 1887 is mentioned in the 1888 *Lustleigh Parish Magazine*.[27] This took place jointly with the second annual fête of the local branch of the Rational Sick and Burial Society in Mr Henwood's meadow, 'a large number of special prizes being offered by the gentry of the district', and so combined social and leisure activities with a new focus on encouraging people to provide for their futures. This was clearly a family occasion, 'the tent present[ing] quite a gay appearance', and over 1,000 people were admitted, with sports and dancing 'kept up till dark; the utmost good humour prevailed'. By 1897, the Show was well established as 'quite the event of the year in the pretty little village',[28] its reputation drawing visitors from the surrounding district, with the benefit of the rail links, and 520 competitive entries being admitted. Exhibitors and nurserymen arrived by train from Torquay and Newton Abbot, and continuing societal distinctions were reflected in specific prize categories for 'cottagers' and 'tradesmen', while for children there were prizes for those attending 'Board or Sunday Schools'. Clearly, the event appealed to many people, doubtless also attracted by sporting contests, dancing and a performance by the Bovey Handbell Ringers. By 1895, the fête, taking place on Whit Monday, was attested as 'a great success',[29] its format mirroring that of 1887, and its sports now including high jump, hurdle races and an egg and spoon race for the children. On Cecil Torr's account, however, in 1900 not everything went according to plan,[30] as 'a gust of wind ripped the poultry tent almost in half ... men were rushing in and being pulled out by screaming females'. Torr also notes a rather sharp-edged commercialism: 'excursion trains kept arriving, innocent passengers paying their sixpences, wondering why the crowd at the gate laughed at them!'

Long-established customs included the ceremony of 'beating the bounds' of Lustleigh Parish as a symbolic underpinning of local 'belonging'; although this had fallen into disuse and was not revived until the twentieth century.[31] Cecil Torr notes another example – dancing around the May Pole at the flower show – but claims credit for re-establishing the custom on May Day itself,[32] when the May Queen (elected by the local schoolchildren) was enthroned on a rock on which her name was carved before the children's tea – 'the main business of the day'.

Amateur dramatics came to Lustleigh in 1879, providing a new type

Figure 6.1: *The Barn Owls Amateur Dramatic Club, Lustleigh, formed in 1879.*
(Courtesy of Lustleigh Community Archive)

of social activity and entertainment, when the Barn Owls Amateur Dramatic Club was formed, taking their name from the site of their performances in the Reverend Frederic Ensor's barn. Formed by a talented actor, James Nutcombe Gould, a local newspaper remarked that 'a theatrical performance far up on the Dartmoor range is indeed a novelty ... of course, all the people of the surrounding district were there'.[33] Described as the 'pervading spirit' of the Barn Owls, James Gould had been a friend of a famous amateur actor, Henry Irving, illustrating how personal interests and enterprise also played an important role in the introduction of new leisure activities. The first performances were *A Phenomenon in a Smock Frock* and *Little Toddlekins*, proceeds being donated to 'widows and orphans of soldiers who had fallen in the war in South Africa'. Both men and women acted in the plays, a domestic drama *The Chimney Corner* in 1880 seeing 'Mr J. N. Gould [as] perfection as Peter Probity, while the party of Patty Probity was well sustained by Miss Mary Gould'.[34] It was noted that the theatre had been much improved, 'the walls completely hidden by flags'. The Bovey Tracey Pottery Band played during the interval and local philanthropy and Christian duty were reflected in proceeds being donated towards the new church organ. Undaunted by more serious fare, the Barn Owls also addressed their talents to Shakespeare's *The Merchant of Venice* and *The Taming of the Shrew*, the latter performed in 1883 at the Dolphin Hotel in Bovey Tracey with the patronage of the aristocracy including the Duke and Duchess of Somerset.[35]

By 1881, an annual ball had become an established feature at Lustleigh's Cleave Hotel, attended that year by 80 people – a number coming from long distances – with dancing to the music of Tanner's Quadrille Band.[36] Other new leisure activities followed, an 'American Bazaar' being held in August 1889, raising £39. 9s. 0d. towards the church bell fund, the items for sale being 'not new things, but ... any old things which people like to spare'[37] – a jumble sale. Misses Morris and Wills provided 'excellent tea and cakes', alongside singing and music. The next year, 1890, an arts and crafts exhibition appeared in the Church House 'which would do credit to many large centres of population',[38] whose object was again to contribute to the church bell fund and to establish an art class in the village. Over 400 people attended plus schoolchildren, with wood carvings 'of high excellence' from as far afield as Tunbridge, together with more local entries from Kingskerswell and the Aller Vale Pottery. Reflecting local interest in empire, there were also 'fine pictures and vase curiosities from all lands'.

Nationally important events were always the cause for a good celebration in the Wrey Valley. In 1856, the end of the Crimean War (1853–1856) was marked by a celebration at Moretonhampstead, with roast beef, plum pudding and plenty of beer, festivities being held in a barn to the accompaniment of fiddlers and dancing.[39] Later in Victoria's reign, a 'Patriotic Concert' was held in Lustleigh in 1899 at the start of the Boer War (1899–1902), raising £13. 12s. 9d. for the Association for Wives and Children of Soldiers and Sailors.[40] It was recorded that the Church House was crowded, with over 200 in the audience, the entertainment, including a recitation of *The Toy Symphony*, being enjoyed 'by people of all classes'. Celebrations of royal events took place throughout the era, providing outlets for expression of patriotism, philanthropy and fun. In 1863, 'the little parish of Lustleigh was all alive with loyalty'[41] for the wedding of the Prince of Wales and Princess Alexandra of Denmark where the morning began 'with the ringing of bells, firing of guns and [sound of] blacksmiths' anvils'. Over 400 people attended, the men enjoying 'substantial food and cider', the women and children 'a plentiful supply of tea and currant cake', followed by 'rural sports and dancing'. For the marriage of the Duke of York and Princess Mary in 1893, the *Lustleigh Parish Magazine*[42] records that every child was presented with a medal and then processed to 'Petherbridge Moor' [*sic*] for 'an excellent tea' and sports. Those in receipt of poor relief were given half a crown each, the magazine ending with the stirring peroration: 'May the respect and affection with which the Royal Family are regarded ever exist'.

Naturally, the milestones of Victoria's reign followed the same enthusiastic pattern, her Golden Jubilee (1887) celebrated with the usual 'repast of beef, plum-pudding and one quart of cider given to all males above fourteen years of age'[43] and 'an excellent high tea for the women and children'. The intrinsic linkage between church and state was reflected in a church service at two o'clock, and the role of local gentry through the gift by Mr Wills of East Wrey of memorial stones. Thereafter, 400 people processed to nearby fields, accompanied by the Bovey Tracey town band, where the children received jubilee medals and sports and dancing took place, with £25 raised towards the cost of steps to the church lych gate as a permanent memorial. A little sniffily, the *Western Times*[44] lamented that 'sports of various kinds and a band of minstrels will have more charms for the villagers than cut and dried platitudes, however eloquently delivered', which perhaps contains a ring of truth as far as some, at least, may have been concerned. Similar festivities and religious dedication attended Victoria's Diamond Jubilee (1897) and her eightieth birthday (1899), with her death in 1901 after a reign of over 63 years being marked only by the 'toll of bells late into the evening'.[45]

Towards the latter part of the nineteenth century, a new social movement appeared in Lustleigh in response to national moral, social and political concerns – that of temperance, alcoholic drink being seen as the core of the problems afflicting many of the lower social orders.[46] In 1898, the chaplain of Exeter Prison gave a lecture at Lustleigh warning his audience of the 'misery which comes sooner or later to the drunkard', although the *Parish Magazine* observed that 'few came to hear the lecture'.[47] Nevertheless, the Reverend G.Y. Comyns remained strongly committed to the cause, preaching a sermon on temperance in December 1898, praying that 'some good effect will follow … by God's blessing'.[48] It clearly had an impact, since a well-attended public meeting that same month, at which the Bishop of Crediton spoke, resolved to establish a local branch of the Church of England Temperance Society, along with its juvenile section, the Band of Hope. The latter soon numbered 40 children, under the supervision of Mrs Wise, whose

Figure 6.2: *The Rechabites, Lustleigh - promoting temperance and social improvement.*
(Courtesy of Lustleigh Community Archive)

song was the optimistic 'My drink is water bright'. In July 1899, it was recorded that a tea was held for members of the band and their mothers at the rectory; at this point, at least, the youngsters were adhering to their pledge.

Temperance was at the forefront of a wider range of new leisure activities which were generally aimed at 'moral improvement' and good use of time. Robert Tombs sees a national response in this to the publication of Darwin's *On the Origin of Species* which challenged the Christian world and saw the Church take the lead in a campaign of religiously inspired improvement activities.[49] For example, 1899 saw a musical concert given in the Church House by the Lustleigh Men's Bible Class, arranged through 'the kindness of Mrs Prior', in aid of local charities.[50] The sum of £3. 1s. 2d. was raised for 13 local families to purchase coal, meat and groceries. A new night school for men and boys over 16 met for the first time in November 1888, the hope being that 'many young men and boys would continue in learning',[51] it was 'fairly attended' and the first book was *Uncle Tom's Cabin*. The Reading Room later spawned new competitive activity, albeit of a genteel kind; 1901 saw its members host the Bovey Working Men's Club to a game of bagatelle, Bovey winning this time by ten points. The 'improvement' theme had other dimensions, too, with varying degrees of success; in 1891 a Mothers' Meeting organised by Mrs Fisher and Mrs Wise tried to interest the village girls in embroidery although 'no one seemed to care about it'.[52] The ever-active Mrs Wise appeared to have had more success with establishing a needlework guild in 1889, its social and philanthropic aims reflected in each member being asked to produce two garments a year for the benefit of the poor.[53] A 'Working People's Cookery class', organised by Miss Vincent in 1890, appears to have been popular, even if the dishes which included 'Sheep's head with onion sauce' must have required quite a strong stomach.[54] Continuing the practical theme, a series of nursing lectures built on Dr Engelbach's earlier 'Ambulance Classes', Mrs Clare Goslett 'earnestly hoping that all classes will attend',[55] a particular concern being with typhoid fever which 'last year cost Lustleigh the loss of some hundreds of pounds'. Again, social, moral and economic concerns were factors underpinning some leisure activities.

Needless to say, not everything always went to plan. In 1891, Messrs Hall and Thompson exhibited their new 'diorama' to a good audience, giving 'a lucid and descriptive account of various countries to general satisfaction'.[56] Sadly, the presenters had to reprimand some noisy young people who interrupted the lecture, leading the *Parish Magazine* to brand their behaviour 'a disgrace … another proof that it is desirable to have a policeman stationed at Lustleigh'. The same technology used in a lecture on 'English Church History' in 1894 suffered a different challenge – this time, the *Parish Magazine* lamented that 'we should have been glad to have seen more present'.[57] An age of social hierarchy and deference was clearly not without its challenges, even in its leisure time; it appears that not all were willing participants.

In conclusion, social life, celebrations and leisure activities in the Wrey Valley reflected multiple interlocking trends during the Victorian era. Notwithstanding its relatively remote and rural location, the valley was never detached from national morality, social issues or economic trends, and the associated 'Victorian values' of religious observance, respectability, freedom and progress, all of which played out in its

Figure 6.3: *Lustleigh Cricket Pitch – an enduringly popular Victorian sport.* (Courtesy of Lustleigh Community Archive)

social life. The coming of the railway in 1866 brought faster change in technology, together with new visitors and ideas. It was a vital factor in the changes in leisure activities, although certainly not the only one; to this must be added the many moral and social imperatives of the time, perhaps most notably the Temperance movement, the pressure for 'self-improvement', the importance of philanthropy, and the greater role of the Church from about the 1870s onwards in many leisure pursuits. As such, whilst some sports and leisure activities declined in importance, a great many others now blossomed – the variety sometimes reflecting the particularly passionate interests and drive of some enterprising local people – which seem to have provided new opportunities for a broader range of participants, including arguably more avenues for women and children – albeit levels of interest were, as ever, variable. The role of local gentry in funding social life and celebrations (sometimes 'in kind' through the provision of land or other resources) was an enduring feature, as very evidently was the localisation of national pride in British global power, the monarchy and enthusiastic patriotism through major celebrations. In all of this, the Victorian era therefore represented a time of both continuity and considerable change in the social life, leisure activities and celebrations enjoyed by the people of the Wrey Valley.

Notes

1. Tombs, R., 2015. *The English and their History*. London: Penguin Books. p.456.
2. Devonshire: hunting. *Sherborne Mercury*, 9th February 1829.
3. Tombs, R., 2015. *The English and their History*. London: Penguin Books. p.485.
4. Moretonhampstead hunting feast. *Western Times*, 5th January 1866.
5. The chase: otter hunts in the Taw, the Teign, the Bovey and their tributaries. *Western Times*, 25th June 1887.
6. District news, Lustleigh: pigeon shooting. *Western Times*, 5th July 1881.
7. District news, Lustleigh: exciting race. *Western Times*, 16th April 1886.
8. Torr, C., 1918. *Small Talk at Wreyland Part 1*. Cambridge: Cambridge University Press. p.25.
9. Torr, C., 1918. *Small Talk at Wreyland Part 2*. Cambridge: Cambridge University Press. p.60.
10. Tombs, R., 2015. *The English and their History*. London: Penguin Books. p.457.
11. Torr, C., 1918. *Small Talk at Wreyland Part 2*. Cambridge: Cambridge University Press. p.60.
12. *Lustleigh Parish Magazine*, February 1901.
13. Cricket: Moreton versus Lustleigh. *Western Times*, 20th September 1880.
14. Crowdy, J., ed., 2001. *The Book of Lustleigh*. Tiverton: Halsgrove. p.111.
15. District news, Lustleigh: railway opening celebration. *Western Times*, 3rd August 1866.
16. Tombs, R., 2015. *The English and their History*. London: Penguin Books. p.465.
17. District news: Newton Whitsun holidays. *Western Times*, 1st June 1871.
18. *Lustleigh Parish Magazine*, July 1888.
19. Tombs, R., 2015. *The English and their History*. London: Penguin Books. p.489.
20. *Lustleigh Parish Magazine*, September 1894.
21. District news, Moretonhampstead: Wesleyan Sunday school. *Western Times*, 9th August 1872.
22. District news, Lustleigh: choral association. *Exeter Flying Post*, 10th July 1872.

23. Moretonhampstead Farmers' Club. *Exeter and Plymouth Gazette*, 27th January 1844.

24. Moretonhampstead Farmers' Club. *Western Times*, 28th October 1848.

25. Le Mesurier, B., 1977. 'Recreation'. In Gill, C., ed., *Dartmoor – A New Study*. Newton Abbot: David & Charles, p.225.

26. District news, Lustleigh. *Exeter and Plymouth Gazette*, 16th October 1891.

27. *Lustleigh Parish Magazine*, August 1888.

28. Lustleigh Flower Show – a successful event. *Exeter and Plymouth Gazette*, 3rd August 1897.

29. Fete at Lustleigh. *Western Times*, 6th June 1895.

30. Torr, C., 1918. *Small Talk at Wreyland Part 1*. Cambridge: Cambridge University Press. p.57.

31. Crowdy, C., ed., 2001. *The Book of Lustleigh*. Tiverton: Halsgrove. p.13.

32. Torr, C., 1918. *Small Talk at Wreyland Part 1*. Cambridge: Cambridge University Press. p.58.

33. Crowdy, J., ed., 2001. *The Book of Lustleigh*, Tiverton: Halsgrove. p.104.

34. Lustleigh: amateur theatricals. *Western Times*, 6th February 1880.

35. Crowdy, J., ed., 2001. *The Book of Lustleigh*. Tiverton: Halsgrove. p.105.

36. Lustleigh: annual ball. *Western Times*, 24th February 1881.

37. *Lustleigh Parish Magazine*, July/August 1889.

38. Art exhibition at Lustleigh', *Western Times*, 18th July 1890.

39. Torr, C., 1918. *Small Talk at Wreyland Part 1*. Cambridge: Cambridge University Press. pp.24–25.

40. *Lustleigh Parish Magazine*, May 1899.

41. Lustleigh: alive with loyalty. *Western Times*, 17th March 1863.

42. *Lustleigh Parish Magazine*, August 1893.

43. The Lustleigh Jubilee celebration. *Exeter and Plymouth Gazette*, 24th June 1887.

44. The Queen's Jubilee, Lustleigh, *Western Times*, 17th June 1887.

45. *Lustleigh Parish Magazine*, February 1901.

46. Tombs, R., 2015. *The English and their History*. London, Penguin Books. p.502.

47. *Lustleigh Parish Magazine*, February 1899.

48. Crowdy, J., ed., 2001. *The Book of Lustleigh*. Tiverton: Halsgrove. p.117.

49. Tombs, R., 2015. *The English and their History*. London, Penguin Books. p.464.

50. *Lustleigh Parish Magazine*, March 1899.

51. *Lustleigh Parish Magazine*, November and December 1888.

52. *Lustleigh Parish Magazine*, April 1891.

53. *Lustleigh Parish Magazine*, August 1889.

54. *Lustleigh Parish Magazine*, January 1890.

55. *Lustleigh Parish Magazine*, December 1895.
56. *Lustleigh Parish Magazine*, March 1891.
57. *Lustleigh Parish Magazine*, March 1894.

All newspaper articles cited are available at <www.britishnewspaperarchive. co.uk> [Accessed between September 2016 and June 2017]. Extracts from the *Lustleigh Parish Magazine* were sourced from the Lustleigh Community Archive, The Old Vestry, Lustleigh, Devon.

7. Mining in the Wrey Valley

Nick Walter

Historical setting

Mineral extraction in the area had been carried out well before the Victorian Age, this being the excavation of tin-rich gravels from the valley bottoms, technically referred to as 'streaming'. The resultant material was washed to refine it, and sometimes crushed, before being smelted in buildings known as 'blowing houses'. One documented site is known at Caseleigh (SX787821) on the Wrey brook, and another one probably existed near Drakeford Bridge on the River Bovey (SX789801). Tin streaming disappeared around the seventeenth century, probably due to the valley deposits being worked out. No tin mining in the modern sense (that is, underground working) is known in the immediate area.

One other economic mineral found locally is a rare form of iron oxide, known technically as micaceous haematite, normally referred to historically and locally as 'shiny ore' or 'shining ore'. The term 'shining ore' will be used here as it was the commonly used term in Victorian times. Shining ore occurs in thin veins in the local granite, the veins (or 'lodes') being almost vertical and trending roughly west to east. The steep hillsides of the Wrey Valley were highly suitable for driving horizontal 'levels' or 'adits' into the hill following the lode from where it outcropped at the surface. This industry was established on a small scale by the start of the nineteenth century, and had developed into a significant local industry by the end of the Victorian period.

Area of interest

Mining activities covered here include the Wrey Valley south of Moretonhampstead, and the associated mining to the south of Slade Cross (SX799812). Activity outside the Victorian era is mentioned briefly where appropriate. References to mining in the early Victorian period are fragmentary, especially for the small-scale and specialist mining in this area, and it is likely that mining on most sites occurred well before any written references. The grid references given for the mines refer to the processing site of each mine. It should be noted that virtually all the sites are on private property, and the underground workings are invariably in a dangerous condition.

Mining of 'shining ore' in the Victorian Age

The early use of shining ore was on a small scale, being used in its raw but refined form. Polwhele's *History of Devonshire*, published in 1797, summarises the uses as follows:

> There is a substance in the parish of Hennock and its neighbourhood, which was thought to be a kind of plumbago; but Dr Priestly and others, who have analysed it, say that it is nothing more than an ore of iron ... This substance is sometimes called the Devonshire sand ... At Bristol, the manufacturers attempted to make crucibles of it ... A few tons were annually sent to London ... as black lead for the cleaning of grates; and the remainder is disposed to the color-grinders, who work it up with their paints. It has been sold at the Exeter Quay, carriage included, from 3 to 8 guineas a ton.[1]

Another early use mentioned in contemporary documents refers to shining ore being used as a writing sand ('pounce'), used to fix ink into paper and soak up blots.[2] The industrial revolution of the mid-nineteenth century saw great advances in technical knowledge and engineering techniques. Widespread use of mass-produced iron and steel generated a need for specialist corrosion-resistant paints. The local ore was ideal as a base for this, the thin pure iron oxide flakes giving physical and chemical protection, and greatly prolonging the life of the paint. That, coupled with the arrival of the railway branch line in 1866, saw an expansion of the mining of shining ore.

However the shining ore was in demand for other uses, as shown by the following extract from the *Mining Journal* of April 1859:

> The Hennock 'shiny ore' had often been worked, but as often unsuccessfully, from the want of adequate means to bring the mines into operation and to manipulate the ore when produced. It is well known that an imitation ' black lead ' or 'Servants Friend' is easily and cheaply manufactured from this article, as well as there being a great consumption of it for lubricating machinery etc. Both of these have been sadly retarded by the irregularity and uncertainty of the supply from these mines.[3]

The above quotes Hennock as a location, as the earliest references to this mining are to Kelly, and to the working at Bowden Hill, west of Hennock. Both sites were at that time in Hennock parish.

The proximity of the railway meant easy movement of the ore to customers around the country, and also overseas, typically to paint makers. By the end of the nineteenth century mines were active in an area stretching from Plumley Mine (SX803807) to Kelly Mine (SX794817). All however were small affairs, rarely employing more than ten men and boys on any one site.

Kelly Mine (SX794817)

Kelly was the largest of the local mines, and was active for many years. The mine is first recorded in 1797, when it was quoted as 'a mine of rich ore, resembling black lead, which has been worked for several years past at a considerable advantage to the proprietor. A sample of said ore can be seen at Messrs. Trewmans and Son, printers of this paper'.[4] However the shining ore product has been found embedded in documents (from its use as writing sand) as far back as 1740, implying small scale extraction had been carried out for many years.

In the first half of the nineteenth century, references to Kelly Mine occur at irregular intervals, usually implying the landowner (at that time the Wills family) were operating the mine on their own account. Production was probably at a low level and not continuous, and the mine workforce likely amounted to only one or two labourers, possibly living on the mine site with their family. What is now the drying shed of the mine has been 'wrapped' around a much earlier roadside cottage, with fireplace and two small rooms. Various pottery finds on the site certainly point to domestic use in the eighteenth and nineteenth centuries. The following newspaper extracts suggest the landowner was selling the ore quite randomly, and open to offers from outside sources to run the operation. In 1836:

> To be granted for tender ... the ORE, commonly called TIN or SHINING ORE, on an estate called Kelly. It is raised in a field and premises adjoining the turnpike-road. The Ore is of excellent quality and can be obtained at a very inconsiderable expense by means of the Adits, Pits etc. by which the same has been hitherto advantageously procured. For further particulars apply to Mr James Wills, Kelly.[5]

In 1841:

> SHINING ORE for SALE, - A quantity of this ore, of superior quality, has been raised at Hennock, Devon. Samples may be had (gratis) on application to Mr Wills, Kelly, near Chudleigh. If desired the proprietor would let the mine for a term.[6]

The reference to Hennock is because Kelly Farm & Mine were in Hennock parish at this time. Chudleigh was the mail and coaching centre prior to the railway's arrival, thus mail for the Lustleigh area would be directed through Chudleigh.

In 1870:

> A very desirable Freehold property, consisting of the Kelly Estate, part of Slade Estate and Bullaton Cott ... There is a valuable mine of the ore commonly called Micacious [sic] Iron or shining ore on the property, which has been profitably worked by the proprietor. There is a large body of the ore which can be easily and cheaply raised, the mine being in thorough working order.[7]

As well as being advertised for sale, newspapers also carried notices from concerns wanting to buy shining ore. One such was in the *Western Times* dated 18 February 1860:

TO OWNERS OF SHINING ORE MINES

Wanted samples and lowest cash price, for 10 or 20 tons shining ore; quality must be first rate.

Address Tabberner and Sidebottom, Druggists, Manchester[8]

Of interest here is why a druggists i.e. a chemists should be using large quantities of shining ore. It may be they were making up and selling their own brand of 'black lead'.

Later in the nineteenth century the mine was put on a more professional footing, with local mining engineer William Henry Hosking leasing the mine by 1877. Even then production was low, with only two or three workers employed. Hosking had many mining interests, and it is likely he was running the mine as his own private project, as opposed to his usual employment as consulting engineer on much larger sites. The lease seems to have expired in 1892 when the mine was advertised to let, and 'containing several valuable lodes and equipped with waterwheel and stamps'.[9] That was not the end of William Hosking locally, as in that year he appears as the manager of Hawkmoor Mine (see below), only half a mile east of Kelly.

Kelly Mine did not remain idle for long, as by 1901 the site had been leased by the grandly named but obscure Scottish Silvoid Company, based in Glasgow and seemingly formed entirely to mine the Kelly ore and market it in Scotland. In that year the mine is recorded as employing 13 workers. This was an exceptionally high number, probably as a result of development work underground and expanding the surface processing works. Kelly Mine saw a major jump in production from that time, reaching a maximum of 202 tons of refined ore in 1907. The mine then continued at work for another 50 years, from around 1918 run by the Ferrubron Company, who ran the larger Great Rock Mine (outside the study area). This company had gradually taken over the other minor sites, which established a virtual monopoly on the supply of shining ore from Devon. Ferrubron relinquished the site in 1946, after which it was leased by the firm of Nicols & New for five years. With the closure of that firm in 1951, mining in and around the Wrey Valley finally ended.

Hawkmoor Mine (SX798817)

The first official record of Hawkmoor Mine is in 1892, but it is probable the mine site had been worked well before that. In 1849 nearby Bullaton Farm was sold: 'For Sale ... all that desirable estate called Bullaton ... one of the best sheep farms in the County. There is an iron mine on the property (which has been profitably worked)'.[10] That could refer either to what is now known as Hawkmoor Mine, or possibly to old workings on the Bullaton property above Kelly Mine. Hawkmoor Mine was active for only a few years after 1892, and the production data is unclear, as the tonnage is lumped in with production from other small mines. An incomplete map of the underground workings held by the Kelly Mine Preservation Society (KMPS) does imply significant production had occurred in that period. Refined ore was carted from the processing site (SX798817) uphill past the mine adits, then south to the road near Slade Cross. Either Lustleigh or Bovey railway stations could have been used.

Plumley and Shaptor Mines

Plumley and Shaptor mines are closely adjacent, situated in the woodlands above what became Hawkmoor Hospital. Processed shining ore from both mines was probably carted to Bovey railway station from 1866.

Plumley Mine (SX803807)

Plumley was certainly in existence by 1892, as documentary evidence exists showing the operation was being extended at that time, the mine being then referred to as Bovey Tracey Mine.[11] The Scottish company of R. & J. Dick were the controlling company in 1892, with the management of the mine in the hands of Alexander Livingstone, resident at Lustleigh, but originally from Scotland. Circumstantial evidence held by KMPS suggests Alexander was sent down from Scotland by Dick's to look after their mining interest. The correspondence below gives a flavour of the issues of the time, with access to water always a critical issue.

1892: Letter from Alexander Livingstone to Mr Harris of Plumley:

Yesterday I took as much of the stream as would fill the pond, so that I was able to try the water wheel and stamps, I consider about half of the whole stream, and this was done by Mr Slatter's consent. Now today Mr Slatter came to me and requested that I should turn the water back to him ... Now Sir it is of great importance to me and my master that this question of water should be settled at once, as my wheel and stamps are almost complete and we hope to get a lot of ore dealt with immediately.[12]

Mr Slatter and the Harris family were local landowners, Mr Edmund Slatter owning the Hawkmoor property and claiming the stream water, and the Harris's owning the site of Plumley Mine. Edmund Slatter later became a mine entrepreneur in his own right, owning the Shaptor Mine site and forming a mining company, the Ferrubron Manufacturing Company.

1897: Letter from Mr J Harris to the *Western Morning News*:

The principal properties from which shining ore is now produced have been in branches of my family for many years, and are now worked by parties under lease. For nearly half a century this mineral has been mined more or less continuously in several places adjoining the high road from Bovey Tracey to Moretonhampstead, most conspicuously on the Kelly estate, where the old working and refuse heaps are still to be seen, less conspicuous, but still in plain view of the main road, on the North Combe and Shaptor Estates, where the largest of the present mines are situated, and from some of which ore was taken longer ago than I can remember, certainly 40 years.[13]

From that it can be deduced that at least Plumley Mine (on the North Combe estate) was active by the 1850s. Production would have been very low, most likely hindered by the difficulty of transporting the ore. Presumably cart or packhorse were used, heading to Exeter for sale and shipment, as referred to by Polwhele in 1797.

Plumley Mine closed around 1907, with the machinery and plant being sold off on the expiration of the lease. The auction included a 14 ft waterwheel, four head stamp battery, pump, weighing machine, 6 tons of steel rails and two turntables.[14] Alexander Livingstone did not live long enough to oversee the mine's closure, as he died in 1897 at the early age of 40. Alexander's death was believed to have been from a mining-related disease, perhaps tuberculosis or silicosis. He left a widow heavily pregnant, and already with six children. Despite being destitute and homeless the family survived, and Alexander's descendants are now to be found in Britain, Europe and the USA.[15]

The photograph is of Alexander and Margaret Livingstone, taken in the 1890s, pictured with some of their children. The location is Shaptor Rock (SX810809), overlooking Bovey Tracey and Lustleigh. Alexander was at this time probably supervising work at Plumley Mine and resident at Brookfield, Lustleigh.

Figure 7.1: *Lustleigh resident Alexander Livingstone, on a picnic at Shaptor Rock whilst Alexander was the manager at the nearby Plumley Mine. Taken c.1896.*
(Courtesy of Lustleigh Community Archive)

Shaptor Mine (SX805809)

The site at Shaptor is only quarter of a mile north of the previously mentioned Plumley Mine, and seemingly opened in 1892, on land owned by Edmund Slatter of Hawkmoor House. Mr Slatter soon became a driving force behind shining ore mining, forming the Ferrubron Manufacturing Company which came to operate most of the local mines. Typical of these mines, the processing plant is situated beside a small stream (a tributary of the Bovey river) with the associated adits and shafts scattered up the hillside following the line of the ore lode. The mine closed around 1911, for most of its life having been overseen by mining engineer William Hosking.

Whereas most mines of this period relied on a waterwheel for their power, at Shaptor it seems a water turbine was the motive power. By the end of the nineteenth century, turbines were appearing in greater numbers, able to provide greater power than a traditional wheel. At the shining ore mines the power was usually needed for crushing ore by 'stamps', which would only need operating for short periods due to the low volume of material. With a suitable holding pond above the mine, a turbine could generate high power for a relatively short period, ideal for the processing of shining ore.

Wray and Pepperdon Mines

Wray (SX770848) (also known as Wray Barton) and Pepperdon (SX776836) (also known as Moorwood) were later sites, active around the middle of the twentieth century, so lie outside the timescale of this study. However both relied on the railway branch line to transport their material, so owe a debt to the Victorian development of the area.

Minor mining sites and trial works

During the Victorian period mining trials were carried out through the Wrey Valley, looking for deposits of shining ore. Some were no more than prospecting pits, others saw major excavations, and some producing of ore before work was abandoned. All have virtually no documented history, references to them often incidental in contemporary newspaper reports.

One such is an unnamed estate advertised for sale as follows in 1849, from the *Exeter and Plymouth Gazette*, 4 August 1849:

> To be sold in Fee, near Moretonhampstead, an Estate consisting of about 70 acres of arable, Meadow, and Orchard Land, with right of common of about 1500 Acres. There is a mine of shining ore and a quantity of capital Timber on the Estate.[16]

The above location is not stated, but matches that of Middle Combe, Lustleigh, which had been advertised for auction the previous year with 68 acres of land and 'a good lode of shining ore on the estate'.[17] Traces of mining are still visible at the site.

Another 'lost' mine is in the vicinity of Caseleigh and Elsford. Cecil Torr, writing in *Small Talk at Wreyland*, refers to Caseleigh Mine, 'which was for micaceous iron'.[18] No supporting documentary evidence has been found, but mining remains exist from just west of Caseleigh Manor, then east to the main road (A382) at SX787821, and uphill towards Elsford Farm. These remains include a processing site on the Wrey Brook, overlying a much earlier tin blowing house. It must be noted that there is no public access to this site.

Further north near Moretonhampstead, references exist to mining at Mardon Down. The exact site has not been traced, but information from the now deceased owner of Stacombe Farm (SX773873) point towards mining for shining ore having taken place in the vicinity of the farm. What are often thought to be mining remains around Headless Cross on Mardon Down are earthworks created by American military activity in the Second World War.

The deposits of shining ore crop out to the surface, and the bright appearance of the oxide would have made it very apparent in any disturbed ground or in stream beds. Prospecting consisted of digging pits and shallow trenches where the ore was noticed, to test the quality and quantity. However, most of the ore veins are very narrow, are too hard for paint use, and of no economic value.

Local miners

At the start of the Victorian age it is very difficult to identify individual miners, and usually impossible to determine where they worked. In the first half of the nineteenth century, mines were active on Central Dartmoor, south of Haytor, and on a very small scale in the Wrey Valley. The later census returns, coupled with official mining statistics, give a better idea of the importance of the industry locally. The peak year for shining ore mining was probably 1901, when a total of 35 miners were recorded at the local mines (13 at Kelly, ten at Shaptor, nine at Plumley, and three at Hawkmoor).[19] This seemed to be a period of expansion of the mines, with several of the mines seemingly undergoing development work, that is, driving access levels, finding ore reserves, and installing processing machinery, all prior to actual production.

A miner recorded in the census as resident in Lustleigh or Moreton-hampstead could easily be working several miles away and living in 'barracks' at the mine during the week. A fine example of this is Tommy Johns, resident in Lustleigh in the latter part of the nineteenth century. Tommy was a mine carpenter at that time, and is known to have worked at various mines around Dartmoor, including Steeperton, Vitifer, and Owlacombe. Around 1900 Tommy, then aged about 60, was the mine carpenter at Hexworthy Mine, on the open moor south of the Forest Inn. At the end of the working week (presumably midday on Saturday) he would return to Lustleigh by walking to either Ashburton or Buckfastleigh, and catch the train to Lustleigh via Totnes and Newton Abbot. This was a good example of professional miners having to go 'where the work was'.[20]

The shining ore miners tended to be mostly local men, who learnt on the job and lived in the vicinity. The Victorian housing estate at Brookfield, Lustleigh, is supposed to have been built to meet the need for housing working-class families, especially miners. Certainly by the 1901 census several of the houses were occupied by miners, one example being Samuel Hill, who was the mine 'captain' at Kelly, his 21-year-old son Jabez also being employed at Kelly Mine. Also living at Brookfield was 30-year-old miner George Rice, with his wife Sarah and 1-year-old son. Boarding with them was miner John Olding, and both men are known to have worked at Kelly. It is reasonable to assume George Rice was related (son?) to John Rice (aged 71), also living at Brookfield and recorded as a copper miner. Assuming John was not retired, then he was probably working at Ramsley Mine near South Zeal, which was a large copper mine active around that time.

Relationships between the landowner, the mining company and the miners seemed to have been very cordial. At Kelly Mine it is known the mine used the farmer's horse and cart to move refined ore to the railway station. The miners are recorded to have helped with the farmer's harvest in the autumn (paid for in cider).

Transport of shining ore

Much of the demand for shining ore was from the larger centres of population, and therefore transport of the weighty material was always an issue. Prior to the railway's construction it is likely packhorse was the preferred method of transport to the nearest port, when coastal shipping was used. At the end of the eighteenth century the ore was reported as sold on the Exeter Quay and dispatched to London, most likely carried by ship from Exeter. Even with the advent of the railway in the South West, coastal shipping was still important. The *Western Daily Press* of 24th July 1860 detailed the arrival at Bristol of the ship *Tavistock*, from Plymouth with mixed goods. Part of the load was '15 barrels shining ore'.[21] The Wrey Valley mines were the only important producer of this material, so probably the ore had come from a local mine, and carted to Plymouth, or possibly to the then nearest railhead of Newton Abbot for transfer to Plymouth dockside.

By the mid-nineteenth century the use of shining ore in paint was well established. The increasing use of iron structures and ships saw a high demand for the specialist protective paints using the ore. Paint incorporating the local shining ore was used all over the world in Victorian times, from the Royal Albert Bridge over the Tamar, to the Eiffel Tower, and in Australia. The material was seemingly so well known that there was no need to explain its use, as shown by an advert in the *Western Daily Press* of 24th October 1878: 'SHINING ORE, 20 Ton, in casks, cheap. – For particulars apply at 7, Gladstone Place, Lawrence Hill Station.'[22] [This was a Bristol address.]

Mining and the railway connection

The railway branch line was opened in 1866, but had been much discussed for several years previously. One of the advantages claimed was the development of mineral resources in the surrounding area. From the *Exeter and Plymouth Gazette* of 1866 comes the following:

It is supposed that the district is rich in minerals including copper, tin and iron, and the shipment of ores can be effected with facility at Torquay, Teignmouth and Dartmouth, and from these ports the Moreton district can be supplied with coal, in addition to that which is brought over the Bristol and Exeter and South Devon Railways.[23]

The allusion to copper could refer to the short-lived copper mine at Yarner, unless there was a hope that the rail line would eventually extend past Chagford to reach the copper mining area around South Zeal. Tin mining never achieved the hoped-for results, although short-lived tin mines were opened up near Chagford (Great Weeke, 1886–1891) and North Bovey (Great Wheal Eleanor, 1876–1883). Tin ore was invariably refined to a high level at the mine, and the actual tonnage of ore sent out would have been insignificant, although the refined ore was of high value.

Figure 7.2: *Underground in a local 'shiny ore' mine.*

References to the iron deposits were probably mainly directed at the large and well-established iron mines just south of Haytor, which produced high-quality ore, typically for dispatch to the South Wales steelworks. These are outside the study area, but used Bovey station as their railhead for many years. However the shining ore mines would have benefited greatly from the ability to move their ore to anywhere in the country. The availability of relatively cheap coal brought by the railway undoubtedly also helped the shining ore mines, which by the end of the nineteenth century invariably had coal-fired furnaces to dry the ore before packing and dispatch.

Soon after the line's opening in 1866, a proposal was made to lengthen the goods siding at Lustleigh specifically to cater for the iron ore trade:

> In reply to a letter from Mr Pridham expressing a desire to have the siding at Lustleigh extended and the cartway raised so as to facilitate the loading of trucks with iron ore … The secretary should enquire what number of tons the parties would guarantee per month.[24]

That never materialised, as probably it was soon realised the shining ore trade was a very specialist and low-volume one, with no need for dedicated facilities.

Ex-miners and railwaymen remember that in the twentieth century the ore was dispatched in barrels, and went as part of mixed goods in open wagons. Probably this was the method used in Victorian times. The highest production figure for Kelly (the largest of the local mines) was 202 tons, in 1907. That equates to around 450 barrels, that is, about nine barrels a week, with production in the nineteenth century less than that. John Harris, writing in 1897, stated that: 'The product is taken to Bovey and Lustleigh Stations, and sent to its various destinations'.[25] With goods trains running every day, the iron ore trade was a significant but not a major part of the goods traffic.

The railway connection was vital for linking the refined shining ore with its customers, which by the end of the nineteenth century could be anywhere. John Harris, whose family owned the Plumley Mine site, gave an insight into the trade as it existed in 1897:

> The ore is largely shipped to Germany, where it is made into paint for use on the bottoms of ships. A firm in London also manufactures from

it a paint called 'Ferroder' for iron structures, such as railway bridges. A considerable quantity is also used in Glasgow by a large firm.[26]

There is a strong local tradition of a German connection with the shining ore mines, but facts are hard to come by. The Scottish involvement in the mines is well proven, with the major manufacturing company of R. & J. Dick of Glasgow operating Plumley Mine, and the Scottish Silvoid Company leasing Kelly Mine in 1901.

Mine ownership

The mine sites themselves remained owned by the landowner, either the local estate (such as Plumley) or the farmer (as at Kelly Mine). Individuals or companies would lease the mine site for a fixed number of years (often in multiples of seven), and pay the landowner an annual rent and 'royalties'. Royalties was a variable sum based on the mine's output, which in Victorian times would be something like 6d. per ton. The mine sites were invariably sited on the steep hillsides of the Wrey and adjoining valleys, so the land itself was of limited agricultural value. Pollution from the mines was very limited, as any overflow from the processing would contain mostly clay and iron, unlike the gross contamination from copper or arsenic mines. At Kelly Mine a small 'slimes pit' trapped most of the waste water, and probably all the mines had a similar feature.

The mine sites today

It must be noted that, unless stated otherwise, the mine sites are on private property and should not be visited without prior permission. Likewise the underground workings, where still open, are invariably very dangerous and should not be entered. After closure, a mine site was usually cleared, with all the equipment sold off, either for scrap or re-use. What remains of the processing site today is usually just the foundations of buildings, overgrown pits and silted up ponds. The often collapsed adit mouths and associated waste dumps are found following the course of the lode into the hillside. On some mines vertical shafts occur, either for hauling and pumping, or for ventilation underground. Brooks (2016) covers the history of the local mines in detail, and what is currently visible.

The site of Wray Mine is on public land and open at all times. Foundations of the processing site are obvious (although much overgrown in the summer), and a walk through the wood will reveal the course of two tramways leading to the underground workings. Do NOT enter these.

Kelly Mine is the best preserved of the local mines, having been subject to extensive preservation and restoration after the mine closed in 1951. The mine site is only open on specific days, see the Kelly Mine website for details (www.kellymine.co.uk).

Summary

Mining activity in and around the Wrey Valley has always been on a small scale, ranging from early tin streaming in the valley bottoms, to the very specialist extraction of shining ore. In Victorian times the shining ore mines saw major expansion, due to two main influences. Firstly, the demand for shining ore increased due to the advance in engineering and the large scale use of iron and steel, which encouraged the development and use of corrosion resistant paints. Secondly, the arrival of the railway eased the problems (and cost) of transporting refined ore to the major customers in the cities and industrial centres. By the end of the Victorian Age the shining ore industry was well established, providing a regular income for the landowners, a steady job for the miners, and hopefully a small profit for the operating companies.

Notes on research

Recent research has been greatly helped by the availability of old newspapers online, through the British Newspaper Archive. It is fully indexed, so can be searched by subject, place names, dates, and so on. It is especially relevant to small mines which rarely made the headlines, and to quarries, which are massively under-recorded historically. The first and second edition Ordnance Survey maps show the mines' locations and layouts in some detail. It should be noted that the Tithe maps are of very little use in tracing these sites, as both mining and quarrying were not relevant to tithe calculations and therefore not normally recorded. However some of the place names on the Tithe lists can contain clues, for example, Mine Copse & Tin Field.

Notes

1. Polwhele R., 1797. *History of Devonshire*. Exeter: Trewman and Son.
2. De la Beche, H., 1839. *Report on the Geology of Cornwall, Devon & West Somerset*. London: Longman, Orme, Brown, Green, and Longmans. p.6.
3. Letter from George Henwood. *Mining Journal*, 23rd April 1859.
4. To be sold. *Exeter Flying Post*, 6th April 1797.
5. Kelley, Hennock, Devon. *Exeter Flying Post*, 15th September 1836.
6. Shining ore for sale. *Mining Journal*, 17th April 1841.
7. Hennock and Bovey Tracey, Devon'. *Exeter and Plymouth Gazette*, 16th September 1870.
8. To owners of shining ore mines. *Western Times*, 18th February 1860.
9. Kelly Mine Preservation Society (KMPS) newsletter, June 2017. p.3.
10. For sale. *Exeter Flying Post*, May 1849.
11. Harris family papers (copy held by KMPS).
12. Ibid.
13. Mysterious mines in Devonshire. *Western Morning News*, January 1897.
14. Auction Tuesday next. *Exeter and Plymouth Gazette*, 24th May 1907.
15. Livingstone family records, personal communication, P. Livingstone-Danby.
16. To be sold. *Exeter and Plymouth Gazette*, 4th August 1849.
17. Lustleigh, Devon. *Exeter and Plymouth Gazette*, 1st July 1848.
18. Torr, C., 1979. *Small Talk at Wreyland*, vol. III, Oxford: Oxford University Press. p.23.
19. Burt, R. et al., 1984. *Devon and Somerset Mine*, Exeter: University of Exeter Press.
20. Greeves, T., 2016. *Called Home – The Dartmoor Tin Miner 1860–1940*, Chacewater, Truro: Twelveheads Press. pp.33–34.
21. Shipping. *Western Daily Press*, 24th July 1860.
22. For sale. *Western Daily Press*, 24th October 1878.
23. The Moretonhampstead and South Devon Railway. *Exeter and Plymouth Gazette*, 8th June 1866.
24. Lang, M., personal communication.
25. Mysterious mines in Devonshire. *Western Morning News*, 8th January 1897.
26. Mysterious mines in Devonshire. *Western Morning News*, 8th January 1897.

General bibliography

Brooks, T., 2016. *Kelly Mine and the 'Shiny Ore' Mines of the Wray Valley.* Monograph.

Burt, R., Waite P. and Burnley, R., 1984. *Devon and Somerset Mines*, Exeter: University of Exeter Press.

Polwhele, R., 1797. *History of Devonshire.* Exeter: Trewman and Son.

Richardson, P., 1992. *Mines of Dartmoor and the Tamar Valley after 1913.* Northern Mine Research Society (NMRS).

8. Quarrying in the Wrey Valley

Nick Walter

Historical setting

The Wrey Valley lies on the eastern edge of the Dartmoor granite, a hard igneous stone used from prehistoric times as building and structural stone. Initially suitable stone would have been just picked from the surface to suit, for example, to form the foundations of Bronze Age huts and to create stone rows. By medieval times, stone was selected and cut to shape for purpose, good examples being found within the structure of all the local churches. All this stone seemed to have been obtained as 'moorstone', that is, stone lying on the surface. Quarrying as we would understand it is first recorded on Dartmoor around the start of the nineteenth century, with granite quarries active at Haytor and near Princetown by 1820. Transport of the stone off the moor was always an issue, resolved at first by the use of horse-drawn tramways at both locations. The picking of moorstone undoubtedly continued throughout the Victorian era, as field walling and minor buildings would only need the stone readily available on the surface.

The quarry age

The quarries most relevant to the Wrey Valley are those at East Wrey (SX782832), Blackingstone (SX784858), and Westcott (SX790873). The large Haytor quarries are also likely to have provided some stone for major building projects in the study area. The advent of the railway would have generated an impetus for the construction of luxury houses and villas for the wealthy upper and middle classes attracted to the area. That required shaped structural stone, with granite being eminently suitable and available locally. By 1800 the use of gunpowder for blasting in mines was well understood, and this technology would have readily spread to the quarrying industry. Blasting would be used at the quarry to break out large sections of granite, which would then be cut to the required shape and size by hand, using either 'wedging' or 'feather and tare'. Minor shaping and cutting would often be done where the stone was to be used. Stone produced at Blackingstone Quarry by Easton & Sons was partly finished off at the firm's workshop in Exeter, the granite being used for prestige buildings, ornamental and street work.

The construction of the railway line to Moretonhampstead brought expectations that granite traffic would contribute to the success of the line. In March 1867 the Moreton and South Devon Railway Company (M&SDR) reported on the completion of the line as follows:

> The entire works and stations are now complete. A siding has been made near the Bovey Pottery to facilitate the conveyance of granite from Haytor to the ports of Dartmouth and Teignmouth … There was every hope that the great work in connection with the Haytor granite would go on, as he heard that in the last few days arrangements had been made for the prosecution of the work. If that granite company should fall into the hands of men of substance and enterprise, that would be a fine thing for the railway. An enterprising firm from Exeter had opened a quarry, granite from which, if the works should be further continued, would have to be taken down to the Bovey station.[1]

The hoped-for granite trade did not benefit the railway to any great extent. The Haytor quarries were little worked after 1867, although some stone is believed to have been carted from Haytor to the railway at Bovey. The quarries around the Wrey Valley seemed to have supplied mostly local demand, with Blackingstone and Westcott probably carting stone to Exeter. The reference to 'an enterprising firm from Exeter' could refer to East Wrey Quarry, as the nearest station at Lustleigh did not have facilities for handling stone.

Blackingstone Quarry

Blackingstone has the earliest record of any local granite quarry. The *Western Times* of 1837 carried the following advert:

> GRANITE QUARRIES - Blackingstone Down
> TO BE LET by Private Contract, for a term of years, all those extensive GRANITE QUARRIES together with a Smiths Shop and other conveniences, on Blackingstone Down, in the parish of Bridford, near the turnpike road, leading from Exeter to Moreton, about nine miles from Exeter. These quarries are well known to contain the best granite in the County of Devon; large quantities have been used in the late improvements in the City of Exeter, and in the erection of the New Market at Crediton. They are now in the occupation of, and worked by Mr Thomas Whitaker, Surveyor, Exeter. Possession of the above premises can be given at Christmas next, and they may be viewed by applying to Mr John Wills, Blackingstone Farm, and further particulars be known on application (if by letter post paid) to Mr Sparke Amery, Ashburton, or Mr Windeatt, Solicitor, Totnes.[2]

From this it can be inferred that the quarry had been already been active for a significant time. A court case in 1850 regarding rights of way heard evidence from a stone cutter of Moreton who recollected working 30 years at Blackingstone. In the same case the quarry owner at that time was named as Jasper Amery, and it was stated some of the quarry workers lodged at the Gregory Arms, Doccombe.[3] Reference was also made to a second nearby quarry at Great Down.

Sometime after 1850 the quarry was taken over by the firm of J. Easton, who had major finishing works in Exeter, and supplied stone for the city. The granite was praised in the following terms: '[it] has a fine base, composed of feldspar, of two colours – light pink and light green … The stone splits easily with wedges, and is worked into copings, kerbs, steps, gate-posts and rollers'.[4] Attracting workers to this remote site must have been difficult, and in 1879 the quarry was looking for quarry workers: 'To Granite Masons – Wanted a few good workmen to work at the Quarries; also one or two Pitching Makers. – Apply to Foreman of Works, Blackenstone [*sic*], near Moretonhampstead; or J. Easton & Sons, Exeter'.[5] Further adverts appeared at regular intervals.

Figure 1: *Blackingstone Quarry, near Moretonhampstead, 1913/14*
(Private Collection)

The quarry remained active throughout the Victorian era, with some stone possibly sent out by rail from Moreton, but much seemingly carted direct. In 1893 the foreman was R. Crabb, as he, together with William Easton and carter George Moore, were prosecuted for 'causing a horse to be worked in lame and unfit state'.[6] All pleaded guilty, with Easton and Crabb fined £1 and Moore 5 shillings. Easton's also worked Haytor Quarry to a limited extent at the end of the nineteenth century.

Blackingstone continued in work well into the twentieth century. At the end of the Victorian era Easton's were employing 27 workers at the quarry. Activity gradually declined after that, with the quarry reverting to private ownership, but with some work continuing to the present day.

Westcott Quarry

This quarry is located at SX790873, close by what is now the B3212 from Moreton to Exeter. The site was active by 1829, then worked by Hutchings and Spry. By 1858 the quarry had been leased by J. Easton &

Son (of Blackingstone). Easton's seem to have ceased work there by 1894, as the quarry was advertised to let, the quarry being

> about a mile and a half from Dunsford Bridge (Teign Valley Railway) with downhill carriage thereto. There is an almost inexhaustible supply of the choicest granite, with Rubble Heap of thousands of tons, suitable and near for building the proposed bridges over the Teign.[7]

What this advert fails to mention is that the Teign Valley railway had yet to reach Dunsford Bridge, with the first work just starting on the extension of the Teign Valley line north of Ashton. It would another 19 years before the line reached Exeter. However, as stated, the quarry would have been a suitable source of stone for the railway construction. A fatal accident at the quarry was reported on in 1904,[8] with Mr Dickson recorded as the lessee. This was probably J.H. Dickson (aka 'Paddy' Dixon [sic]) who around the same time opened large quarries at Bridford, and was heavily involved in the construction of the Teign Valley Railway. Westcott Quarry is last heard of in 1913, when advertised to let.[9] The site is now hidden deep in woodland.

East Wrey Quarry

East Wrey Quarry is situated on the hillside above the Wrey Brook, at SX782832. The opening of the quarry may have coincided with the railway construction (1864–1866), implying it originated to supply granite for the railway engineering works, such as the bridges, culverts and viaducts. The granite at East Wrey was subtly different in appearance from that of Blackingstone, the East Wrey stone recorded as 'darker granite studded with clear quartz crystals'.[10] The quarry seems to have been taken up by Mr John Greep, as in 1887 it was advertised to let, and stated as

> has been successfully worked for many years past by Mr John Greep, who is now declining on account of ill-health. There is an unlimited supply of the very best granite, and the Quarry is in good working order. It is situated about two miles from both the Moreton and Lustleigh Railway-stations, with downhill carriage thereto.[11]

The quarry probably continued active but at a low level, as in 1897 the East Wrey estate was for sale, and included 'a partially developed quarry working at the present low rental of £9 per annum'.[12] By that time it was worked by the local Painter family, with William Painter recorded as a granite mason employing his sons, and with several other masons and a stone carter recorded resident in Lustleigh and the adjoining housing of Brookfield.[13] In 1898 the quarry was advertising for a worker: 'BLACKSMITH Wanted for tool sharpening: Apply to Painter Bros., Eastbury [*sic*] Granite Quarry, Lustleigh'.[14] Around the end of the Victorian era the quarry was taken over by A.R. Knight of Newton Abbot, although the Painter family were recorded as still involved up to 1914, when Scott Painter is referred to as the foreman at the quarry.[15] Knight's used the quarry to supply monumental stone, especially monuments and gravestones, and as Knight & Triggs continued working the quarry until the 1950s.[16]

A mystery quarry

> TO BUILDERS, CONTRACTORS, GRANITE MERCHANTS, etc. etc.
>
> A VALUABLE GRANITE QUARRY having been opened on the line of the Newton and Moreton Railway, quarter of a mile from Lustleigh Station, and the Granite having been pronounced by Mr Montfrics, Agent to the Marquis of Bute, Pwlly Pant Quarry, Caerphilly, South Wales (to whom references as to quality may be made) to be superior to any he has seen in Devon, Cornwall, or Scotland, the Proprietor of the said Quarry is willing to negotiate on liberal terms with any individual or company who may be disposed to work it. Samples of the stone, plain or polished, will be sent to any part of the kingdom on receipt of six postage stamps, on application to the proprietor, The Rev. J. N. GOULD, Stoke Rectory, Teignmouth.[17]

The above advert of 1868 may refer to East Wrey Quarry, however the Reverend J.N. Gould is recorded as a landowner compensated for the loss of land at Knowle (SX790805),[18] and the Gould family certainly owned the Knowle estate at the time. One possible location for this site is at SX79018061, marked as 'Quarry' on the 1905 Ordnance Survey Map.

As at East Wrey, the quarry may have originated to supply stone for the railway construction. The area around Knowle is also the most southerly point on the railway route where granite occurs on the surface.

The perils of quarrying

From the *Exeter Flying Post* of the 3rd May 1876 comes the following cautionary tale:

> FATAL ACCIDENT WHILST BLASTING – Mr Coroner Hooper held an inquest at the Topsham Inn, South-street, Exeter, on Saturday, touching the death of Thomas May, a quarryman, sixty-one years of age. Deceased resided at a place called Ducksmow, Moretonhampstead, and was in the habit of working the quarries for a Mr Easton. On the 1st April last he went to his employment as usual, and, having finished his day's work, he, according to agreement, went to a farm at Bridford, occupied by Mr Tuckett, to blast a rock, of a black ironstone formation. The deceased and Mr Tuckett bored a hole in the rock about fourteen inches deep, and the deceased than proceeded to charge it. Having placed the blasting powder in the hole, with some straw, he filled it up with rubble. This he drove into the hole with an iron bar. Deceased said to Mr Tuckett that he thought he had pretty well finished when the charge suddenly exploded, split up the rock, and threw the deceased some distance away. Mr Tuckett, who was standing on the top of the rock, was thrown down by the explosion, but was not burnt, and he immediately went to May's assistance. The same evening the deceased, who was badly injured, was taken to the Devon and Exeter Hospital, where he died last Friday evening from inflammation of the lungs, resulting from the injuries received. The jury returned a verdict of 'Accidental death'.[19]

The railway connection

Despite the optimism about the benefits the railway would bring, it seems the quarries did not directly benefit. There is no record of substantial granite exports on the railway, with the quarries only supplying building and monumental stone as far as the Exeter works of Easton's, presumably mostly transported by cart. However the surge in building houses for the wealthy classes moving into the area must have generated business for the local quarries.

Inspection of any of the surviving railway structures will reveal the widespread use of granite, with worked stone highly visible in viaducts, bridges, culverts and the station buildings. One contemporary record tells of the railway gangs intending to break up massive granite boulders near the line, but sparing them after a petition from the local residents.[20] Granite was a heavy and expensive material to move any great distance, so likely the railway gangs would obtain their building stone from the nearest possible site. Probably a combination of moorstone, quarry stone, and excavated stone was used. The resident stonemason at Castle Drogo (Wesley Key) believes that Blackingstone and East Wrey quarries both supplied stone for the railway construction.[21]

The 'moorstone' industry

The taking of moorstone from the fields and hillsides continued throughout the Victorian period. In 1871 John Perdon of Lustleigh is recorded in the census as a 'rock blower'. As John was an agricultural labourer in the previous census of 1861, he may have learned a new trade whilst supplying granite for the railway. There is a local tradition that stone from Lustleigh Cleave was used to build the railway, and in the Hammerslake area (where John Perdon lived) there is evidence of stone breaking taking place. Helen Harris (1992) states that granite was extracted at Yeo, Chagford: 'In the 1890's Exeter Corporation used granite from fields there for cutting kerbs and channels for the city's Fore Street'.[22] Thus the two ways of taking granite continued side by side for many years.

Summary

The granite industry was already well established by the start of the Victorian era, albeit to supply strictly local needs, and often using readily available surface stone. The improvement in transport systems, that is, turnpike roads and railway, did mean easier movement of stone, although in this area only resulted in supplying granite to Exeter. The railway construction itself used vast quantities of worked granite, with at least some of the demand being met by quarrying. A subsequent opening up of the area, and resultant house building for the wealthy incomers ensured the local quarry industry remained viable throughout Victorian times.

Notes on research

The quarrying industry is poorly documented, all the local quarries being worked by individuals or long-defunct companies who have left no known records. Contemporary local newspaper reports are the best source, most now easily available online through the British Newspaper Archive. However these reports usually only cover employment vacancies, change of ownership, or fatal accidents. Day-to-day activities and working conditions are noticeably absent. For a general overview of the granite industry refer to *South West Granite* by Peter Stanier (Cornish Hillside Publications, 1999).

Notes

1. Moretonhampstead and South Devon. *Western Times*, 1st March 1867.
2. Granite quarries – Blackingstone Down. *Western Times*, 9th September 1837.
3. Kelley v. Ackerley. *Exeter Flying Post*, 21st March 1859.
4. Devonshire granite. *Exeter and Plymouth Gazette*, 2nd September 1886.
5. To granite masons. *Western Times*, 15th May 1879.
6. Moretonhampstead Petty Sessions. *Western Times*, 6th January 1893.
7. Granite quarry to let. *Exeter and Plymouth Gazette*, 30th November 1894.
8. Fatal accident at Bridford. *Exeter and Plymouth Gazette*, 7th March 1904.
9. To be let. *Exeter and Plymouth Gazette*, 30th May 1913.
10. Stanier, P., 1999. *South West Granite*. St Austell: Cornish Hillside Publications. p.3.
11. To granite workers. *Exeter and Plymouth Gazette*, 4th January 1887.
12. South Devon. *Devon and Exeter Gazette*, 12th March 1897.
13. 1901 census, Lustleigh and Bovey Tracey.
14. Blacksmith wanted. *Exeter and Plymouth Gazette*, 18th May 1898.
15. Lustleigh Community Archive, WW1 roll of honour.
16. Stanier, P., 1999. *South West Granite*. St Austell: Cornish Hillside Publications. p.19.
17. To builders, contractors, granite merchants etc. *Exeter and Plymouth Gazette*, 19th June 1868.
18. Kingdom, A.R. and Lang, M., 2004. *The Newton Abbot to Moretonhampstead Railway*. Newton Abbot: ARK Publications. p.297.

19. Fatal accident whilst blasting. *Exeter Flying Post*, 3rd May 1876.
20. Owen, J., 2000. *The Moretonhampstead Branch*, Settle: Waterfront Publications. p.16.
21. Key, W., personal communication, July 2017.
22. Harris, H., 1992. *The Industrial Archaeology of Dartmoor*. 4th ed. Newton Abbot: Peninsula Press. p.77.

Historical newspaper articles sourced from the British Newspaper Archive, available at <www.britishnewspaperarchive.co.uk> [Accessed between April 2016 and August 2017].

9. Changes in the built environment and landscape of the Parish of Lustleigh

Michael Kearney

Introduction

To establish the impact on Lustleigh's built environment of, amongst other things, the arrival of the railway in 1866, a before and after comparison has been made using land and building records prepared for the civil parish in the years 1838 and 1905. Aligning closely with the start and end of Queen Victoria's reign, the two dates were in fact chosen for research convenience.

The Tithe Commutation Act of 1836 had enshrined in law a practice of commuting tithes payable – that is replacing the system of payment in kind still commonplace at the time with a conventional money 'equivalent'.[1] To this end, in-depth surveys of building and land use were made of all tithe paying parishes in England. Lustleigh's survey, which produced the standard combination of tithe map and supporting written apportionments (written details of land ownership, acreage, use and so forth), was completed in 1838.

In 1905 the second edition series of the Ordnance Survey (OS) 1:2500 sheets for Devonshire were issued. A helpful record in themselves for comparison purposes, the sheets' usefulness is augmented by the supplementary field book details (similar to the tithe apportionments) produced between 1910 and 1915 as part of what became known as the Lloyd George, or Domesday, Land Valuation Exercise.

Parish boundaries

The Parish of Lustleigh has developed and grown since the end of Victoria's reign. The transfer of Wreyland from Bovey Tracey in the 1950s was one of a series of boundary changes which presents Lustleigh civil parish as it is known today. Since similar before and after records for adjoining settlements are available, in order that like is compared with like this study focuses on that tract of land which now comprises Lustleigh, but which between 1838 and 1905 was a combination of the old Lustleigh parish, part of adjoining Bovey Tracey, and Sanduck.

Source material

A few words now (from a surveyor) on the building and land surveys conducted. The 1838 Tithe map for its time was a remarkable production in terms of level of detail, speed of delivery, and aesthetic appeal. However, due to the inconsistent application by local surveyors of the national terms of reference, the Tithe maps proved not to be as uniform in content as had been hoped, nor as comprehensive as the apportionments which accompanied them.[2] Parish by parish maps varied greatly in scale, accuracy and size.

Two grades of map merged. The first-class Tithe maps represented the highest standards of accuracy achievable at the time. Signed and sealed to this effect by the Tithe Commissioners this category amounted to some 17 per cent of the total.[3] The balance, the second-class variety, of which Lustleigh Parish is one, were a mixed collection, known to contain discrepancies and duplications. Whilst sufficient for commutation purposes of the 1836 Act, the second-class maps were never regarded as definitive records of land boundaries or building size.

The 1905 Ordnance Survey plans, on the other hand, achieved the reliable and precise representation of all features charted, although, interestingly, despite considerable technological advances in surveying, photography, and the whole process of map production, the second edition series was still not deemed sufficiently accurate to be acceptable as the principal means of resolving, for example, boundary disputes.[4]

The upshot is that a perfectly exact comparison of on the ground conditions, 1838 v. 1905, using the source materials discussed, is a practical impossibility. Whilst the sets of records have been invaluable in painting a reasonably detailed picture of the building development progress that took place, and its effects on the landscape, the data produced and which follows should be regarded as rather more indicative than definitive.

The railway

Perhaps the greatest agent of change in nineteenth-century England was the coming of the railways.[5] The scale of development was immense: from 2,000 miles of track in 1840, the 14 years to 1854 saw a 300 per cent increase in mileage covered. By the turn of the century, the aggregate track length had reached 23,000 miles.[6]

The 12-mile run of the Newton Abbot to Moretonhampstead Railway (the new line) which passed through Lustleigh was completed by 1866. Traditionally, Victorian railway development had responded to society's demand for coal, with communication between colliery and city initially paramount. Facilitated coal transport, along with greater ease of moving produce and materials in and out of Moretonhampstead and Lustleigh, certainly would have occupied the minds of the new line railway promoters. But, for the essentially rural, sparsely populated area the new line was to serve, the perception of a huge public desire to travel on this state-of-the-art technology (the potential for 'passenger fare profit') more likely would have been uppermost in speculator investor's minds.

The mass appeal of the railways in mid-Victorian times is perhaps hard to envisage in a travel age now so dominated by car and aeroplane. The extraordinary civil engineering lengths to which the builders went, and the very considerable long-term inconvenience and physical disruption the building of tens of thousands of embankments and cuttings and viaducts caused, were all to be conveniently subjugated in Mammon's interests. Keeping up with the neighbours was a key driver, the benefits of a very much faster information exchange (newspapers arrived on the day of issue, national mail deliveries achieved 24-hour turnaround) seduced populace and businesses alike. And, for many, the complex steam locomotives, with their attendant technological paraphernalia, were the science fiction spaceships of the time.[7] Such an all-encompassing intrusion into rural communities impinged from the start on the way people lived, and worked, what people ate and read, how people thought, and, by extension, upon the sort of buildings in which people lived and spent their time.

For South Devon, greatly enhanced inward (and also outward) tourism was expected to be one of the first benefits of railway arrival; there was an early expectation too of (passenger profit fare) opportunities arising from what was seen to be the possibility of daily commuting from the rural idylls to the business centres of Exeter, Plymouth and Torquay.

Much of which, it was hoped by those speculators whose interests went beyond railway development *per se*, would lead to other sources of profit, in for example the property development sphere, where, domestically certainly, but also in the case of those other buildings needed to satisfy the inevitable onrush of entrepreneurial activity, demand was expected to be considerable.

Housing

Figures 9.3 to 9.7, which follow, illustrate the extent and distribution of non-civil engineering development which took place in Lustleigh during the Victorian era. The figures are referenced to the annotated plan, Figure 9.8 in the appendix to this chapter.

It will be seen that there was a total of some 5,700 sq. m. of new development in the parish during the study period. This equated to a 42 per cent increase overall in the size of the built environment. The significant majority of new work concerned domestic construction activity.

For context, applying current design standards, building work of this scale might now produce a respectably sized, mixed housing estate of say 15 four-bedroom detached houses, and maybe 30 or so three-bedroom semis. With service access and garden space added, this theoretical development would take up something in the order of 8 acres (3¼ hectares) of land.[8] Superimposed on the village today, the new estate would consume the cricket ground (and pavilion), the orchard (stretching from the grounds of Underwood across to and including the village hall) together with many of the listed buildings in the Conservation Area between.

Lustleigh's housing boom had begun.

Concentrated and intensive development was of course for the most

Figure 9.1: New buildings begin to appear on the slopes above the centre of Lustleigh village. Reproduced from a Chapman & Son Postcard (Courtesy of Lustleigh Community Archive)

part avoided. The reality of dispersal of the new buildings throughout the parish meant that once the construction dust had settled, the effect on the appearance and flavour of the village was to prove rather less marked than had been initially imagined in some of the more negative local quarters.

The 1838 Tithe map depicts Lustleigh very much as a Celtic village – that is, a small centre around a church, with farmsteads and hamlets scattered for several miles around. Despite the later development tentacles that stretched out from the village centre towards the outlying farmsteads, and with now a railway line running through its very midst, this Celtic character, in 1905 still, for the most part, prevailed.

Dispersal involved the majority of the larger new homes (the so called villas) being built beyond what might loosely be described as the village centre. This is hardly surprising, given the paucity of central village land suitable for new construction. In any case, the trend, seen elsewhere in Devon (in Exmouth, for example) saw villa development away from the older core settlements, where streets were narrow and irregularly laid out. Higher-ground plots, with the opportunity for large gardens, were favoured: additionally these afforded uninterrupted rural views, building orientation as to preference, and clean air. As with elsewhere, with the drawbacks of living immediately adjacent to an active line becoming known, the railway was serving to discourage grander house building any closer to the trains than strictly necessary.

What smaller-scale housing development there was, however, did take place in, or very near to the heart of the village. Given the potential for heightened sensitivity here, it is surprising that there seem to have been few protests about the impact of the new upon the centuries' old, which by the turn of the century, had virtually doubled the housing-stock floor space in the village centre. Possibly this reflected the fact that Lustleigh, for a settlement of its kind, was not unique in either the scale or type of residential development that was happening. Typically the combination of railway accessibility and desirable living environments was seeing building-stock increases in many settlements hitherto largely untouched by meaningful development. This village trend, in Devon at least, was especially obvious in those places where the new railway connections were proving sufficiently sound to London, primarily, and, to a lesser extent, to the business centres of Bristol, Taunton and Bath.

Second- or holiday-home ownership had been a growing aspiration amongst the business classes for some time, and the thrust to relieve at weekends the pressures of urban existence (to escape to the country) flourished once the railways arrived. In time, the relative pleasures of country living, were such that permanent converts were made of weekender owners. The worm was turning: for some, country houses were to become the principal residences, with the railways affording occasional visits back to the cities for whatever cultural replenishment was required.

Reputations for the better retirement destinations grew accordingly. Lustleigh fared especially well here with former senior Navy and Army personnel, and some of those returning from service in the colonies, developing themselves or buying new-enough villas of a quality that incoming residents of comfortable means were able to demand.

The smaller-scale building that took place away from the grander designs reflected different inspirations. The needs of local industry and commerce, their fortunes enhanced by the railway, had highlighted the problem of a shortage of properties for working people to rent. This demand had intensified with the growing labour needs of the mine workings at Kelly and in the quarries; even some of those in service in the larger houses now vied with farm hands for any accommodation deemed remotely affordable.

A long history of stalled construction and re-financing culminated eventually in the phased building of the terraced houses at Brookfield, which went some way to relieving the immediate pressure. More were needed, and in due course built. But the principal additional worker-related developments that took place (local authority housing at Pethybridge, and, nearer to the village centre, on land across the road from the War Memorial)[9] were to be left to later times, and differing political influences.

Limitations

By the turn of the twentieth century a development inertia had begun to settle in. The railways by then had become well established, and some of the early entrepreneurial energy the arrival of the tracks had spawned inevitably had waned. Some of the promoters' initial enthusiasm had been found wanting also.

Speculators' optimism about commuting synergy benefits had, over the years, proved to be wide of the mark, though not before a period of local nervousness in the non-investor camp. Cecil Torr, to choose one example, had from the start anticipated the worst, asserting that the arrival of a new line would lead to the hillsides being laid out for commuters with 'winding roads and villas' in the 'accepted Torquay style'.[10] Torr had cited as examples of the expected excess two such villas, a claim, which if correct, given the scale and value of buildings concerned, might have gone some way to justify the new line investors' hoped-for opportunity for bolted-on profit.

The fact that parts of one of the properties Torr is thought to have had in mind, St Andrews, pre-dated railway arrival, and the other, Combe Hill, was built without a shred of evidence to support the commuting premise, rather points to what in time became established reality: the trains that ran on the new line were simply too infrequent to permit business affairs to be conducted remotely for anything approaching a normal working day.

Figure 9.2: St. Andrews, one of the new 'villas'.
(Courtesy of Lustleigh Community Archive)

There were construction problems too, particularly when the better villa sites had gone. Considerable outlay was needed for the work: few, if any of the houses would have been built speculatively. What capital was employed seldom was done so without risk: the remaining sites, particularly the higher ones, were not always easily accessible, frequently were densely wooded, and most had ground conditions which invariably were difficult to establish reliably pre-construction. Moreover building contractors familiar with newer techniques and materials were not local, *known* people. Specialist rates and travelling charges inflated prices further.

By the end of the study period the Lustleigh housing boom had reached its zenith. More private houses were to follow as the twentieth century advanced, with the Lower Knowle Road, and land below Pethybridge seeing most activity. But with the enough is enough mantra of the rural lobby hardening a national political will, a growing raft of restrictions (and eventually Town and Country Planning legislation) was to emerge, greatly limiting opportunities for future domestic development of any size or form.

Lustleigh's built-environment status quo was fast approaching.

Figure 9.3: *Adjacent SE, and E parish boundaries*

OS reference	C I.5 (1905)	Tithe (1838)	CI.1 (1905)	Tithe (1838)
Parish location. (For *Ref.* see plan at Figure 9.8)	Adjacent SE boundary, N of Pullabrook Farm (*Ref.* A)		Adjacent E boundary, Slade Cross to Kelly Farm (*Ref.* B)	
Footprint (sq. m.)	890	560	1070	470
Change 1838–1905	+59%		+128%	

Figure 9.4: *Adjacent S parish boundary, and S of village centre*

OS reference	C.12 (1905)	Tithe (1838)	C. 8 (1905)	Tithe (1838)
Parish location. (For *Ref.* see plan at Figure 9.8)	Adjacent S boundary, Trendlebere Down (*Ref.* C)		S of village centre, inc. Hisley and Rudge (*Ref.* D)	
Footprint (sq. m.)	0	0	4,080	3,180
Change 1838–1905			+28%	

Figure 9.5: *Centre of village northwards, and NE of parish*

OS reference	C.4 (1905)	Tithe (1838)	X C. 16 (1905)	Tithe (1838)
Parish location. (For *Ref.* see plan at Figure 9.8)	Centre village, northwards to South Harton and Caseley (*Ref.* E)		NE of parish, Eastwrey Barton to Sanduck (*Ref.* F)	
Footprint (sq. m.)	10,230	5,820	1,050	827
Change 1838–1905	+76%		+27%	
Notes	1. Various commercial and educational buildings, being housed in, or later converted to 'domestic' property, are included in the calculations: Post Office; Bakeries; Mill; Smithy; General Store; School House 2. Ecclesiastical buildings are excluded: Church of St John the Baptist; the Old Vestry, etc.			

Figure 9.6: *Adjacent W, and NW parish boundaries*

OS reference	C.3 (1905)	Tithe (1838)	X.C. 15 (1905)	Tithe (1838)
Parish location. (For *Ref.* see plan at Figure 9.8)	Adjacent W boundary, near Foxworthy (*Ref.* G)		Adjacent NW boundary, near Fursdon (*Ref.* H)	
Footprint (sq. m.)	595	520	1,580	1,490
Change 1838–1905	+11%		+6%	
Notes	1. Commercial Mill property included in the calculations – as Figure 9.3.			

Figure 9.7: *NW of parish, and totals*

OS reference	X C. 11 (1905)	Tithe (1838)	TOTALS (1905)	TOTALS (1838)
Parish location. (For Ref. see plan at Figure 9.8)	NW extremity of parish (*Ref.* I)		Entire parish	
Footprint (sq. m.)	0	0	19,495	13,757
Change 1838–1905	0%		+42%	

Nature of the new homes

Domestic properties in Devon villages such as Lustleigh, between the sixteenth century and mid-Victorian times, architecturally reflected vernacular traditions.[11] Generally, buildings were long and low, and comprised granite/cob walls which mostly were rendered and colour washed. Thatched roofs were ubiquitous, and chimney stacks, where initially incorporated, or added, substantial structures of ashlar granite.

The siting of doors and windows in the elevations of these buildings were to suit use, and internal layout; buildings were not consciously architecturally designed, as such. The effect was one of picturesque irregularity. Typical examples of the style are seen at Littleholm, Spring Cottage, and Lynnfield.

The coming of the railways corresponded with a radical shift in rural house design. Railways quickly were to supplant the canals for ease and cost-effectiveness of transporting heavy (building) materials.[12] Areas adrift from the core canal network, but now reached by trains, saw the greatest change most quickly, but eventually most of the country was to take advantage of modern, sturdier, building methods that emerged from the readier availability of key materials such as bricks.

Lustleigh's version of the late-Victorian architectural shift showed some variations to the wider theme.

Local supplies of granite, the principal walling material, had not diminished, and little point was seen in mass transport over distance of competing materials, when a familiar, proven masonry form remained on the doorstep. Imported bricks for wholesale use did, in time, play a part (see Melrose Terrace for example) but generally, and certainly for the larger domestic buildings that were to arrive, granite was to remain the norm, though now the material was worked to retain its natural beauty and no longer concealed with render. To soften the effect of the exposed masonry further, brickwork of gentle reds and yellows was used to dress window openings.

These features apart, Lustleigh otherwise was to embrace the developing national trends in quasi-rural domestic construction.

Late-Victorian properties differed from their predecessors in being designed; architects now inclined towards symmetry of appearance, significantly greater scale, and an individuality borne of attractive detailing. There were contemporary improvements in the building process itself too, and much more energy was now given over to internal appearances: floor and wall tiles were chosen for beauty as much as practicality; and plasterwork, hitherto merely an internal finishing necessity, was to become a thing of elaborate and creative decoration.

It was with roofing, however, that Lustleigh's concessions to construction progress were clearest. Stout slates from the Welsh quarries had found their way to the West Country in the earliest days of railway connection. The logical widespread adoption of slate as the principal, rural, roofing material (in both domestic and commercial constructions) followed. Thatch, the time-honoured covering, whilst undoubtedly offering beauty, water tightness and good standards of insulation was bedevilled by two fundamental drawbacks, in the end successfully exploited by the promoters of the solid-covering competition: Welsh slate did not burn, and, once *in situ*, given minimal maintenance, had a planned lifespan of, minimum, 60 years (cf. Norfolk reed thatch, which could be expected to last, at best, for no more than three decades).

Typical examples of the new designs that were to evolve predominate *en route* to Ellimore, Pethybridge, Mapstone and Caseley. For some of the clearest versions, stay in the foothills and see Wreyland Villa, Rockvale, and Hillside.[13]

Non–domestic development

Farming

Farming, the predominant commercial undertaking in the parish, in built environment terms, saw little change in Victorian times. Certainly a marked contraction took place in the number of individual farm businesses, but in Lustleigh, as elsewhere in Devon, there appears to have been no commensurate reduction in land used for agricultural purposes, nor material change in the associated buildings' infrastructure.

Dr Paul Brassley points to various external impacts on Devon agricultural practice during the nineteenth century, but concludes that despite modernising influences elsewhere, Victorian Devon farmers continued to produce food from the resources of their farms, largely using 'muscle power'. 'A farmer from 1800,' Dr Brassley asserts, 'would have understood most of the processes and activities on the average farms of 1900.'[14]

The few instances where farm building development did take place largely concerned modifications for the addition of habitable space, a reflection, no doubt, of the shortage of work-persons' accommodation in the parish. The related increase in building footprint size is included in the calculations in Figures 9.1 to 9.7.

Tourism

By the 1860s the arrival of the railways had meant London to the West Country travel times were measured in hours rather than days. The shortness, ease, and comfort of the new means of travel quickly led to widespread building activity in many seaside resorts, then, and now, a greater tourist pull than the delights of the countryside. Coastal towns in Cornwall, for example, were subject to rapid growth, with hotel and guest-house development leading the way.

The effects in Devon, were less clear cut. Tourism here, in a county having the relative advantage of greater proximity to the larger cities, had already it seems encouraged in some quarters a sense of a certain pre-eminence. Some of the perceived consequences of railway connection were not always welcome. A principal, openly voiced fear (the potential negative impact of a mass influx of a lower-class clientele into respectable and successful destinations) appears to have been effective in grinding many an initiative to a (temporary) halt; the line extension to Torquay, for example, was for years the subject of successful deferment.

Overall the railway-driven tourist benefits for Lustleigh were to prove less successful than the pioneers of the Newton Abbot to Moretonhampstead line had predicted. Visitors to the parish traditionally had been day-trippers, with walking in the Cleave the single most popular activity of those that came. These predominantly one-day visits had spawned the occasional tea-room and tea-garden business, but not much else. It was not, surprisingly, until the turn of the twentieth century that visitor passenger numbers had begun to show an appreciable increase, particularly during the summer months.[15] The small-scale teashops saw some benefit, no doubt. But the nature of visits it seems did not change; still few visitors remained for longer than their walk required, and overnight stays were very much the exception, not the rule.

Whether chicken and egg played a part is debatable. Had an enterprising Lustleighite funded a new hotel and guest-house development to attract discerning tourists from farther afield, the profile of the tourist visitor may very well have altered to wider advantage. That the extent of tourist accommodation adjustment to the arrival of the railways was the conversion of Gatehouse Farmhouse to the Cleave Hotel, alongside similar opportunistic lower-scale provision of rooms to let in established households, meant, as with agriculture generally, there was no discernible impact on this aspect of the built environment.

Religion and education

Apart from the building and civil engineering work associated with the railway itself (see below) the only notable non-domestic construction activity in the parish was the erection in 1853 of the Baptist Church, and in 1876, of the new school.[16]

Predating the railway, the Baptist Church appeared during a time of increasing acceptance of the right for Nonconformist religions to pursue their beliefs in registered premises of their own.[17] The impending arrival of the railway would have had no bearing on the construction of this substantial building on a prominent plot fringing the village centre.

Equally, the development of the new school building was rather more the result of the wider Victorian aspiration for free education for all, than any local initiatives or ideals that might have been said to be due to the new, railway inspired, age of information. Replacing limited facilities in the Old Vestry, and occupying a site immediately overlooking the Church of St John the Baptist, the new school was to become a dominant feature of village life until its closure in 1963, and subsequent conversion to domestic accommodation.

Railway infrastructure

The principal physical changes that were to take place to the landscape in and around the village of course arose from the railway civil engineering undertakings themselves. Few parishes could have been so wholly physically affected by the coming of the railways as was Lustleigh. Not here the benefits of greatly improved communication afforded by a nearby line, none of the typical grudging acceptance of nineteenth-century progress attendant to tracks that brush village extremities, but by no means directly interfere.

No, for Lustleigh, from southern boundary to north, the intervention was total. Bisecting the parish, and with the new station at the village heart, no part of the neighbourhood was immune from the effects of the construction work: the 'once gentle landscape' soon was to be peppered with embankments and viaducts, waiting rooms, platforms, a related network of platelayers' huts, lock-up coal bunker buildings, paraffin lamp stores, all in addition to the tracks themselves.

Cecil Torr's grandfather articulated the understandable apprehension that preceded the vast project. 'Raw and glaring' cuttings, he feared, would soon ruin the surrounding landscape.[18] But in the nature of things where vegetation plays a part, the scars, though considerable at first, proved only a temporary inconvenience. Within a decade (admittedly a significant timeframe in a Victorian community having an average life expectancy in the forties) some satisfactory restoration had been achieved. A delighted Cecil Torr reported 'cuttings and embankments ... [to be once again] ... overgrown and covered with verdure ...' 'One can hardly realise,' Torr added, 'how hideous it looked ...'[19]

Indeed as the land settled, and weathering mellowed the initial sharpness of the construction stonework, there seems to have been a shift towards the view that, aesthetically, the railway had in fact improved the landscape. Torr, considering some of more obvious incursions, was now full of praise. Had, he asserted, the well-proportioned viaducts that strode across the countryside with 'Roman grandeur' been transported to Italy and attributed to 'Roman or Etruscan builders', in all likelihood 'artists would have flocked to paint them'.

A final indication of the acceptance of the new arrangements, can be found in what was to become the positive adoption of the railway itself, and some of the villas it spawned, as a means of attracting tourists to the parish. By the turn of the century, almost as readily as the traditional images of thatched cottages and rolling hills, newspaper, pamphlet, and postcard promotion had now begun to feature shots of bustling station platforms, and the fine viaducts above Caseley Court and Lustleigh Mills.

Legacy

Initially feared, for a time despised in the more reactionary circles, by 1905 the railway had become integral to village life, an essential twentieth-century lifeline to the wider world. Now there was a strong sense of community pride in its best kept station, and in the majesty of the fine stonework infrastructure, already satisfyingly at one with the surrounding landscape. Following centuries of construction inertia and civil engineering inactivity, in something less than 40 years the new line had delivered a hitherto unimaginable degree of change to Lustleigh's built environment and landscape.

The epitaph for the railway is therefore as sad as it is remarkable: in little more than another four decades the line connecting Newton Abbot with Moretonhampstead would suffer such a sustained commercial decline that the closure to passenger traffic that eventually came actually preceded Dr Beeching's early 1960s axe.

The legacy of that Victorian time of energy and action is mixed.

Certainly, in terms of housing, the scale and nature of nineteenth-century development had put Lustleigh and its environs squarely on the map of desirable places in which to live. The new-found reputation for quality property in agreeable surroundings has, if anything, grown with time.

How those driven Victorians would have viewed the fate of their considerable civil engineering undertakings is another matter. One modest twenty-first century cycle route project apart, little else has been done since the line closure to maintain, less still enhance, the towering embankments, and elegant arches. Nowadays, not always in the more remote parts of the parish, the impression is becoming one of crumbling stonework cheek by jowl with cuttings almost irreversibly overgrown with untamed vegetation.

That today's financial and investment challenges are greatly removed from their perhaps more straightforward Victorian equivalents is not in question. There is no doubt either that in times of such competing demand for public funds, the upkeep and improvement of civil engineering structures in a remote Devon parish inevitably is a lowest priority issue – at best.

All of which presents an unfortunate reality for some of Lustleigh's established and finest structures: as is the case with so much of the rest of our Victorian (and more recent) built heritage, in the absence of the intervention of private or charitable money, once essential assets of a former time, inexorably will degrade to a point at which restoration becomes no longer achievable, whatever the outlay.

It may take a decade or two yet, but it would seem now inevitable that Cecil Torr's once striding viaducts are about to face the fate of the line that conceived them.

Appendix

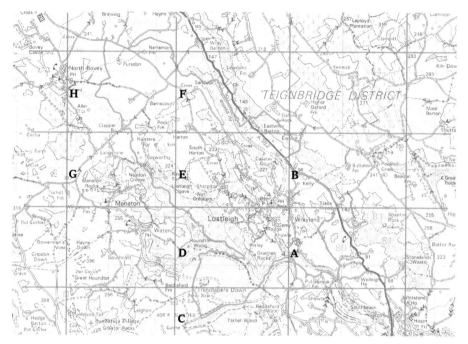

Figure 9.8: *Plan of Lustleigh civil parish.*
Crown copyright and database rights 2018 Ordnance Survey 100024842

Notes

1. The National Archives, 2017. *Research Guide on Tithe Records*. [online] Available at: <www.national archives.gov.uk/help-with-your-research-/research-guides/tithes/> [Accessed 7th May 2017].
2. The National Archives, 2017. *Research Guide on Tithe Records*. [online] Available at: <www.national archives.gov.uk/help-with-your-research-/research-guides/tithes/> [Accessed 7th May 2017].
3. The National Archives, 2017. *Research Guide on Tithe Records*. [online] Available at: <www.national archives.gov.uk/help-with-your-research-/research-guides/tithes/> [Accessed 7th May 2017].
4. Seymour, W.A., 1980. *A History of the Ordnance Survey*. Folkstone: William Dawson & Sons. p.203.
5. Stewart-Beardsley, R., 2014. *Landowners and the Great Western Railway: A Study of Rural Change in Five Rural Thameside Parishes 1831–1901*. Available at: <www.history.ac.uk/history-online/theses/thesis/landowners-

and-great-western-railway-study-rural-change-five-rural-thameside-parishes/> [Accessed 2nd April 2017].

6. Turnock, D., 1998. *An Historical Geography of Railways in Great Britain and Ireland*. Aldershot: Ashgate Publishing. p.115.

7. Zola, E., 1977. *La Bete Humaine*. London: Penguin Books. p.11.

8. Chown, I., 2012. Houses and flats. In: Littlefield, D. ed. *Metric Handbook Planning and Design Data*. Abingdon: Architectural Press. pp.8.1–8.21.

9. Dartmoor National Park Authority, 2011. *Lustleigh Conservation Area Character Appraisal*. [pdf] Available at: <www.dartmoor.gov.uk/__data/assets/pdf_file/0004/864166/Lustleigh-2011.pdf> [Accessed 5th June 2017].

10. Rowe, J., 2001. The railway. In: Crowdy, J. ed. *The Book of Lustleigh. Portrait of a Dartmoor Parish*. Tiverton: Halsgrove. p.79.

11. Dartmoor National Park Authority, 2011. *Lustleigh Conservation Area Character Appraisal*. [pdf] Available at: <www.dartmoor.gov.uk/__data/assets/pdf_file/0004/864166/Lustleigh-2011.pdf> [Accessed 6th June 2017].

12. Freeman, M.J., 1999. *Railways and the Victorian Imagination*. New Haven, CT: Yale University Press. p.56

13. Dartmoor National Park Authority, 2011. *Lustleigh Conservation Area Character Appraisal*. [pdf] Available at: <www.dartmoor.gov.uk/__data/assets/pdf_file/0004/864166/Lustleigh-2011.pdf> [Accessed 28th May 2017].

14. Brassley, P., 2017. In the footsteps of the Victorians: exploring the Victorian heritage of Dartmoor. Lecture at Parke, Bovey Tracey. 11th March.

15. Kingdom, A.R. and Lang, M., 2004. *The Newton Abbot to Moretonhampstead Railway*. Newton Abbot: Ark Publications (Railways), an imprint of Forest Publishing. p.137.

16. Dartmoor National Park Authority, 2011. *Lustleigh Conservation Area Character Appraisal*. [pdf] Available at: <www.dartmoor.gov.uk/__data/assets/pdf_file/0004/864166/Lustleigh-2011.pdf> [Accessed 6th June 2017].

17. Cutts, B., and Green, J., 2001. Lustleigh Baptist Church. In: Crowdy, J. ed. *The Book of Lustleigh. Portrait of a Dartmoor Parish*. Tiverton: Halsgrove. p.56.

18. Rowe, J., 2001. The railway. In: Crowdy, J. ed. *The Book of Lustleigh. Portrait of a Dartmoor Parish*. Tiverton: Halsgrove. p.77.

19. Rowe, J., 2001. The railway. In: Crowdy, J. ed. *The Book of Lustleigh. Portrait of a Dartmoor Parish*. Tiverton: Halsgrove. p.77.

10. Lustleigh schools and schoolchildren in the reign of Victoria

Alexa Mason

At ten to nine on a warm July morning in 1900, children are walking to school along rough footpaths and narrow lanes, across fields and through woods. Those living in 'the town' that clusters round the church have a short, steep hill to climb, but the children from the distant scattered farms are running downhill. They have had chores to do at home, and must not be late, so some arrive to line up in the playground that is on a level with the church tower quite breathless. The infants are called to order by the pupil-teacher and herded into their classroom. The older boys and girls, in their separate lines, file silently through their separate doors only to meet in the big room where they are all taught together, girls on one side, boys on the other, the different 'Standards' marked only by a slight separation of the desks. The room is crowded and already stuffy, for the school was built 24 years ago for 80 children and now has 118 on roll.

Some are looking forward to the day, for as well as the 'Three Rs' there will be a singing lesson for the whole school, technical drawing for the boys, sewing for the girls and the head master, Mr Sing, is to show one of his chemical experiments to Standard III. Others, unable to look out of the high windows and already sweating in their jackets and woollen stockings can only long for 'Recreation Time' in the dusty playground at the front of the school. Some are already thinking with dread of the lavatories in the back yard, for the smell is appalling in this hot weather. All of them, however, know that this little school, at the heart of the village of Lustleigh, is where they are expected to be.[1]

Twelve years before the Education Act of 1880, which made attendance at school compulsory, the Reverend H. Tudor, Mr T. Wills and Mr J. Wills (all Trustees of the then Lustleigh Endowed School) attended a lecture at Newton Abbot Town Hall given to the Devon Central Chamber of Commerce by the Reverend J.M. Hawker of Ideford on 'The Education of the Labouring Classes'. He explains at the start that he means only the agricultural sector.

The Reverend Hawker begins promisingly by defining education as

> not merely book learning or committing a number of facts to memory ... but the *drawing out*, into their full development the power and the faculties of the mind, so that the talents that God has given to each one ... are not wasted or left unproductive. By education I would signify that which teaches the young to do what they have to do thoroughly ... not to go around when there is a short cut, or to make two strokes where one will do; to exercise forethought, the sheet anchor of farming; to know that civility costs nothing and that courtesy is the oil of the wheels of life – in short to do their best in all matters, great and small.

> Now in the matter of agriculture, a great part of this education must be learned by actual practice and it must be allowed that boys ought to be allowed to go to work on the land at a very early age if they are to gain a real knowledge of farm labour. No amount of book-learning can ever make up for the keenness of observation, the practice under difficulties, the handiness of new and unlooked for circumstances which are all almost insensibly taught to a lad who is sent to work at nine or ten years of age.

Hawker says he is aware that he is advocating a system which 'debars a large class from that cultivation of the intellect whereby men are raised above the brutes of the field' but claims that this is far from his purpose, that the daily work on the farm is itself cultivating the intellect and that 'beneath an apparent slowness and dullness of speech there is often considerable shrewdness and activity of mind'. Hawker claims that between the ages of 6 and 8 years it should be possible to teach children to read with ease, to write with a legible hand and to know the basic rules of arithmetic. He has been an Inspector of Schools for the County and is of the opinion that there are enough schools already to achieve this purpose. 'It is not the quantity that are required, but the quality.'

The speaker mentions the right of children to have education 'within their reach' and then goes on to complain of poor attendance, mentioning in passing the 'nominal weekly sum' that is the usual fee. Children will be kept at home 'on the most frivolous of excuses'. There are some who will not be sent at all 'despite all coaxing and scolding'. He then moves on to the question of compulsory education and doubts that this is enforceable. 'Many of us know how steadfastly in this country the Vaccination Acts have been neglected and set at defiance.' He talks of the 'carelessness and apathy of the ordinary agricultural labourer' with regard to the education of his children. His bold remedy is to put the answer in the hands of the farmers. If they

> would refuse to engage any boy or girl who could not bring a certificate of competency to read, write, cypher, and in the case of the girls to do plain sewing also, they would put a far severer screw upon the parents than any legislative enactment.

He mentions that boys applying for the Navy or the Railways are required to be literate.

Hawker is very anxious about adolescent youngsters and is appalled by their general ignorance and illiteracy. He thinks evening classes in rural areas have not done much to help, as employers do not like the youngsters to be away regularly from the farmhouse, perhaps getting together and getting up to no good on the way. Hawker wonders whether a Scottish system of peripatetic school teachers making regular visits to farmhouses for after-work learning, and work left to be completed between visits, could be adopted in rural areas. He also refers to the new 'delicate and costly' farm machinery and 'scientific applications' that require a better educated labour force.

Being a clergyman, he moves on to the religious element of education and a proposed Conscience Clause and believes that 'its forms are likely to breed strife'. He points out that in a town there are several schools, usually including National, Church of England (C of E), Wesleyan, and so on, whereas in rural parishes there will be only one (often C of E). He himself did not compel a dissenting child to learn the Catechism or object if they worshipped elsewhere. Any religious difficulties should not get in the way of 'those who are in earnest in the work of Education'.

There were two whole hours of discussion after the talk. It appeared that this was a time of great national interest in the education question, with speeches in the Lords and conferences in Manchester, Tunbridge Wells and Birmingham. There was mention of the new teacher-training schools, the possibility of compulsory education (which they thought would fill the prisons) dismissed by some, approved of by others. Dr Barham stood to say that children had rights in the same degree as other members of the community and he considered that those rights ought to be protected. 'Should ... [parents] ... have the liberty to keep their children in a state of mental starvation?' Comparing this country with others, Dr Barham had no doubt that England, with a few exceptions, was the worst educated country of the whole, and he did not see why compulsory education should not be as successful in this as it had been in other countries. He was in favour of secular education, believing that sufficient religious education was given at the Sabbath schools.

There was discussion of the Conscience Clause with the Reverend R.R. Wolfe approving the compromise. He was against a 'rate' for educational purposes, trusting to private purses or 'assistance from the Government'. Mr T. Wills (from Lustleigh) was in favour of government aid. Dr Heydon spoke at great length of the evils of an ill-educated underclass. The Chairman (Mr C.J. Wade) in his closing speech condemned sectarianism. He would like a plan whereby all local districts should have to provide a certain amount of money, and the government, out of the Consolidated Fund, should provide a considerable portion, 'so as to secure free, independent supervision and free independent action ... [then] they would soon do away with sectarian teaching in their schools'.[2]

We will see many of the points raised at this lecture vividly illustrated when we look at the progress of the new Lustleigh Board School, established after the 1870 Act which laid down the framework for the schooling of all children between the ages of 5 and 12 in England and Wales. The process of learning, absenteeism, religious education and funding will all be important in the running of the village school, and it is significant that a delegation of Lustleigh worthies were present at this event. It is also interesting that many clergymen and doctors gave their views, indicating their established interest in local education. The active roles of clergy, 'gentry' and farming landowners in promoting the education and well-being of young people are constant throughout the period, though their motives are not always entirely altruistic.

Figure 10.1: *The Old Vestry which was built as an Endowed School in 1825.*
(Courtesy of Lustleigh Community Archive)

1825.
BUILT BY SUBSCRIPTION,
AND ENDOWED WITH LOWTON MEADOW
IN *MORETON*,
FOR SUPPORTING A SCHOOL FOR EVER,
BY THE REV. WILLIAM DAVY,
CURATE OF THIS PARISH
UPWARDS OF FORTY YEARS.

Figure 10.2

In the earlier part of Victoria's reign, Lustleigh already had a small school, a building now known as 'The Old Vestry,' tucked into the corner of the churchyard. Despite its current name, it was in fact built as a school, though the clergy did use one of the small rooms as a vestry. The plaque on the wall by the door reads 'Built by subscription/and endowed with Lowton Meadow in Moreton/for supporting a school forever/by the Rev. William Davy/curate of this parish'.

William Davy, curate of Lustleigh for 40 years for an absentee rector and also theological author, horticulturalist and philanthropist, had his own printing press, producing a leaflet to explain his motives entitled 'Apology for giving Lowton Meadow to the Parish of Lustleigh'.

Whereas from my long service in that church I have a strong regard and hearty desire for its present and future welfare, and being from repeated proofs too unhappily convinced of the uneconomical and profligate disposition of my immediate successors, and being willing in my lifetime to do the greatest and most lasting good with the little property I have in fee, I do hereby, with the consent of my son (who by good conduct and kind providence is sufficiently provided for) offer to give to the officiating minister and churchwardens of the parish of Lustleigh all that one close or meadow called Morice or Lowton Meadow in Moreton Hampstead to have and to hold the same with the rents and profits thereof from and after the 25th of March 1824 in trust forever for the support and maintenance of a school for poor children in the parish of Lustleigh aforesaid in the house to be erected in the parish town for that purpose.[3]

In his deed of gift, 4th August 1825, the Reverend Davy states that the setting up of the school is

for the education and instruction of the poor children, being parishioners of the said parish, on the principals of the established Church of England, in reading and needlework, in learning their catechism and other proper and useful learning for poor children …

Spelling and basic arithmetic were also taught, and the school and the land managed by eight 'feoffees' or trustees appointed by Davy.[4]

There appeared to be general feeling that such a school would be an asset to the village.

The parishioners are very anxious to accept Mr Davy's liberal offer and to establish this school and have had several meetings on the subject and one on the 25th March instant when all present except one landowner and his tenant wished the proposed school to be erected, ample money for which purpose can be procured by Voluntary Subscriptions among the Parishioners. As the school is to answer for a Vestry also in the Parish there being none at present it is hoped there will be no objection to its being built on part of the churchyard, considering there is no other place to erect such a desirable establishment. There will be no entrance from the school to the Churchyard for the Children, but only for the

Clergyman on Sundays. We the undersigned being the Rector, Curate, Churchwardens and Inhabitants of the said Parish of Lustleigh do hereby signify one entire consent and approbation to the erecting and building a house for the said School and Vestry on the north-west corner of the said churchyard.

John Mudge, Rector
W, Davy, Curate
T. Amery and W. Amery Churchwardens
James Jackson and John Cuming Overseers

'I have examined on view the spot intended to be appropriated for the erection of a School room and Vestry room and deem it in every respect eligible as the Churchyard is copious and the population small.'
P Whipham, Rural Dean

(other signatories – T. Hickman, A. Hill, J. White, R. Rowe, T. Crideford, G. Wills, W. French, J. Amery, G .Wills, W. Hole, J. Wills)[5]

However, there may have been some reactionaries in the parish, as there is a reference in a book of 1851[6] that claims that earlier, in 1822, Reverend Davy had offered to endow a school, 'to which liberal offer the parishioners would not accede, in consequence of their objections to the education of the poor'.

Cecil Torr of Yonder Wreyland recollects that in the early school there used to be no more than a dozen children. The endowment was not large enough to make it a free school and there were fees. If parents could not manage it there were often benevolent folk in the village who would pay for them, though many children may have slipped through the net during the 50 years it was open. (When Church House was a poor-house, any children living there were paid for by the parish.) It was a mixed school with the children taught all together by a dame, whose discipline was enforced by a stick, and she lived in the small four-room building. As far as is known there was neither toilet nor kitchen as such.[7] As mentioned above, children were not allowed access through the churchyard but had their own door on the road side of the building. One wonders where they played at break-time. (They would of course have gone home at lunchtime). Perhaps they were allowed to go to the green, under the shelter of the elm trees.

Not all parishioners welcomed the school. Torr says he remembers 'an old lady saying it would be horrible if her maids could read – she would not be able to leave her letters lying about. That was before the Education Act of 1870'.[8]

There is little material available to give an accurate insight into the management of the school day, but contrary to Cecil Torr's memories (and he does seem to remember with the golden glow of nostalgia) there was one time when pupils numbered about 50, and during the changeover of control from Endowed to Board school, 40 children were crammed into the little granite building. By 1875, Susan Ann Knapman is the sole teacher of the school, having begun her duties in 1869 at the age of 20. Her Majesty's Inspector of Schools (HMI), in his first report for the school, reveals

> These premises are so small and low as to be quite unhealthy for the number of children taught in them. The Schoolroom has cubic feet air for seventeen children and the little closet upstairs has air for seven more. Under these circumstances, and with a total absence of apparatus it is wonderful that the young mistress could do even what she has done. The attainments of the children however are very small, especially in reading and arithmetic. The little infants are well grounded. There should be an increased supply of books for the Lower Standards and the ordinary School apparatus and maps should be provided. An Admission Register, Log Book, Portfolio and regular Cash Book should also be provided, and secular singing should be taught.

The authorities were prepared to give the Board time to provide more suitable accommodation and were also prepared to continue the grant for this year, provided the stipulated average attendance was maintained. The above-mentioned apparatus and books had to be provided at once. The rector, the Reverend Ensor, was the current chairman of the newly established Board.

One can imagine the daily toil of Miss Knapman, only 26 years of age, with 40 children of all ages, struggling to teach and keep control in cramped and no doubt insanitary conditions. In both cold and hot weather it was probably nearly unbearable and, as the completion of the new building dragged into 1876, it is no wonder Miss Knapman resorted to her cane for 'gross disobedience'.[9] In June an unusually sympathetic HMI commends her for her hard work and improvement in

Figure 10.3: *Photograph taken around 1900 with the Board School in the background.* (Courtesy of Lustleigh Community Archive)

attainment despite the poor conditions, and recommends to the Board the appointment of a monitress to help in Standards I and II.[10]

Doubtless to Miss Knapman's great relief, the new school above the church, built on land owned by Thomas Wills,[11] opened in 1876, described by HMI as 'an ornament to the village', including accommodation for the mistress, a playground and outside 'offices' behind the building.[12] The school roll nearly doubled, to 80. This was despite the fact that the building was supposed to accommodate 75 children (which included 20 from Wreyland, at that time in the Parish of Bovey Tracey).

The Elementary Education Act of 1870 had set the framework of schooling for all children between the ages of 5 and 12 years in England and Wales. The most rural areas of Devon had few schools at all and many of those existing, such as Lustleigh, had totally inadequate buildings.

The government therefore set up Board Schools, to be managed locally, but eligible for aid from the Public Works Loan Commissioners for building work. In Lustleigh, a Board was elected with local landowners and gentry as members and the rector, the Reverend Ensor, as chairman. From now until the end of our period, the children of farm workers, domestic servants, tradesmen, craftsmen and shopkeepers were educated in this building above a massive granite wall, overlooking the church and 'the town', walking to and from school in all weathers and at the mercy of teachers of varying abilities and inspectors with sometimes unrealistic expectations.

After the infants were provided with separate accommodation in 1892, the building had few alterations. As was thought proper, the windows were too high for inattentive pupils to look out of, the playground was impacted stony earth and the lavatories were outside at the back of the building. No mention can be found of heating, though there probably was an enclosed stove in the main classroom and the infant's room. No lunches were provided and children went home for a midday meal, though those from outlying cottages brought lunch with them. Arriving at school soaked through was obviously a problem, especially for the little ones, and they were often kept at home in very wet weather.

Absenteeism was the scourge of the head teacher's life, and a perpetual headache for the Board. The grants awarded to the school by the Department for Education depended upon attendance figures and the results of HMI's reports on attainment. The more time a child stayed away from school, they less they learned, or could remember in order to satisfy the inspector. Time after time, in the school log book, every head teacher bewails the number of absent pupils.

Although teachers were not supposed to express personal views in school log books, many needed either to let off steam or to convey to the Board that poor results are not their fault. In 1890, even after the rector has offered to chase up the offenders on the master's list, Mr Derbyshire records after the summer holiday, 'Twenty-two children are absent … It is impossible to do well when the attendance is so bad'. Eight days later 25 children are away without good excuse. 'How the school is to do well in the face of such attendance is a puzzle. Very small attendance this afternoon, owing to a wedding.'[13] Mr Derbyshire's log entries during his time at the school (1885–1891) are almost exclusively about absenteeism.

In 1895 Mr J. and Mr. C.G. Wills, Board members, come to the school to harangue the pupils about the loss 'both financially and educationally the school suffers, through the extreme irregularity'.[14] (This is in spite of the fact that the yeoman farmers of the board are some of the worst offenders in employing pupils without their Labour Certificates.)[15] The master, Mr Sampson, records in the log a couple of weeks later that 'in the majority of cases the absentees are mostly the most backward children. (By which he means they are behind in their work rather than having special needs.)

> I beg to call to H.M.I's attention to the extreme irregularity which prevails throughout the school and to point out to his notice the very small proportion of children who even make a full week's attendance. It is ridiculous to judge the results of a teacher's work on the Examination Day when he is handicapped by such an attendance.

Strong words, but probably necessary, and it is notable how attendance goes up for the annual inspection, thus disguising the problem. Like many of the Lustleigh head teachers he must have hoped his words would also filter back to the Board.

Earlier, during the brief tenure of Mr. J. Badcock, two non-attendees were, not unusually, working on farms in the spring of 1884, 'John Hole for Mr Amery of Higher Combe, 3 days a week and 2 for his father' and his brother, William Hole 'for Mr Carlyon Hind at North Harton for the whole of the time he has been away'. It was reported to the Board and at the meeting on 9th June Mr Amery said that 'he was not aware that the boy he employed had not passed the Fourth Standard'. Mr Carlyon airily stated 'that he had employed the boy without his knowledge'. The sympathetic Board acknowledged that the excuses were unsatisfactory, but as it was a first offence in both cases, decided to take no action.

In 1896 Mr Sampson is in conflict with the Board over their loose interpretations of the regulations concerning labour certificates, for example Frank Coles is working as a part-time gardener despite not having passed the necessary standard. Mr Sampson tactfully asks for the regulations to be given to parents, but notes that a Board member has taken his own 11-year-old daughter to assist at home, although she has no certificate. Mr Sampson's successor, Mr Sing is moved quite soon after arrival to ask the Board to appoint an attendance officer, but there is no record of them having done so.

It is interesting to note from the log the variety of reasons for absence given by children or parents. (It was rare for a parent to send a note and sometimes siblings gave a more truthful account to the master than he might have received otherwise.)

1. Elizabeth Osborne is absent assisting in a Gentleman's house', 1887.
2. Helping with the hay harvest, 1878.[16]
3. Potato digging, 1878.
4. 'Samuel Squires and Frank and Fred Osborne have miched', that is, have played truant. The parents were informed and Mrs Osborne informed Miss Knapman that her boys had been 'severely punished'. Four days later Frank and Fred 'miched' again. Their mother was not satisfied with the punishment meted out by Miss Knapman and 'taking them out of the school, soundly flogged them herself'.[17]
5. Visits to relatives, 1882.
6. 'Strained eye-sight', 1884.
7. 'Stormy weather', 1885.
8. 'Mary and Emma Squires do not attend as they ought to, their mother keeps them at home to mind the baby', 1885.
9. 'Stephen Clarke again kept at home, his mother says, upon enquiry, "to look after the garden"', 1885 (in June he is cutting hay for Mr Amery).
10. January snow and storms, together with 'dangerous' roads keep children and assistant teacher away, 1886.
11. Potato dropping, 1886.
12. Whitsun. Parents regard this as a rightful holiday. (Later the Board gives in and grants it annually), 1886
13. 'William and James Hole are absent, the reason is probably that they do not like to come on account of their father being in trouble.' Two days later they are back, Mr Derbyshire having been to see their mother at North Harton, 1886.
14. Choirboys' 'treat', 1886.
15. Alice Cheeseman plays truant from school to play with Mrs Mortimer's little boy the whole afternoon. She tells her uncle, who was probably *in loco parentis*, that she was at school, and he removes her and sends her to another school, Mr Derbyshire

      commenting irritably that Alice's uncle believed her story 'in the face of *facts*', 1887.

16. Running errands for mothers who have taken in lodgers and looking after siblings when they go to market, 1887.
17. 'Gone to Newton Abbot Christmas Market', 1887.
18. Collecting washing for mothers, 1888.
19. Funerals, 1889.
20. 'Gone to the circus in Bovey.' 1893.
21. 'Pupils absent because of visit by the Duke of York', 1899.

The reasons that do not change from year to year and crop up continually are bad weather, helping with agricultural or garden work, and illness, and Lustleigh was only one of the many small rural schools to struggle to keep their grants in the face of these constant factors. Indeed it was a country-wide problem, for a visiting cleric from East Anglia in 1879 was actually impressed by the attendance in Lustleigh School and asked for a copy of the school rules and the 'scale of payments'.

The Reverend Davy's bequest prizes[18] were used almost exclusively for good attendance. Considering all the above, it is remarkable that every year there were at least a handful of children eligible for these awards. It is noticeable that under the excellent headship of the John Loftus Sing (1896–1901) attendance improved dramatically, with certificates to prove it every quarter. In 1900, ten children out of 118 had not missed a single day. It is possible that parents were at last conceding the benefits of a regular education, and becoming aware of the slowly increasing opportunities for youngsters to find work other than in agriculture or domestic service. Let us hope that, unlike Mrs Osborne, not too many parents felt they had to beat their children into compliance.

The health of children at this time was still generally precarious, with what we now refer to as childhood illnesses often leading to more severe diseases or death. Mentions are made in the log of whooping cough, chicken pox, measles, scarlet fever, typhoid, smallpox, croup and diphtheria, the latter being the cause of death of at least three children in one outbreak. Twice children are mentioned as being unable to walk to school because of the pain of 'broken chilblains'. Inadequate footwear and clothing must also have been a factor for absenteeism among the poorest pupils.

The Medical Officer of Health always responded to the reports of infectious diseases and imposed strict quarantines on families, with the result that as the illness passed from sibling to sibling, quarantine lasted for months. Parents of healthy children were naturally reluctant to send their offspring to school to mix with others that might be incubating the germs.

The diphtheria outbreak and recurring sore throats were blamed on the continuing poor water supply and drains. The 'new' school had been functioning for 22 years and the number enrolled increased from 80 to a 115. So by July 1898, despite a new ventilation shaft for the sewers and some improvements in the latrines, it is not surprising that HMI's report criticises the school's sanitary arrangements which rely on the school house (that is, the master's house) pump and well. The Board are told to secure a more regular and reliable source of water.[19] However, they are in no hurry to do so as the whole village is waiting for a new supply. By September the drains are choked and need urgent attention.

Time passes. Vile smells come and go, drains are blocked and unblocked, and in October 1900 Mr Sing complains 'owing to the failure of the water in the School House well, no flushing has been done since last week and the smell from the offices is very unpleasant'. The same month his wife retires from her duties due to ill health, not specified but quite likely to be connected to the bad sanitation, and by Christmas both have gone. Her Majesty's Inspector of Schools reports continue to feature the sanitary crisis and in the report of 1902 says that new water supplies and sewers for the village are 'expected shortly'. Perhaps the local term 'dreckly' would have been more accurate. No mention is made in the log of a caretaker or who is responsible for the cleaning of the school, but in the autumn of 1886 Mr Thomas Wills came to the school to see the master, Mr Derbyshire, to complain of 'the dirty state in which the school was kept'. No comment or explanation is recorded and Mr Wills makes two more visits 'to see how the school was going on' in the next few months. Again, Mr Derbyshire does not elaborate.[20]

The only accident recorded on the school premises is soon after Mr Derbyshire's arrival. James Hole is obliged to take his brother home after he has been struck on the head by a stone in the playground. There is no mention of the stone-thrower being in trouble.[21] This does not mean that children did not have accidents while at school, as every head had a slightly different approach to what he or she felt should be recorded. It is surprising, however, that there is only one or two mentions of head lice, as it must have been common, and became a pre-occupation in the school a few more years into the twentieth century.

In 1878 Miss Knapman recorded two instances of children being removed from the school because of ill health. Eliza Osborne ('the poor child is deficient') was taken away as both mother and teacher thought that 'the pressure of lessons has increased her malady'. The following month Enoch Willcox left the school 'on account of a weakness of constitution which appears to be inspired by school attendance'. Miss Knapman might not have felt able to express opinions in her reports, but there is an acuteness in the use of the word 'inspired'.

It seems from the census that no doctors lived in Lustleigh during our period, and the Cottage Hospital at Moretonhampstead was not opened until 1901. Sending to Moreton or Bovey Tracey would have been difficult for the labouring classes, even if they could afford the fees. The wife, later widow, of the Reverend Ensor[22] 'was always sent for before the doctor', to assist and advise. She owned a book 'by a well-known surgeon' written specifically to advise the country clergy and their families of what to do in the case of an emergency.

If a doctor was not affordable or a knowledgeable member of the gentry was unavailable, parents could always fall back on old wives' tales and superstition. Cecil Torr has some interesting and amusing anecdotes on this subject. His grandfather wrote in June 1848 that measles were rife and 'the old women here say we may expect to see measles in the growing of the moon: they tell me they never knew of a case on the waning of the moon'. On 23rd July he remarks that 'the old women had proved right so far'.[23]

Children's health and cures were not just dictated by their grandmothers' superstitions. In July 1847 a local doctor said that a visitor who had been taken ill whilst visiting Wreyland had brought it on herself by 'imprudently sleeping with her window open one hot night', and children were advised not to get dressed in the mornings with the bedroom window open.[24]

Torr, who always enjoyed a chat with local elderly worthies, also records that

A man here who was born in 1852, tells me he had whooping cough when he was four years old, and that he was treated for it (if not cured of it) by being laid on a sheep's forme. A forme is the imprint that a sheep makes on the grass by lying in one place all night; and when the sheep gets up in the morning, a sort of vapour rises from the warm ground underneath into the cold morning air. He was taken out into a meadow in the early morning and was told to lie face-downwards on a forme and breathe this vapour in, not merely through the nostrils but with open mouth. He breathed it in until the ground was cold and there was no more vapour to be breathed (a matter of about five minutes) and then he was taken home to bed.[25]

As late as 1902, the year after Victoria died, sick children were being treated by magical folklore methods. A village child with a rupture was treated thus:

The father had split an ash-tree on the hill behind this house, and had wedged the hole open with two chunks of oak, Then he and his wife took the child up there at day-break; and, as the sun rose, they passed the child through the tree, from east to west. The mother then took the child home and the father took out the chunks of oak and bandaged up the tree. As the tree-trunk healed, so would the rupture heal also.

Cecil Torr asked the man why he did it and was told, 'Why, all folk do it'. When asked if he thought it did much good, he replied, 'Well, as good as sloppin' water over'n in church'.[26]

As we have seen, the masters and mistresses of the school were not immune to illness themselves, and very occasionally had to take time off, for severe colds, 'ulcerated' throats, or 'severe pains in the head'.[27] In 1895 the 'certificated' wife of Mr Sampson is overwhelmed by the amount of work in preparing the girls' sewing for examination, her husband accusing assistant mistress Miss Arnold of 'gross insubordination' in refusing to help her. Miss Arnold replies that 'she has nothing to do with the big room' (that is, her sole concern is with the infants.) The Board responds by telling Miss Arnold that her terms of engagement state that she should assist in the whole school 'as required'. Miss Arnold is obviously reluctant to comply and Mrs Sampson takes to her bed 'quite broken down by the extra time (nearly four hours every evening) she has to give to the needlework'. At this point the older girls were very irregular in attending, and one wonders how much of their prepared examination work Mrs Sampson was trying to do herself.'[28,29]

As has already been demonstrated, the stress caused by the system of grants depending on attendance during the year and performance at the examinations was considerable, and over this period the head teachers had varying degrees of help during their service. (For names see Appendix 1.) During Miss Knapman's first four years of running the Board school, every single HMI report states that she needs help in the form of monitors, but the Board does nothing until 1879 when HMI Mr Burrows report is glowing: 'This is a remarkably good school. The children are brought up in the habits of cleanliness, good manners and obedience, and the elementary attainments are sound and satisfactory'. Despite this, HMI is insistent that monitresses be appointed. The Board comply and appoint Susan Nicholls, Elizabeth Osborne and Selina Westcott and, by the end of the October, HMI Burrows is visiting the school to give them 'special instruction in their duties'.[30]

Miss Knapman, a talented teacher, suffered from ill health, although only in her late twenties. In 1877 she is taken ill during the Christmas holidays, which are extended to three weeks. On 11th January the Board re-opens the school with the chairman, the Reverend Ensor, in charge, 'and all the voluntary teachers and governesses'.[31] After the death of her mother in November 1880 she is away from 8th April to 9th May 1881 and an 'experienced Mistress', Miss Damerell, took charge. On her return, Miss Knapman, 'not having felt very strong' retained Miss Damerell's services – at her own expense (but with the relieved approval of the Board).[32]

Voluntary teaching was probably appreciated by Miss Knapman and her successor, Miss Colton, who naturally had no partner to help them, married females not being allowed to teach. From the beginning rectors and curates in Lustleigh took positive roles at the school. The ladies of several of the 'important' families in the village also took an active interest.[33] These names dwindle and almost disappear by the end of the century as teaching improves and proper aid is given by the assistant teachers and monitors.

Miss Ida Gould and her sister Lilian give lessons in singing for at least eight years, with varying degrees of success. Teaching the children to read music is a failure, but sometimes HMI praises the singing 'by note', particularly in the infant class. Sometimes, however, upon examination, the singing is not good enough for a grant.[34] A Miss Hayes teaches geography regularly for a few years, as does Miss Morris, who also tries her hand at scripture. The Reverend Ensor's daughter puts in an appearances as a teacher of religious instruction for a time. After the arrival of the married Mr Derbyshire, lessons by these well-intentioned ladies seem to cease. Only Mrs Wyse, wealthy widow and general benefactor to the village, with a particular interest in matters concerning the children, is mentioned in the later years. First referred to in 1890, she visits to 'look at the needlework', perhaps because the standard has been criticised in that year's HMI report. She is now Chairman of the Board, having headed the poll at a recent Board election and replaced the Reverend Harry Tudor, (only fourth in the list.)[35] It does not seem that she taught needlework at any time, but advised and encouraged those that did. In her capacity as chairman she inspects and approves the registers and attends both HMI and diocesan inspections with the Reverend Tudor. In 1899, she very generously gave the school a piano, which must have been of great help to the obligatory singing lessons.

The quality of the teaching at the school no doubt varied, and certainly the equipment available in the early years was limited. Having endured the overcrowding and dreadful facilities of the old school, the young Susan Knapman seems to have done remarkably well. The sudden increase in the roll must have been a shock and some of the older children as a result became unruly and boys continued to be occasionally caned for swearing and disobedience.[36] Miss Knapman seems to have been popular with the children's parents. When Susan was away ill on the first occasion (1878), the temporary teacher, Miss Nosworthy, kept Ellen Singleton in for bad behaviour. Ellen's mother then kept her daughter away from school 'until Miss Knapman should return'.

Miss Nosworthy only lasted a few weeks and was replaced by Miss Treleaven, who writes, 'I have had very hard work during the last week on account of the neglect of the former teacher (Miss Nosworthy) who took charge of the school and did not attend to her duties'. Miss Treleaven stayed on for the rest of the summer term and the efficiency of the school was once more on track, with HMI Burrows, after a 'visit without notice' saying that the school was 'satisfactory in every way' and the 'discipline is so much improved'. His full report after the examination in the summer notes improvements in many areas but says that work in the infant class is only moderate. However, he reveals a soft spot for Miss Knapman, 'who in a mixed school with a considerable and increasing attendance and many very rough and backward children is quite unable to devote enough time to the infant class. Efficient and qualified assistance is urgently needed'.[37]

The code governing the inspection of schools was rigid, and HMIs were all-powerful, so that the annual inspections were nerve-racking affairs, prepared for with cramming, and dressed up on the day with as many children as could be mustered in Sunday-best clothes and shoes.

Miss Colson uses the log book to record lessons she has taken in addition to the 'elementary', including geography and grammar. Geography class subjects include 'The Rivers of the East and South Coast of England' and 'drawing a map of India'. The one boy in Standard V was able to draw from memory a map of Ireland with its rivers and ports. Other subjects included grammar – 'The Analysis of a Simple Sentence' (Standards V and VI). Copy writing, history (a collective lesson on the Gunpowder Plot on 3rd November 1882), and boys as well as girls in the infants are learning to knit. They will soon 'be taught Position Drill so as to commence sewing'. Object lessons were introduced into the Infant class.[38] The mistress also mentions receiving poetry books, grammar textbooks and atlas copybooks, together with a clock face with movable hands to teach the infants to tell the time.

Individual classes are 'kept in' for careless work or unnecessary noise, though this must have been as tedious for the mistress as the pupils, and in 1883 HMI praises Miss Colson for her discipline and organisation. Mr Badcock's brief reign from September 1884 to April 1885 is recorded in the log book by a series of request for supplies and little else.[39] His entries on other matters become rare and brief. Having probably exhausted the school budget he departs suddenly in the Easter holidays, when his post is taken by Mr. J.H. Derbyshire who finds the standard of attainment not to his liking: 'Not one of the scholars knows anything about notation and numeration'. He finds Standards II to IV 'very backward' and hastily returns three children to the infants before the examination 'as they are not even able to read'. At first he has some discipline problems[40] with the older boys and has to resort to the cane, but soon they cease testing him and order is restored with a good comment about discipline and instruction in the HMI report of 24th August.

In addition to object lessons, the Department of Education required the learning and recitation of poetry, one poem per standard, to be learned by all, but attention to these more pleasant tasks did not disguise the fact that after a good start Mr Derbyshire was failing to make the grade – or had come up against an inspector with unrealistic expectations, which was often the case with small rural schools. The report of 1886 is critical of the teaching of the older children. HMI writes,

> It is with hesitation that the payment of any grant is recommended. The knowledge of Geography is neither accurate nor intelligent. The specimens of sewing made on the day of examination are only moderate. My Lords will look for a more satisfactory report another year. The defects in instruction noticed by H.M. Inspector should receive the teacher's careful attention.

This must have been galling for Mr Derbyshire, especially as it was the duty of the head teacher to copy the report into the log book himself. The report next year acknowledged the level of illness there had been, but found little to praise. In 1888, HMI noted some improvements in singing and sewing, and assistant teacher, Miss Osborne, must have been pleased to hear that 'The Infants are in very good order and carefully taught'.

The report of 1894 is perhaps unsurprisingly not entered into the log in Mr Derbyshire's own hand, but by Mr W. Wills, Clerk to the Board. Mr Derbyshire's morale must have been very low, as he was unable to express any opinions or justifications in the log, though he would have done so to the Board. Her Majesty's Inspector of Schools', Reverend Wilkinson, report begins well, but becomes harsh in its criticisms:

> Order is satisfactory, and a very fair percentage of passes has been obtained in the Elementary Subjects; but the results of examination rather tend to show that the Master does not aim at really good results, the instruction in Grammar being absolutely valueless, the children showing no intelligent interest in their work. The Fourth is a very weak Standard in all respects, the writing on paper is very poor, Arithmetical problems are hardly touched and the Reading and Writing are slovenly and unintelligent.

Her Majesty's Inspector of Schools also draws attention to the fact that there are seven children of 7 years and four children of 8 years in the infant class, which shows that either they have very poor attendance (which should be enforced) or that 'full justice is not done to them when they do attend'.

Even Mr Derbyshire's discipline is faltering. The next year, 'May 6th 1890. Punished William Squires for talking; after I had done so, he kicked me and used foul expressions towards me … On the boy refusing to express his sorrow for using bad language, I sent him home'.

That year's report also being poor, and the Good Merit Grant being withheld, by the end of the winter the master has sent in his resignation and he and Mrs Derbyshire leave the following March to be replaced by Mr and Mrs Newberry, with two daughters to put on the roll, which now begins to rise once more, reaching 116 by June 1891. Again, they seem to make a good start, but by their second inspection Mr Newberry was not awarded a grant for either English or geography and was criticised sharply for putting low achievers into lower classes for the day of the examinations. The boys are now being taught technical drawing, but this is not being offered for examination. Following this report, attendance drops, Log entries are sketchy and the following February (1893) the log is not kept at all for a month and the master is recorded as being absent on business. The school was obviously in crisis and by 10th April Mr and Mrs Newberry were gone.[41] They were replaced by temporary teachers, Mr and Mrs Ash, who held the fort until the arrival of Charles Sampson, certificated first class, and his wife, also a certificated teacher, with three children to be registered at the school.[42]

Mr Sampson immediately finds discipline lax, especially among the boys 'who take very little notice of their teachers'. There were huge gaps in the elementary subjects.

> Children in Standard IV are not sure of the multiplication table and the spelling of simple words is wretched … the discipline is … very poor; the children seem never to have been taught what coming to school means or how they should behave when they get there.

These are telling words. The Sampsons find the equipment 'scanty and worn' – there are pages missing from readers and no answers to the arithmetic cards. The specimen sewing work to be presented at the imminent inspection has not been completed and there has been little practice for the tasks that will be set on the examination day.[43]

Mr Sampson commences by concentrating on discipline and

obedience, and his wife must have worked miracles in a very short time, as that summer HMI praises the needlework. Making few allowances for the recent change of regime, he finds the school failing in most other areas, so the Sampsons set to with energy to remedy the defects, testing the progress of the pupils every month. Alas, bad weather and sickness take their toll, and when on 28th June 1894 HMI made a special visit there were only 54 children present of 106 on the register. The school was then immediately closed for a month, there being typhoid and whooping cough in the parish.

On 26th July as many children as possible were assembled at the school for further inspection by HMI. The infants underwent a full examination. Children in the main school were only examined if they had missed the last examination or wished proficiency certificates to enable them to leave school. Recitations and songs were performed, and grammar was tested in the upper standards.

Credit is due to Mr Sampson and his wife for a reasonable report, in which improvements in discipline and the efficiency of the teaching were noticed, and English, geography and needlework had improved enough to be awarded the full grants. There was a dip in the attainments of the infants, no doubt because the new assistant, Miss Arnold, was settling in after the departure of the long-serving and popular Miss Osborne.[44] The numbers in the infant class were increasing, and Miss Arnold, who we have already seen in conflict with Mr Sampson, complains to the Board, who order Mr Sampson to provide one of the older girls to help her in the mornings. Mr Sampson is angry at her having gone over her head and at losing a pupil very close to the examination.[45] Despite the friction, Miss Arnold does well with the infants, 'Reading, Spelling and Needlework being exceptionally good'.

There are no clues in the log to Mr Sampson's sudden resignation at the beginning of the autumn term in 1896. He seems to have been making progress at the school and there is no mention of ill health, and again, a temporary teacher is found by the Board to serve for a month until the appointment of Mr John Loftus Sing, who begins his duties on the 5th October, with his wife, Mrs F.E.L. Sing who is 'to assist with the Standards and to take charge of the needlework'.

Mr Sing appears not to have read previous entries in the log book, for in his first entry he writes,

> We find, much to our surprise, that the children have made no progress whatever since their last examination, particularly in the higher standards ... No needlework has been done since June and there are no materials for starting in the school ... A whole year's work will have to be done in nine months.[46]

There was a lack of materials in general, books were 'in a wretched state' and there were very few unbroken slates. Mr Sing sends a long list of requirements to the Clerk of the Board, and draws the attention of the Board to the poor state of the classroom furniture.

He also pays particular attention to discipline, including arriving and leaving the school in an orderly manner, and he changes the timetable to make it comply with regulations. With the permission of the Board, Mr Sing introduces morning and evening prayers to the classroom and sets himself the task of going back to basics in the teaching of arithmetic. In February 1897 he does his own thorough examination of the whole school and records 'substantial improvements ... and slow but sure progress'. There is the first mention of the teaching of science in school, and Mr Sing brings in his own equipment and apparatus to use in class. Object lessons include porous bodies, filters, soluble substances, adhesive and fusible substances. Standard III are now receiving lessons in physics, botany and zoology. Horizons are broadening for the 'rough' and 'backward' children of Lustleigh.[47]

A year of hard work reaps its reward, with the first all-round excellent report for many years. The infant class is awarded the highest Variable Grant, (£26. 8s. 0d.) and the mixed school, £64. The Reverend Tudor and Mrs Wise, who had attended the inspection, must have been extremely relieved. Attendance is greatly improved and the message, at last, seems to be getting through to parents and agricultural employers that schooling is a priority as well as a right for Lustleigh's children.

Infections are still rife however, and there is a virulent outbreak of diphtheria. Considering the contemporary rate of child mortality there are fairly few records of deaths on the school register. Mr Sing is the only head teacher to record deaths of children as something more than a simple, stark fact in the log.

24th January 1898, 'By the sad death last night of Mabel Parker, 12, after only one week's illness, the school has lost one of its best and most promising pupils'. And 18th May of the same year, 'Death has robbed the school of another scholar, Jessie Coles, 5, who died yesterday'.

This was the year that he lost a pupil in happier circumstances. Douglas Livingstone, son of the mine manager at Plumley, having attained the dizzying heights of the VIth Standard, left Lustleigh to go to grammar school in Torquay.

This must have been a feather in Mr Sing's cap, and is only one of his achievements at the school, which is now receiving consistent, good reports from HMI and having steady average attendance figures. He teaches pupil-teacher Dora Hill, after school at his house throughout her apprenticeship, to a an excellent examination result, employs Joseph Sprague as a pupil-teacher before she leaves, so that the boy can observe and start his out-of-school lessons, introduces physical education (PE) to the timetable, and rewards his children with magic lantern shows during school time.[48]

One concern for the head master, now that he has got the school running smoothly, is the number of children arriving at school for the first time at 7 years old, or from other schools.

> The children who were on last year's roll are making very satisfactory progress, but some ten scholars ... have been admitted quite recently, and these are miserably behind the others, in fact most of them are utter failures. On the whole, owing to these new-comers, the school is much inferior to what it has been at a corresponding period of previous years, and these two or three dull scholars in each class will need a lot of attention and pushing before the school reaches last year's standard.

However much modern teachers might deplore words such as 'dull' and 'failures', and reject the technique of 'pushing', there is no doubt that Mr Sing gave his pupils a great deal of time and attention.

At the very end of Victoria's reign, in January 1901, Thomas Williamson takes over the headship, with his wife, Rose, as assistant. Mr Williamson is the very first new incumbent not to make implied criticism of his predecessor. There are 122 children in the register, 40 of these in the infants. The school is popular, running efficiently and receiving its full grants – but the new water supply still has not reached the village, and consequently, the school 'offices'.

The census returns for Lustleigh and advertisements in the local newspapers reveal that other forms of education were available in the village for those with the means to pay. In 1851 Thomas Amery at Higher Combe was employing 19-year-old Caroline Nosworthy as a governess, and 55-year-old Maria Luscombe was similarly employed by Edward Cuming at Fursdon. (The same census shows Elizabeth Coade, 41, as a schoolmistress. It is possible that she, and Susan Ann Ireland, ten years later, are predecessors of Susan Knapman at Parson Davy's school).

In 1871, as well as Miss Knapman, the census records a William Kirby, curate and schoolmaster, living with his wife, and three boys between the ages of 11 and 12, described as 'boarders'. A few years earlier (1868–1869), there had been notices in the local papers advertising a 'Middle Class' school, probably equating to a preparatory school, in Lustleigh ('one of the most Healthy Spots in the Country'). The standard of education was stated as 'that of the Oxford and Cambridge University Local Examinations' and pupils were offered a 'sound commercial and classical education'. Parents are told to contact 'The Principal', and it is reasonable to suppose that this establishment belonged to the Reverend Kirby.[49] Such schools, common in towns, were usually run as family businesses and were not subject to government inspection.

Miss Colton's assistant, Susan Nicholls, shows up in the 1881 census, living with her parents Sam and Elizabeth. In 1891 Walter Newberry (35) and his wife Catherine, (40) are at the schoolhouse and there are governesses (Rachel Macintosh, 27) at Rock Vale and at Higher Combe (Mabel Willnot, 19).

Thanks to the charitable ladies of Lustleigh (who also ran clothing clubs for the school)[50] there were some opportunities for older youngsters to improve their education, with winter evening classes offered at the Old Vestry in literature (for boys and men), free-hand drawing (boys), Bible classes, and fine needlework and embroidery (girls). Further self-improvement might be looked for at lectures such as 'Homely Talks for Mothers and Girls of all ages at the Church House, admission one penny'.[51]

The wealthy of Lustleigh of course had governesses, tutors, preparatory schools and public schools at their disposal, Harrow being favoured by both the Torr and Amery families.[52]

Sunday schools were always an influence in the period, and an excellent way of keeping children out of the way while mother cooked the Sunday dinner. Those who attended regularly could be sure of their invitation to various 'treats' during the year. Magic lantern shows with a tea were very popular,[53] as were day trips to the seaside. Even a trip to Chudleigh Rocks (which is 'down the road' to a present-day motorist) gave pleasure and excitement to the children. Christmas brought further entertainments, noted in the *Parish Magazine* of February 1890,

> Mrs Wise during the last month gave a beautiful Christmas tree to a number of the Sunday School Scholars. A Conjurer from London, Mr Strode, gave the children of the Day and Sunday schools an Entertainment in the Church House.

Mrs Wise also managed the Sunday School, often on her own, and even ran a little afternoon Bible class at her own house, Coombe, for 'the smaller children being too far away to attend …'.[54]

Choirboys had their special treats too. They played cricket and were coached by the rector's son in the rectory field and had matches with boys from other villages.[55] They had their own treats, one in September 1898, according to the *Parish Magazine*, taking them from Totnes to Dartmouth by boat and Dartmouth to Paignton by train. Mrs Wise may well have paid for such trips out of her own pocket, for she trained the boys, and continued to take supportive interest in them after they left the choir.

Throughout the Victorian period the church and the chapels played an important part in the day-to-day lives of the village children. Up at the school, the Reverend Ensor was not only chairman but a sort of school chaplain, visiting regularly to give religious instruction, as did the Reverend Tudor and a succession of curates. A Board school, under the 1870 Act was supposed to be non-sectarian, not to impose any religious education other than Bible reading and not to require inspection by the diocese. However, Lustleigh's clergy certainly went further in their instruction than was strictly required, with the consensus of the Board (of which they were active members), for example, promoting the introduction in Mr Sing's reign of prayer times. The Board also consented to a yearly diocesan inspection, and a comment from the Reverend Tudor on a laudatory report, given by the Reverend R.J. Boggis in January 1891, is revealing: 'We are of the opinion that education without religious teaching is a very imperfect education, and likely to prove a curse rather than a blessing'.

The diocesan reports as printed in the *Parish Magazine*s (edited by the Reverend Tudor) are universally approving of the religious knowledge and general behaviour of the children. In the school log book it is noticeable that visits by the Rector are increased in the month before diocesan inspection.

The general behaviour of children out of school was not always as it should be, however, and the Reverend Tudor used his platform as *Parish Magazine* editor to castigate the miscreants. In March 1895 he writes,

> Complaints, we are sorry to hear, are made that a few foolish boys and girls collect sometimes outside the railway station, and annoy persons by their bad behaviour and bad language. We hope this foolish conduct will cease. It would be a disgrace if anyone was summoned before the magistrates for bad conduct.

April 1896, and the reverend's concern was recurring vandalism – broken tiles on the roof of the Old Vestry. (Possibly children had been trying to pitch stones over from the road to the churchyard.) 'If the parents have to pay the expense of replacing these tiles,' he thunders, 'it is hoped the boys will be punished.' In August he is again concerned about youthful failings,

> We are grieved again to hear of bad behaviour in Church on the part of two or three young people ... the children who eat nuts in Church are reminded that St Paul says we ought to eat in houses, not in Church.

Although some children did make the occasional visit to family members in other villages and the nearer towns, sometimes even as far as London, their social life was mostly contained within the village. It would have been an eye-opener for them when, in 1898, the Chapple family of 'Brookside' hosted four young relations from Australia; Sidney, aged 12 years, Gertie, 9, Willie, 6, and George, aged just 4. They stayed from April to August, attended school, and must have had many tales of their life in Australia and their epic journey to Devon.

If they could afford the small admission fee, there were regular concerts at the Church House to attend, and occasionally the children were themselves performers. In March 1894 an entertainment of 'Songs, Recitations, Dialogues etc.' was given. The rector hoped that

Mr. and Mrs. Sampson, who are taking a great deal of trouble in getting the children perfect in their different parts, will be rewarded with a very good attendance, especially of the parents of School children. The proceeds, after paying expenses, will be awarded with prizes to the best behaved and most diligent children.[56]

The report in the next issue of the *Parish Magazine* is of

success due to painstaking practice … It was pleasant to see that the youthful performers enjoyed the evening. The room was more crowded than we have ever seen it and we were glad to see many parents of the performers present.

In Mr Sampson's time, a school choir entertained visitors to the Lustleigh show in a marquee.[57] The show was always eagerly anticipated by the children, with its brass bands, games and sports as the fête of the Lustleigh branch of the National Sick and Burial Society often ran alongside it. In the show itself there were always a small number of competitions especially for the children. Classes included a nosegay, darning, making a boy's shirt, a model of a flower garden, a piece of hemming one yard long on a piece of calico, a bunch of wild flowers.[58]

In September 1891 the *Parish Magazine* reported,

The boys' drawings were admired and the dressed dolls competition for the girls was a success. They looked 'bright and cheerful and were most of them so well dressed that it was no easy matter to award the prizes; one had work done with a beautiful ornamental feather stitch.' E. Maunder and D. Hill got prizes. The models of gardens showed that boys had learned the use of rules and compasses, prizes were gained by P. Wills, C. Arnold and L. Hill.

When their out-of-school hours were not devoted to household and garden chores, farm work or infant-minding, the children were free to use the fields, woods and streams as their playground. It is known that they 'scrumped' apples from the orchards, and went bird-nesting because there were admonishments against these pastimes in the *Parish Magazine*. No doubt any chances to earn pocket money or contribute to the family income in the holidays were seized upon. A notice in the

Parish Magazine announces that 'Edwin Arnold would be glad to act as messenger or guide to Cleave, Manaton &c., &c.'.[59] Master Arnold was 10 years old and his mother was a widowed midwife, unable to work because of illness. This enterprising lad lived at Stable House in the centre of the village and so was well-placed to catch the tourists.[60]

Edwin's customers may have had to concentrate hard on his directions, as all the schoolchildren had broad Devon accents. Her Majesty's Inspector of Schools's reports often deplore 'indistinct articulation'. Later in the twentieth century, Cecil Torr records examples of local dialect that would not have changed since his grandfather's day. He appreciates the local idioms more than the school inspectors.

> Happily, the school has not taught them English that is truly up to date. They have not learned to say, 'The weather conditions being favourable, the psychological moment was indulged in.' They still say 'As 'twere fine, us did'n.' And their pronunciation is unchanged: beetles are bittles, beans are banes, and Torquay is Tarkay.[61]

Figure 10.4: *Lustleigh Board School in the early years of the 20th Century.*
Reproduced from a Chapman & Son Postcard (Detail)
(Courtesy of Lustleigh Community Archive)

By the turn of the twentieth century, parents and land-owning employers had at last conceded that education for all was a beneficial step for all concerned. The training of teachers had improved considerably, and so had the quality of teaching. A new Act (1902) was about to come into being) establishing Local Education Authorities that would replace the Boards and end the 'grants-according-to-results' system which caused teachers so much misery. There were also more varied employment prospects for the school leavers. In the village there were a number of shops needing assistants, and craftsmen and women requiring apprentices, and the train made it possible for youngsters to go to work outside the village. A number of lads also joined the armed forces.

If the Reverend Hawker and any of those present at that purposeful meeting in Newton Abbot were still alive in 1901 to note the effects of the Education Act of 1870, they would no doubt have approved of some of the progress made, even though the main method of imparting knowledge was still through memorising and copying. With the new Education Act would come those opportunities for further education (for some) dismissed by the gentleman of the Devon Chamber of Commerce. Victoria's reign had been long and progress in education in the rural areas had been gradual, but prospects were now brighter for the young people of Lustleigh.

Notes

1. See Amer, F.M., 'The childhood of a Devon maid' for descriptions of the journey to school. Lustleigh Archive.
2. *Exeter and Plymouth Gazette*, 17th April 1868.
3. Torr, C., 1921. *Small Talk at Wreyland* (hereafter *STAW*), vol. 3. Cambridge: Cambridge University Press. p.3. The 'town' is the centre of the village, around the church.
4. Ibid. Original document is in Lustleigh Archive.
5. 'Old papers dated 1825' reproduced in *Lustleigh Parish Magazine*, October 1892.
6. Fraser Halle, D., 1851. *Letters Historical and Botanical*. London: Houlston & Stoneman. p.14.
7. Torr, *STAW*, vol 3. pp.40–41.
8. Only children who had passed the examination for Standard IV could be awarded a Labour Certificate allowing them to leave school, but only if they had a job to go to.

9. May 1876, *Lustleigh School Log Book* (hereafter *LSLB*), vol. 1. Exeter Records Office, cat.no.1275C/1/EAL/1 *LSLB*.

10. Ibid., June 1876.

11. '[Be]ing a piece of land known as Little Hill'. A quarter of an acre belonging to the Gate House tenement, sold for £50. Indentures and Conveyances. Lustleigh Archive.

12. 'Offices' = lavatories. At first unisex, later separate girls' lavatories were built.

13. *LSLB*, vol. 1. September 1890.

14. Ibid., vol. 2. Cat. No.175C/1/EAL/2, 11th March 1895.

15. Labour Certificates were only awarded to scholars who had passed Standard IV.

16. The summer holidays were invariably referred to as 'The Harvest Holidays'.

17. Surprisingly little truancy, for fun, or out of dislike for school, is recorded in the log.

18. Lowton Meadow was sold when Davy's Endowed School was closed and the proceeds used to fund the new school's prizes (see Torr, *STAW*, vol. 3. pp.42–43).

19. HMI report 1899. *LSLB*, vol. 2.

20. *LSLB*, vol. 1. 1886–1887.

21. Ibid., 1885.

22. Eulogy of Mrs Ensor. *Lustleigh Parish Magazine*, August 1910.

23. Torr, *STAW*, vol. 1. pp.6–7.

24. Ibid.

25. Ibid., vol. 2. p.56.

26. Ibid., vol. 1. p.6.

27. Ibid., *passim*.

28. Ibid., June–July 1895.

29. Sewing was an important subject for the girls as they would be expected to make all the clothes and do all the mending for their eventual families. Techniques to be learned included, button-holing, darning, marking, turning a tuck, and cutting out material for garments.

30. *LSLB*, vol.1. October 1879.

31. See later information on voluntary assistance from clergy and gentry.

32. *LSLB*, vol. 1. January 1878 and April 1881.

33. See Appendix 2 for a list of names.

34. HMI report for 1883. *LSLB*, vol.1.

35. *Western Times*, November 1899, 'Lustleigh School Board election'. The votes were cast as follows; Maria Elizabeth Wise, widow, 60 votes; Francis Stoneman, gardener, 52; John Wills, yeoman, 49; Reverend Harry Tudor, vicar, 45; Chas. Germon Wills, gentleman, 33; William Henry Parr, farmer,

37. The first five were duly elected. Fifty-nine ratepayers voted out of the eligible list of 92. (Female householders could vote and stand for office.)

36. Teachers were not obliged to record punishments in the log book and few do so. This does not mean that no punishments were meted out as a matter of course.

37. HMI report 1878. *LSLB*, vol. 1.

38. These were set by the Department of Education. The objects for illustration and illumination for 1883–1884 were: 1. Daisy 2. Whale. 3. Nightingale. 4. Needle. 5. Wheat. 6. Sheep. *LSLB*, vol. 1.

39. *LSLB*, vol. 1. 29th October 1884, '6 dozen Royal Readers, 6½ dozen Home Lesson books, one gross of slate pen holders, 1 gross of exercise books, 2 quires of blotting paper, 1 ream of foolscap paper, 2 dozen yards of calico. 4 packets of knitting needles, 5 packets of sewing needles. January 5th 1885 1 gross of copy books, 1 gallon of ink, 2 dozen India rubbers, 4 dozen primers, 1 dozen slates, 25 atlases, 1 set arithmetic cards, 3 lbs wool, 2 dozen reels sewing cotton, 1lb knitting cotton'.

40. Boys are punished for 'impudence' and 'bad language'.

41. They may have remained in the parish, as their daughters seem to have stayed in the school, one as a monitress.

42. All would receive, unsurprisingly, Good Attendance prizes.

43. *LSLB*, vol. 2. 7th July and 29th September 1893.

44. *Totnes Weekly Times*, 19th June 1894. Miss Osborne left to get married, the ceremony taking place two days after she left the school. She was presented with an inscribed clock and a 'testimonial'.

45. *LSLB*, vol. 2. 26th May 1896.

46. *LSLB*, vol. 2. October 1896.

47. *LSLB*, vol. 2. 1898.

48. 'Stopped usual work to give illustrations of "Recitation Scenes" by Magic Lantern'. *LSLB*, vol. 1. 3rd November 1889.

49. *Western Times*, 3rd January 1868, 7th July 1868, 12th March 1869.

50. Clothing clubs (in Lustleigh's case, run by philanthropic ladies of the parish) required from poor families a regular contribution towards the basic children's clothing and shoes provided by the club.

51. *Lustleigh Parish Magazine*, 1888–1891.

52. Lustleigh census.

53. *Lustleigh Parish Magazine*, 1895: 'It is requested that all the children who come to the Tea and Magic Lantern Show … on December 28th will remember that this and the Summer Treat at Teignmouth, will have been to encourage regular attendance at the Sunday and Day Schools, and that next year any child who has been irregular in attendance at School, unless the reason has been illness, may not be invited. People who subscribe to the

expenses of such treats, naturally wish to promote regular attendance and good behaviour'.

54. Eulogy. *Lustleigh Parish Magazine*, July 1923.
55. *Lustleigh Parish Magazine*, August 1888.
56. There was also enough profit to put towards a school trip to Teignmouth by train on the 1st September, when they dined on meat, bread and buns, washed down by tea and ginger beer.
57. *Totnes Weekly Times*, 10th August 1895.
58. Reports on the show from the *Western Times*, 8th August 1890, and *Exeter and Plymouth Gazette*, 10th August 1894.
59. *Lustleigh Parish Magazine*, June 1891.
60. 1891 census.
61 Torr, *STAW*, vol. 1. p.55.

Bibliography

Sellman, R.R., 1967. *Devon Village Schools in the Nineteenth Century*. Newton Abbot: David & Charles.

Torr, C., 1921. *Small Talk at Wreyland*, vol. 1. Cambridge: Cambridge University Press.

Torr, C., 1921. *Small Talk at Wreyland*, vol 3. Cambridge: Cambridge University Press.

Appendix 1: Head teachers and assistant teachers of Lustleigh Board School 1875–1907

March 25 1875 to July 1881 **MISS SUSAN ANN KNAPMAN certificated teacher** (previously teacher of the Endowed School, where she began in 1868) Temporary mistresses when Miss Knapman ill, M.M. NOSWORTHY and A.TRELEAVEN. Monitresses, SUSAN NICHOLLS, ELIZABETH OSBORNE, SELINA WESTCOTT.

September 5th 1881–September 29th 1884 **MISS D. COLTON certificated teacher second class.** Assistant Mistress SUSAN NICHOLLS (aged 18 in1881). Stipendiary Monitress later Assistant Mistress, ELIZABETH OSBORNE appointed 1882 (aged 18).

September 1884–April 1885 **MR J. BADCOCK certificated teacher first class** assisted by his wife MRS. M. BADCOCK, certificated teacher. Assistant Mistress ELIZABETH OSBORNE.

April 1885–July 1891 **MR J.H. DERBYSHIRE** certificated teacher assisted by his wife MRS DERBYSHIRE, Assistant Mistress ELIZABETH OSBORNE.

July 1891–April 1893 **MR WALTER NEWBERRY** certificated teacher first class, assisted by his wife MRS CATHERINE NEWBERRY, Assistant Mistress ELIZABETH OSBORNE, Monitress V.NEWBERRY(Daughter)

June 1893–September 1896 **MR CHARLES SAMPSON** certificated teacher assisted by his wife MRS SAMPSON certificated teacher. Assistant teacher ELIZABETH OSBOURNE leaves to marry. MISS ARNOLD appointed (1894) Monitress DORA HILL.

September 7th–October 5th **MR JOHN TUCKER temporary Master**

October 1896–January 1901 **MR JOHN LOFTUS SING** certificated teacher with Parchment, assisted by his wife Mrs F.E.L. SING, Assistant Teacher MISS CLACK (transferred to the Infants) DORA HILL pupil-teacher 1898, appointed as assistant Mistress 1900. 1900 Miss ELIZABETH MITCHELL pupil-teacher

January 1901–1907 **MR THOMAS WILLIAMSON** certificated teacher assisted by his wife MRS ROSE WILLIAMSON. Assistant Teacher DORA HILL leaves 1901

Appendix 2: Lustleigh parishioners as voluntary teachers with dates of mention in the school log book 1875–1901

1875–1887	Reverend Ensor	*Scripture*
1877–1885	Miss Ida Gould	*Singing*
1877–1880	Mr Buckworth (Curate)	*Scripture*
1877–1890	Miss Hayes	*Geography*
1880	Miss Sanders	*Reading*
1880	Miss Ensor	*Scripture*
1880–1883	Miss Lilian Gould	*Geography*
1881	Reverend Clapp (Curate)	*Scripture and Geography*
1881–1891	Miss Morris	*Scripture and Geography*
1883	Miss Jabet	*Needlework*
1885	Mr Serceton (Curate)	*Bible classes*
1886	Mr Oxenham (Curate)	*Bible classes*
1886–1901	Reverend Tudor	*Religious Instruction*

Appendix 3: The six Standards of Education laid down by the Revised Code of Regulations 1872

Standard I

Reading –One of the narratives next in order after monosyllables in an elementary reading book used in the school.

Writing – Copy in manuscript character a line of print, and write from dictation a few common words.

Arithmetic – Simple addition and subtraction of numbers of not more than four figures and the multiplication table to multiplication by six.

Standard II

Reading – A short paragraph from an elementary reading book.

Writing – A sentence from the same book, slowly said once and then dictated in single words.

Arithmetic – The multiplication table and any simple rule as far as short division (inclusive).

Standard III

Reading – A short paragraph from a more advanced reading book,

Writing – A sentence slowly dictated a few words at a time from the same book.

Arithmetic – Long division and Compound Rules (money).

Standard IV

Reading – A few lines of poetry or prose selected by the Inspector.

Writing – A sentence slowly dictated once, by a few words at a time, from a reading book such as is used in the First class of the school.

Arithmetic – Compound rules (common Weights and Measures)

Standard V

Reading – A short paragraph in a newspaper or other modern narrative.

Writing – Another short paragraph in a newspaper or modern narrative, slowly dictated.

Arithmetic – Practice and Bills of Parcels

Standard VI

Reading – To read with fluency and expression.

Writing – A short theme or letter or easy paraphrase.

Arithmetic – Proportion and Fractions (vulgar and decimal).

Source: Elementary Education Act 1870. *Wikipedia*, 10th August 2017.

11. 'With Great Spirit'

The contribution of the Divett family to the growth of Victorian Bovey

Viv Styles

In Bovey Tracey in 1831, out of a population of 1,697, there were 237 men over the age of 21 engaged in agricultural labour. By 1881 the population had risen to 2,127 and 140 were recorded working as agricultural labourers.[1] In percentage terms, men over 21 employed in agricultural labour fell from around 14 per cent to less than 7 per cent. Census returns can provide evidence of this and it is possible to track these changes through families over time. For example, looking at the Manley family in 1841,[2] Elias Manley, aged 60, and his son James, aged 24, are both working as agricultural labourers. Ten years later Elias is still working as an agricultural labourer but James is now working as a 'Potter's Labourer'. By 1861 James had progressed to 'Potter' and continued working at the pottery until his death in 1872 when his son, another Elias, was also employed at the pottery. This shift in employment practice from agriculture to manufacture and service is well documented across Britain, and there is a perception that Victorian Britain was dominated by a class of prosperous industrialists who exploited the working classes in order to accumulate wealth. In the light of this assumption, the purpose of this essay is to investigate the contribution of the Divett family to Victorian Bovey Tracey.

In June 1841, the census enumerators recorded a population of 1,823 with around 300 people employed in agriculture with 45 farmers and 57 people of independent means, only five of whom were over 80 years of age.[3] The Tithe map of 1840 shows that the majority of the inhabitants lived along the through roads, then Main Street, now Fore Street, East Street, St Mary Street and College. The abundance of clay deposits and lignite in the area meant that raw material was transported to the Staffordshire potteries throughout the eighteenth century. From the mid-century, enterprising potters were setting up potteries of their own to exploit local materials, and the remains of an early salt glaze kiln were discovered in Fore Street in 1934. This kiln can now be seen on site at Bovey Tracey Heritage Centre. Nicholas Crisp began manufacturing pottery at Indio House from 1766 and investments made under the management of William Ellis meant that the pottery flourished for some years, making fine tableware. In 1800 a rival works was set up by Mead and Lemble which became known as the Folly Pottery, later owned by John and Thomas Honeychurch. The pottery struggled to survive and was put up for sale by public auction on 2nd May 1836. The advertisement in the *Western Times* stated,

> This pottery may unhesitatingly be designated one of the largest and most complete in the West of England, situated 14 miles from Exeter, and 28 from Plymouth, on the Great Western Road, and possesses local and other advantages which no other ever possessed – Its situation being in the LAND OF CLAY, from which nearly all the potteries in Staffordshire draw their supply and having thereon an inexhaustible COAL MINE, with a railroad from the pit to the kiln's mouth.[4]

The advertisement goes on to explain that materials to and from the premises were conveyed by 'the Haytor Company's Rail Road, which passes through the property to the Teignbridge canal'. This is evidence of the route and usage of the granite tramway, built by George Templer in 1820 to transport granite from the Haytor quarries to the Stover canal. The reference to a coal mine relates to the lignite pit nearby, lignite being an intermediate stage between peat and coal. Lignite was a readily available and cheap source of fuel for the kilns, but temperatures reached were lower than could be achieved with black coal.

Despite this enticing advertisement, the pottery remained for sale until 1842 when it caught the attention of Thomas Wentworth Buller and his brother-in-law, John Divett. Buller was the second son of James Buller, an Exeter Member of Parliament (MP). Thomas Wentworth Buller joined the Navy in 1806 and served in the Mediterranean as well as the Americas, achieving the rank of Commander in 1817.[5] Commander Buller married Ann Divett, the only daughter of Edward Divett, of Bystock, in 1827. Ann's brother, John, was also a second son, born at Withycombe Raleigh in 1810. Educated at Eton and Trinity College Cambridge, he served as one of the Tithe commissioners alongside Thomas Buller.[6] In 1833, John Divett married Henrietta Emma Buller, sister of his already brother-in-law Thomas. John's brother, Edward Divett, was the Liberal MP for Exeter, who kept his seat from 1832 until his death in 1864. Their father, Edward, came from a Quaker family of leather and wool merchants and became a partner in a London bank. He purchased a 250-acre estate at Bystock near Exmouth in 1801, which was inherited by his eldest son Edward, in 1819.[7]

Buller and Divett went into partnership and set up a new business on the Folly Pottery site in 1843, trading as the Bovey Tracey Pottery Company. They expanded the site and continued to exploit the local lignite supplies as well as supplementing the fuel with coal brought into Teignmouth, transported along the Stover canal and from there to the pottery. The Bovey Tracey Pottery Company was a major supplier of mess ware, commissioned for use on ships of the Royal Navy. It is a matter of conjecture whether Thomas Buller used his Navy connections to secure the contract. M. Billing's *1857 Directory and Gazetteer of the County of Devon* stated, 'There is a pottery, upon a very extensive scale, and carried on by Messrs. Buller, Divett and Co. with great spirit, giving employment to a great number of hands'.[8]

Although an active partner in the business, Thomas Buller lived with his wife Ann and family at Whimple, in East Devon, until Thomas' death in 1852. He was described in the *Western Times* as a 'man of great energy, uprightness and resolution'.[9] Patent applications in the Devon Heritage Centre demonstrate that Buller was not just an investor, but was also keen to develop the technical operations of the pottery. In 1849, he was granted the patent for various inventions including

an improved mode of manufacturing earthenware articles which are termed by the trade 'cockspurs' and 'pins' and are employed for the sustaining of plates and dishes apart from each other in the 'saggers' while they are undergoing the firing operation.[10]

The Pottery, Bovey Tracey.

Figure 11.1: *The Bovey Pottery about 1908.*
(Courtesy of Bovey Tracey Heritage Centre)

Thomas' son, Wentworth Buller, inherited the proprietorship of the company and worked with Jabez Hearn Mugford to manage the pottery production and development of the manufacture of 'kiln furniture'. In the 1860s this aspect of the business transferred to Hanley in Staffordshire and Bullers Limited became one of the world's foremost manufacturers of electrical insulators.[11] Wentworth Buller was instrumental in bringing gas lighting to Bovey Tracey in 1857, the apparatus for manufacturing gas being erected under the supervision of Jabez Mugford, the 'indefatigable manager of the works'.[12]

John Divett, his wife Henrietta and their daughter Mary, moved to Bovey Tracey and took up residence in Bridge House in what is now Fore Street. The house was occupied in 1841 by Noah Flood. It seems the property was known locally as Noah's Ark because of the area's tendency to flooding. John greatly expanded the house and added a stable block which is currently occupied by the Devon Guild of Craftsmen. John also bought farmland at Langaller and much of the land he owned was traversed by the now disused granite tramway. Les Brealey, a senior resident of Bovey and a former builder, maintains that setts from the tramway can be seen in the building inside the Devon Guild, and can point out evidence where the sett flanges have been levelled for use in its construction. Reused granite setts can be spotted throughout the town. Bridge House remained the Divett family home until Mary's death in 1914.

By 1847 the *Western Times* was reporting on the 'extensive works at the Potteries', commenting that 'great proficiency in the manufacture' has taken place, implying that this is because it is being superintended by workmen from Staffordshire.[13] The 1851 census[14] bears this out, with numerous families stating births in Staffordshire. New buildings were constructed to house the pottery workers, including cottages in Brimley and accommodation on site simply called Folly Pottery. Robert Steele, a potter, and his wife Sarah, a burnisher, were both born in Shelton in Staffordshire. James Fletcher and his wife Ann, both potters, were born in Hanley in Staffordshire. Migration can clearly be seen in the example of the Harper family; Henry Harper, aged 33, was born in Scotland and his wife Jane, aged 31, was born in Liverpool. Elizabeth, aged 11, Mary, aged 6, and Henry, aged 5, were born in Scotland. Joseph, aged 3, was born in Hanley, Staffordshire, and the youngest, Thomas, aged 1, was born in Bovey Tracey. All but the two youngest are listed as 'potter'. William Robinson, recorded as the 26-year-old manager of the pottery, was born closer to home, in Whimple, presumably known to Thomas Buller in his home town and brought in to this responsible position.

By 1861 the address is now Bovey Tracey Pottery and around 22 families are listed here, representing 126 individuals. Many of those who appear in the 1851 census are still employed at the pottery, for example the Fletchers' two children Jane, aged 16, and Bovey Tracey born Theodore, aged 14, are also potters. William Robinson remains as manager, now married to Frances who has no occupation listed. Many more families have moved from Staffordshire and are living nearer to the town. In the cottages known as Pludda are Henry and Maria Pope, born in Staffordshire, and both working at the pottery, he as a potter and Maria as a warehouse woman. Elijah and Mary Sherrat lived next door, he a packer and she a burnisher both from Staffordshire. The Cartledge family were all born in Stoke-on-Trent, except the youngest, Henry, who was born in Bovey Tracey. Further along the row, James Hancock, John Steer and John Winckle were all potters born in Staffordshire. Occupations listed were spur makers, spur pickers (spurs being kiln furniture of the type developed by Thomas Buller), clay mixer, holloware maker, brick maker, coal heaver, painter and labourer as well as potter. The term 'potter' is used for any age between 5 and 60, but it is striking how many young men and women in their late teens and twenties found employment at the pottery. It is also notable that John Freagle, aged 50, a potter living with his 80-year-old mother at the Bovey Pottery in 1861, is recorded as blind.

The *Western Times* published an extensive description of the Bovey Pottery in January 1850[15] as part of a series of articles on the manufacturing industries of Devon, reporting that,

> Mr. John Divett, and Capt. Buller, of Whimple, possessed both the energy and the capital necessary for such an undertaking. The requisite machinery and buildings were erected, skillful [sic] workmen were brought down from the potteries, and though there were some failures at the outset – difficulties were overcome, as difficulties will be overcome, by increased attention and perseverance; the place assumed a busy bustling aspect, the manufacture increased rapidly, the surplus labor [sic] of the neighbourhood was in great measure absorbed, a profitable field of employment was opened for young and old of both sexes, and at the present time pottery both common and costly, the plain and the ornamental is manufactured to an extent which but few people have any idea of.

The author of the article undertakes a thorough tour of the pottery and describes the production processes in great detail, illustrating the division of labour:

> The potter's wheel consists of an upright cylinder on the top of which is a circular horizontal disk of wood. A rotary motion is given to this disk ... by means of a wheel and a band ... It is turned by a female, who drives it fast or slow, or promptly stops it, according to the direction of the thrower, whilst another female is required to take the various articles, when shaped, from the wheel. The thrower seats himself at his little table, the wheel being in the centre and level with it.

The throwers and turners were paid by piece work, earning around £2. 0s. 0d. a week, out of which they had to pay their wheel turners. Work

classed as unskilled labour, coal diggers, labourers and those engaged in
the preparation of the clay, earned between 10 and 15 shillings a week.
Women's earnings varied between 6 and 12 shillings a week, younger
women earned less. Girls earned from 1/6d. to 4 shillings whilst boys
could earn up to 10 shillings a week. The article reports a weekly wage
bill of between £100 and £150. It goes on,

> The benefit arising from the distribution of so large a sum through this
> rural district is too obvious to be insisted upon: if anyone doubts let
> him take the opinion of any shopkeeper in Bovey Tracey what effect the
> shutting up of the pottery would have on the weekly receipts.

The author notes there is no school connected to the factory, but there was
a library and reading room, 'to which all hands have access' consisting
of around 200 volumes mostly on scientific and historic subjects. The
pottery had its own cricket team and later a Bovey Pottery Brass Band.

Around this time Canon Courtenay, vicar of the parish Church of St
Peter, St Paul and St Thomas, proposed a second parish church to be built
at his own expense, to meet the spiritual needs of the pottery workers
living on that side of town. The first stone was laid on Shrove Tuesday
in 1852 for the building of St John's Church at the junction of Newton
Road and Ashburton Road.[16] St John's cottages followed to house the
clergy. Various newspaper articles throughout the 1860s and 1870s
accuse Canon Courtenay of ulterior motives in building this church,
maintaining that he built it to indulge his high church leanings and there
is open hostility towards 'tractarianism'. There is little evidence to show
that the church was used or welcomed by the pottery workers, however,
a new cricket house, opened in the field behind the church seems to have
been warmly received. In 1858, the *Western Times*[17] reported on a 'most
brilliant holiday' on the 5th November, to celebrate the opening of the
new cricket house. The programme announced a tea and a dance which
was attended by around 200 people, with grand fireworks to finish the
evening. Apparently the 'Bovey folks' had never witnessed such a grand
spectacle before.

> Since the progressive character of the works at the Pottery, nothing has
> been spared, either in liberality or energy, by the indefatigable proprietor,
> J.Divett, Esq., to further the interests of the inhabitants of Bovey, and

assist them to place themselves on a par with the neighbouring towns around. Domestic comforts – comfortable homesteads – moral teachings – and healthful recreations, have been suggested, planned, carried out, and well-appreciated.'

The 'indefatigable' John Divett was becoming a central figure in the life of the town. He is credited with engineering the leat to divert water from the Becky Falls stream to the pottery,[18] and as well as being a landowner he was also a shareholder in the Great Wheal Vor United Mines.[19] He served as a magistrate at the Newton Abbot Petty Sessions, helped to establish a branch of the Western Provident Association, a life assurance society, in Bovey, interested himself in the state of the roads, and was a keen participant in the annual flower shows. The British School, for children from 'non-conforming' protestant families ('Independents, Baptist and Wesleyans') was opened in Mary Street in 1866, thanks largely to his support,

> The great difficulty was a site, and in this, disappointment followed disappointment, until a true friend was found in John Divett, Esq., 'whose unostentatious and gentleman-like conduct,' to use the language of the committee, 'deserves from the people of Bovey warm and constant gratitude,' granted the present site at a nominal consideration and contributed valuable materials towards the building.'[20]

John Divett also supported the establishment of a proprietary college in Newton Abbot.

His role in bringing the railway to Bovey is well documented elsewhere, but he was a prime mover in this from his chairmanship of the early public meetings in 1861. The meeting heard 'with great satisfaction' the announcement of the projected railway and 'pledged themselves to give the undertaking their united and cordial support'.[21]

A picture is emerging of a prosperous and thriving, but changing town and sometime during the 1860s the annual flower show became a 'Horticultural and Industrial Show'. The Flower, Fruit and Vegetable Show by the Bovey Tracey Horticultural Society was supplemented with an 'Exhibition of Objects of Industry, Art, Antiquities,' thereby demonstrating the town's changing identity. This is demonstrated in an article in the *Exeter and Plymouth Gazette*[22] in 1867, the author of which is clearly uncomfortable with what he (or she) was seeing in Bovey. The article describes Bovey as lacking 'breadth, picturesqueness and freshness'.

> The inhabitants of a purely agricultural village have probably no substantial advantages over those of a country parish in the immediate vicinity of some system of manufacture; the latter often earn a greater amount in wages, and have facilities for the improvement of their lot which to the labourers on the land are impossible; but as a general rule, the pursuit of any business, on a large scale, other than agriculture, gives a certain aspect to a village which is no improvement upon the picture ordinarily presented by rural life.

The author goes on to say that Bovey Tracey has some of the characteristics of the East-end district of a large town, describing narrow lanes and a lack of domestic comforts glimpsed through open doorways. There is only one open space at the junction of three lanes, and there, 'surrounded by semi-dilapidated buildings and some indications of squalor and poverty, where there is nothing whatever in keeping, is a handsome Town Hall which would do credit to a town of ten thousand inhabitants'. The author hopes this will be an indication of further improvements to the 'picturesqueness' of the town.

The Art and Industry exhibition was repeated the following year, with large contributions from Bovey Pottery, including,

> The 'Moustache cup and saucer' – the tea cup with a band laid across the top, leaving a space sufficient to drink from, the band just mentioned preventing the labial appendage from dipping into the tea. It is the brightest idea in the ceramic art out [sic].[23]

By 1875, the pottery is described in glowing terms in the *Western Morning News*, and following the coming of the railway, appears to be something of a tourist attraction,

> The pottery is close to the railway. It consists of a large irregular group of buildings, above which rise a number of great brick cones well besmoked. These are the kilns. ... we are not surprised to learn that in its various departments over 250 hands, men, women and children,

find constant employment. When trade is dull the holiday time of the week may be longer, but the full staff is kept on. And as nearly all the hands have been brought up in the pottery itself, it is not difficult to understand how important such an establishment – the largest of its kind in the West of England – is to the immediate neighbourhood. Thanks to the railway, during the summer months large numbers of tourists find their way to Bovey; and many of these will gladly avail themselves of the ready courtesy of the proprietors to stroll through the works.[24]

No doubt this courtesy was designed to help sales, as visitors were also able to visit the showroom, where 'great piles' of earthenware of all kinds could be seen.

There is evidence that John was taking an active part in the life and affairs of the town well into his sixties, continuing his work as a

Figure 11.2: *"A handsome Town Hall which would do credit to a town of ten thousand inhabitants", Bovey Tracey Town Hall built in 1866.*
Note the Co-op store in the background.
(Courtesy of Bovey Tracey Heritage Centre)

magistrate, becoming a Senior Magistrate with a reputation for 'clear and unbiased judgement'.[25] He engaged in political activities as a member of the Liberal Party committee in the polling district of Newton Abbot, as well as attending public meetings when anything of note was discussed in the town. There is evidence of growing tensions between established agricultural practices, new industrial developments and the growth of the tourist industry in the area. In August 1882, there was an inquiry into the use of traction engines in Devon, following a proposed change in the by-laws to restrict the working of these locomotives on public roads between the hours of 10 a.m. and 6 p.m. There were representatives from residents who objected to the use of traction engines as well as from the owners of the engines, and the debate lasted for three hours with no discernible outcome recorded. Canon Courtenay declared the engines to be a 'bad thing' and a general nuisance but he supposed they must exist, proposing a fixed timescale for their use. The traction engines could not be passed easily in narrow lanes and frightened the horses. Mr Joll, proprietor of the Dolphin Hotel, declared that the traction engine at Haytor was a great inconvenience to tourists and 'kept a large number of them from visiting Haytor Rock and other places of interest over the hills'. Mr Collings, one of the engine owners, argued that by using his locomotives, farmers could transport lime to their farms at a cost 25 per cent cheaper that by cartage. John Divett commented that this was a benefit to the community. He said he was the largest employer of labour in Bovey, at the pottery: 'At the same time, he admitted that agriculture was the staple industry of the neighbourhood'.[26]

The following year, 1883, saw grand celebrations in Bovey Tracey to mark the occasion of Mr and Mrs Divett's fiftieth wedding anniversary. At a luncheon attended by 120 people, they were presented with a 'handsome hall time piece' supplied by Messrs Ellis, Depree and Tucker of Exeter and with an inscribed gilt plate to say it was a gift from their 'employees, those connected with the pottery and the parish of Bovey Tracey'. An illuminated address was signed by around 350 subscribers. The *Western Morning News* reported considerable warmth towards the couple; Mr W.R. Hole, in the Chair, gave the toast of the day and remarked, 'By far the greater portion of the wedded life of Mr. and Mrs. Divett had been spent amongst the people of Bovey, and they had earned, and justly earned, the esteem and affection of all who knew them'. Mrs Divett's good deeds were well known and fully appreciated in the parish.

In reply, John Divett alluded to the success of the potteries and, 'referred with pleasure to the hearty and loyal co-operation which he had received from all employees and from the manager, (Mr. Robinson)'.

In turn, Mr Robinson, was reported as saying that Mr Divett was a kind and considerate man and went on to give instances of employees who had worked at the potteries for many years; 19 had been there for more than 35 years and 22 for more than 30 years. Whilst this could be evidence of nowhere else to go, it does seem to indicate that the pottery provided stable, long-term employment under a benevolent owner. Mr Handel Corsham, Mayor of Bath, spoke in high terms of the 'kindly relations' existing between Mr Divett and his employees. Canon Courtenay suggested that they could hardly go into any cottage in Bovey in which there were not 'memories and gratitude in connection with kindnesses done by Mr. and Mrs .Divett and members of their family'.[27] Here, Canon Courtenay was presumably referring to John and Henrietta's daughter, Mary, who lived throughout this time with her parents in Bridge House, and also to John's niece, Adela Divett. Adela was the youngest of six children born to Edward Divett (Liberal MP for Exeter from 1832 to 1864) and Ann Ross. Her mother died in 1856, when Adela was only 8 years old. She was orphaned at aged 16 when her father died in 1864. Her uncle John took on guardianship of Adela and she appears on the census returns as living in Bovey Tracey in 1871. Adela is recorded attending meetings of the South Devon Archery Club with her cousin Mary in 1866,[28] bringing to mind the painting entitled *The Fair Toxophilites* by William Powell Frith which is in the collection of the Royal Albert Memorial Museum in Exeter.

'Living on her own means', the 25-year-old Adela had a house built for herself in 1873, St Mary's in Ashburton Road, on land between St John's Church and the cricket ground. Adela seems to have maintained a close association with St John's Church, and therefore with Canon Courtenay, contributing funds to build the church vestry, now the Lady Chapel. In 1873, she commissioned a stained-glass window, which can be seen today, to the memory of her parents, Ann and Edward Divett. *White's Gazetteer 1878–79*, credits the founding of the cottage hospital at Heathfield to Miss Divett and this is also supported by Veronica Kennedy in her history of St Mary's house.[29] In a letter to the editor of the *Western Morning News* in June 1875, Adela described herself as the treasurer of the Bovey Tracey cottage hospital and wished to correct errors in the figures of funds received.[30]

The 1881 census records Adela living in St Mary's with six servants, but the following year, aged 34, she travelled to India and married Captain Francis Beaufort in Ambala in the Punjab area of India. Returning to live in Bovey, she sold her house to Canon Courtenay[31] and moved across the road to The Hove, a house no longer in existence. Adela and Francis had four children; the eldest, Francis Hugh, born 1883, was killed in action on 16th May 1915. There is a memorial tablet to his memory on the Ashburton Road side of the exterior of St John's Church, not far from the stained-glass window dedicated to his grandparents. Adela was widowed in 1891, her husband Francis was buried in St John's churchyard.

About 18 months after celebrating her Golden Wedding Anniversary, Mrs Henrietta Divett died. Her funeral was attended by around 100 employees from the pottery and business in the town was suspended.[32] Less than a year after that, John Divett died at his home, Bridge House, at the age of 75. The cortège left Bridge House and as it passed through the town, shops were closed and blinds were drawn, 'whether occupied by rich or poor', as 'a token that Bovey Tracey had lost one of its most valued and respected inhabitants'.[33] Around 150 pottery workers and farm labourers led the cortège and a large number of mourners followed the coffin, which was carried by the oldest pottery worker and farmhands. According to the *East and South Devon Advertiser*, more than a thousand people witnessed the interment.[34] It appears that Mary Hole, aged 86 and the oldest inhabitant in the town, died during the funeral service.

John left the pottery to his daughter Mary and his nephew George Ross Divett, who was living in West Kensington. The will was 'proved' under £40,000, with property in Smithfield and Clerkenwell left to George.[35] Mary continued to live in Bridge House but there is little evidence to connect George with managing the pottery in Bovey Tracey. He may have moved to the area at some stage as there is a county council election pamphlet dated 1892 signed by George Ross Divett and giving an address of Chapple.[36] Mrs Ross Divett gave instructions for the sale of Chapple Farm in 1894.[37] The death of George Ross Divett is recorded in Newton Abbot in 1894 and reported as a loss to the Newton Abbot Liberal Party.[38]

Jabez Mugford's connection with the pottery ceased when John Divett died, and perhaps without these firm hands at the helm, it seems that the pottery went into decline. In 1891, the men employed in mixing and working the clay went on strike because of a 25 per cent reduction in pay coupled with a 25 per cent increase in labour. There was an attempt by the manager, the appropriately named Mr Clay, to draft in three workers from Staffordshire. Apparently, these men were unaware of the strike and downed tools as soon as they found out, declaring they would not be 'blacklegs' and had been 'duped'. A meeting of around 250 employees raised a subscription, enabling them to pay the train fares so the men could return to Staffordshire.[39]

The Union District Secretary, Mr Gardner, tried to meet with Mr Clay who refused to see him,

> but ultimately a letter was taken to the proprietress [Mary Divett], and a meeting of that lady, the manager, the men and myself took place. As a consequence, matters were satisfactorily arranged and the workers have no cause to regret belonging to the Union. Many of the workers who have become grey headed in the service of the firm, have too much respect for the lady and her predecessors to desire anything but what is right and honest. They are not, however, prepared to let a manager that has not been employed in the firm more than 12 months, reduce their wages 25 percent, with increased labour to boot, without having a voice in the matter, especially after so many years of peace and good feeling.[40]

William Robinson, aged 66, was now working as a cashier at the pottery[41] and it seems that his management and the expertise of Jabez Mugford were sorely missed. Jabez Mugford's death in 1894 merited several column inches in the *Western Times*, which gave a fulsome summary of his 'interesting career', describing him as the faithful and trusted friend of the late John Divett.[42]

Several hundred local workers and their families were dependent on the pottery and supporting businesses, so it must have been a devastating blow to the town when the pottery continued to struggle and by the beginning of 1894 had been declared bankrupt and was closed. In November 1894, the *East and South Devon Advertiser* reported that Charles Davy Blake of Newton Abbot, a ball clay supplier, had purchased the freehold, and commented that 'the news will be heartily welcomed by the inhabitants of Bovey Tracey, as the closing of the works for the past few months has occasioned much distress amongst the late employees'.[43]

The new Bovey Pottery Company was incorporated on 22nd December 1894 under the directorship of T.B. Johnson of Bristol.[44] The Divett family's association with the pottery was over. Mary, now aged 60, still owned Langaller Farm as well as the rights to the lignite pit. She owned land around Bridge House and purchased land in Ilsington. Mary was a manager of the National Schools, a member of the Newton Board of Guardians and the Rural District Council and she was the only woman to sit on the local Parochial Committee. In contrast to her father, she was a 'strong Unionist' and gave assistance at election times by lending her carriage to the Party.

Mary petitioned the Newton Abbot Board of Guardians for Ilsington to be attached to the Bovey Tracey Medical Officers district, rather than Ashburton and in 1887 she highlighted the case of Mary Nosworthy, of Ilsington, accusing Dr Adams of medical neglect after he issued a death certificate for the woman who had not been seen by him for four years.[45] She appeared less sympathetic in discussions about whether to give bread and gruel to tramps who presented themselves at the Newton Abbot Workhouse declaring that they were 'tourists who were travelling at the expense of the public' and if they were only given bread and water it might deter them from coming to the workhouse.[46] She gave permission for her land behind Bridge House to be used for the installation of a septic tank, but had cause to regret this later when she complained of the smell.[47]

Mary died in 1914, at the age of 80, leaving her property to her nephew, Raleigh Buller Phillpotts, who moved to Bovey Tracey from Whimple. The *Western Times* listed the names of around 100 mourners.[48] She was described as a 'ready subscriber to every local institution and gave valuable help to the aged poor in the town; and her kindness will be greatly missed by them'.

There is a relatively modest headstone to Henrietta, John and Mary in the cemetery in Bovey Tracey but, as the town grew, their legacy appears to have been largely in connection with the coming of the railway. As a wealthy man in his own right, John Divett could surely have lived on his own means and even as an owner of the pottery, need not have moved to live in Bovey. However, he appears to have made a significant contribution to the growth of Bovey Tracey in the Victorian period and genuinely appears to have been a benevolent and fair employer, with a strong interest in the well-being of the community. The workers may have been exploited – there was clearly evidence of poverty in the town, but there is no evidence that they perceived themselves to be exploited, until after John's death, when the clay workers went on strike in 1891.

The last words are from John himself, reported as spoken at his Golden Wedding Anniversary celebrations in 1883,

> There were many who might suppose that Mrs. Divett and himself were 'original inhabitants' of Bovey, but that was not so. He had come to Bovey many years ago, and had finally become a resident. He liked Bovey, and Bovey seemed in a manner to have liked him. (Applause.) He felt he could quote the words of the song, and say–
>   'All countries so fair and beautiful
>   This little valley I prize far above.'[49]

Notes

1. GB Historical GIS / University of Portsmouth, Bovey Tracey CP/AP through time | Population Statistics | Total Population, *A Vision of Britain through Time*. Available at: <http://www.visionofbritain.org.uk/unit/10051459/cube/TOT_POP> [Accessed 23rd May 2017].
2. Ancestry.com. HO107; Piece: 253; Book: 13; Civil Parish: Bovey Tracey; County: Devon; Enumeration District: 12; Folio: 11; Page: 16; Line: 12; GSU roll: 241324. *1841 England Census*. [online database] Available at: <http://www.ancestry.co.uk> [Accessed: 23rd May 2017].
3. Mountford, W. (2004). A snapshot of Bovey Tracey in 1841. In: Kennedy, V. ed. *The Bovey Book*. Newton Abbot: Cottage Publishing. p.15.
4. *Western Times*, 16th April 1836.
5. Ancestry.com. *British Naval Biographical Dictionary, 1849* [online database]. Original data: O'Byrne, William R., 1849. *A Naval Biographical Dictionary: Comprising the Life and Services of Every Living Officer in Her Majesty's Navy, from the Rank of Admiral of the Fleet to that of Lieutenant, Inclusive*. London: John Murray. Available at: <https://search.ancestry.co.uk> [Accessed 23rd May 2017].
6. *Western Times*, 20th November 1852.
7. Information supplied by April Marjoram from her research into Edward Divett MP.

8.   Billing, M. (1857) *Directory and Gazetteer of the County of Devon, containing a descriptive account of every town, village, hamlet, etc.* Birmingham: M. Billing's Steam-Press Offices.

9.   *Western Times*, 20th November 1852.

10. Devon Heritage Centre. *Patent Granted to Thomas Wentworth Buller for his invention for improvements in the manufacture of earthenware.* Reference number: 4622M/T/16.

11. Adams, B. (2005). *Bovey Tracey Potteries Guide and Marks.* Bovey Tracey: House of Marbles.

12. *Exeter Flying Post*, 3rd December 1857.

13. *Western Times*, 9th October 1847.

14. Ancestry.com. HO107; Piece: 1870; Folio: 554; Page: 16; GSU roll: 221018. *1851 England Census.* [online database] Available at: <http://www.ancestry.co.uk> [Accessed 23rd May 2017].

15. *Western Times*, 19th January 1850.

16. Western *Courier*, 3rd March 1852.

17. *Western Times*, 13th November 1858.

18. *Western Times*, 6th November 1894.

19. *London Evening Standard*, 29th September 1871.

20. *Western Times*, 24th July 1866.

21. *Western Times*, 12th October 1861.

22. *Exeter and Plymouth Gazette*, 6th September 1867.

23. *Exeter and Plymouth Gazette*, 21st August 1868.

24. *Western Morning News*, 26th May 1875.

25. *Western Times*, 30th September 1885.

26. *Exeter and Plymouth Gazette*, 11th August 1882.

27. *Western Morning News*, 27th April 1883.

28. *Western Times*, 14th September 1866.

29. Kennedy, V., 2006. *St Mary's Bovey Tracey: A Brief History of a House and Family Home.* Bovey Tracey: Bovey Tracey Heritage Trust.

30. *Western Morning News*, 30th June 1875.

31. Kennedy, V., 2006. *St Mary's Bovey Tracey: A Brief History of a House and Family Home.* Bovey Tracey: Bovey Tracey Heritage Trust. p.4.

32. *Western Morning News*, 24th October 1884.

33. *Western Times*, 25th September 1885.

34. *East and South Devon Advertiser*, 26th September 1885.

35. *Exeter and Plymouth Gazette*, 26th January 1886.

36. Original pamphlet in the archive of Bovey Tracey Heritage Centre.

37. *Exeter and Plymouth Gazette*, 21st September 1894.

38. *Western* Times, 1st February 1895.

39. *Totnes Weekly Times*, 20th June 1891.

40. *Totnes Weekly Times*, 27th June 1891.
41. Ancestry.com. RG12; Piece: 1696; Folio: 64; Page: 7; GSU roll: 6096806. *1891 England Census*. [online database]. Available at: <http://www.ancestry.co.uk> [Accessed 23rd May 2017].
42. *Western Times*, 6th November 1894.
43. *Exeter and Plymouth Gazette*, 21st August 1868.
44. Adams, B., 2005. *Bovey Tracey Potteries Guide and Marks*. Bovey Tracey: House of Marbles.
45. *Exeter and Plymouth Gazette*, 6th May 1887.
46. *East and South Devon Advertiser*, 28th March 1903.
47. *Western Times*, 17th November 1903.
48. *Western Times*, 20th March 1914.
49. *Western Morning News*, 27th April 1883.

Newspaper references are from <http://www.britishnewspaperarchive.co.uk/> ©The British Library Board [Accessed 23rd May 2017].